ANOTHER DOOR OPENS

A FIGHT FOR A LIFE

Betty Ann Williams

edited and adapted
by

Peter Tye

"HOME is the most powerful word in the English Language. Everyone has the right to have a place to call home"

William Shakespeare

IN LOVING MEMORY

My dearest Mother
Ethel May Williams (nee Bryan)
1909 to 2001

My little Sister
Rosemary (Rosebud) Margaret
1947 to 2017

My big Brother
Bryan Thomas
1941 to 2004

Their memory inspired me to pen this memoir.
I only wish they were still here to help me write it.

Perhaps they are?

CONTENTS

Page:

Front Cover Picture

© Medici/Mary Evans

Cover Design
Peter Tye

INTRODUCTION

My mother, Ethel May, had a hard but rewarding life. The hard part was dealing with all the tribulations which were forced upon her at such an early age. For many children it was a fact of life in Edwardian society where another child born into a poor family could tip the balance from poverty to abject destitution. Her premature birth, coupled with the early death of her father, placed her mother in the invidious position of having to offer her for adoption to make ends meet. On the face of it she made a wise choice, but a catalogue of events when Ethel May approached school age led to the authorities stepping in and sending her to an authoritarian school for prisoners' children. The rewarding part of her life was caring for others, but that initially came about through fighting to keep a roof over the heads of her three children. It was a fight she initially lost and my two siblings and I were put into orphanages. However, eventually we were all together again and following Ethel's example my sister and I started and ran our own very successful care home businesses. Life was difficult at times, but we found that with patience and determination, as one door closed another inevitably opened.

My intention was to cover my mother's life and my own in one volume, but after going through all my mother's notes and diaries, I decided that her story deserved to be a book in its own right, So 'A Fight for a Life' is the first in a trilogy. Would, Ethel May have put up such a fight to exist, had she known how things were to unfold? I have to begin with that question and promise I will let you have her honest answer before the conclusion of this book.

Betty Ann Williams

Headington Workhouse 1900

1

A FIGHT FOR LIFE

Ellen Bryan wept silently. Her young heart was breaking. She was encircled by the gripping waves of pain from ever strengthening contractions as she was carried from her warm, comfortable home, during the afternoon of 1st February 1909 and placed inside the freezing, bare St. John ambulance. Her pitiful tears were not only for herself on that bitterly cold day as the horse drawn vehicle was battered by the blizzard, but also for her devoted husband and the fact she knew, only too well, premature babies rarely, if ever, survived.

As her beloved Arthur, obviously a sick man, watched anxiously in the driving snow, a thoughtful attendant turned up his coat collar and shouted over the wind.

"Will you be accompanying your wife to the workhouse sir?"

"I can't!" an anguished Arthur shouted back. "I have to look after our young child."

As much as he yearned to comfort his cherished Ellen, Arthur accepted that it was his duty to stay behind and care for Ruby, their one and a half year old daughter. Earlier he overheard the home-birthing nurse explain to Ellen that surgical intervention could be required and as he knew something of the primitive nature of such interventions, he was well aware of the danger and that Ellen may never return to him and their precious Ruby Florence. He watched the horse-drawn ambulance moved off at a slow pace into the raging blizzard, it was lost to sight within seconds, but he remained rooted to the spot, swamped within his own thoughts as he stared mournfully into the swirling snow.

Ellen and Arthur Bryan married young and always wanted a large family. On discovering that Ellen was pregnant again, they were delighted to be providing a companion for their much-loved daughter. They had often discussed the risks in childbirth which were severe and terrifying. Only half of mothers and babies survived a normal delivery, let alone a premature one, where, more often than not, forceps or other surgical interventions were employed. Everybody knew someone who had died from a complicated pregnancy and Ellen's best friend, Monica, had had a baby son stillborn only three weeks before.

The depressingly gloomy Headington Workhouse, into which Ellen was about to be rushed, was built in 1837 to house 200 waifs, strays and

10

inebriates in Headington, Southwest Oxford. The hospital wing had been added some decades later and housed a thirty bed 'open to non-residents' maternity ward. But the appalling conditions within the ugly, monolithic block were still contaminated by the squalor and deprivation of the despised Victorian workhouse.

As the horse-drawn ambulance came to a clattering stop, it was besieged by a sea of destitute paupers and street-sleepers. They crowded around the rear doors as they opened, begging for coppers. The St. Johns driver and his attendant were well used to this and carried a few sweets that could be tossed out to hastily clear a way through for their sick or dying patients.

An overpowering stench of ether, carbolic soap and human excrement swept over Ellen. She remembered it well and what a cold, soulless place the birthing room was from the traumatic delivery of Ruby, eighteen months before. The unit suffered from a lack of basic sanitation; hardly any life-enabling equipment and little in the way of effective medication. To give birth in that place was a hazardous procedure, with high mortality rates for both mother and baby.

This time her baby was expected to be one such child. Ellen was there due to complications brought about by a very early onset of labour. It was pronounced by the home-birth midwife, who had been attending Ellen since 2am, that the child would perish within its mother if nothing was done to assist in its removal. The St. Johns ambulance was summoned to take her to the closest medical unit, which happened to be the workhouse.

Upon her arrival at the maternity unit, she was met by a young assistant nurse and escorted directly into the delivery room where a physician and a senior midwife were waiting. Her night garments were replaced with a rough, open-backed, white surgical gown. A brown, rubber tube was inserted into her rectum and two pints of a warm water and soap enema was poured into her bowel by the midwife who told her what to do.

"Try and retain the enema liquid within your body as you go to the bathroom, Mrs Bryan; then sit on the toilet until you feel empty."

When she failed to return after ten minutes, the junior nurse was dispatched with a wheelchair and bedpan to collect her. Ellen had to be helped to clamber onto the steel framed delivery couch where her legs were spread apart and strapped to the upright posts.

The assistant nurse shaved her pubic area, washed her with carbolic soap and then covered her genitals in white lard. Her contractions became severe and fast, but as the baby's heartbeat could not be found, it was thought Ellen would be delivered of a still-born child.

As she entered the transition stage and the physician prepared for a forceps delivery, the vastly experienced midwife, who had no wish to see yet another tiny baby grabbed around the head and pulled out by an impatient physician. intently encouraged her.

"Come along now Mrs Bryan, push, my dear, push with all your might."

The midwife's encouragement had the desired effect and within three pushes a tiny, rather blueish baby arrived without the physician's intervention.

"You have a baby girl Mrs Bryan" said the relieved midwife, who had witnessed two brutal forceps interventions already that day.

Ellen managed a faint smile, but looked anxiously on as the midwife passed her daughter to the doctor and not to her. The frail baby was held, upside-down, by her feet, to receive the ubiquitous finger taps on her tiny bottom. This made her instinctively throw her arms wide with fingers outstretched; but they dropped back and dangled, lifelessly below her head. She failed to cry and struggled for breath, eventually becoming still and to all appearances, lifeless.

The room fell silent as the midwife took the inert child from the doctor, gently laid her on a warmed towel and began to rhythmically rub her body with Vaseline. But when this did not appear to be having the desired effect, she stopped and looked towards the doctor for instructions. The doctor, knowing it was most unlikely that this perfectly formed, but tiny scrap of humanity would survive, gave the midwife his instructions.

"Give the child a dropper of warmed sugar-water, wrap her up and remove her to a quiet side room." He reduced his voice to a whisper as he added directly into the midwife's ear. "If she is strong enough she will endure the night. If not, we must allow her to depart this world in peace."

The younger nurse, who was not yet hardened to the death of a child, shed silent tears as she gently wrapped her charge in a winceyette blanket, passed a few drops of the sweet liquid into the infant's mouth and placed her in a linen cot.

The doctor smiled sympathetically at Ellen, but said no more, leaving the room to assist in another confinement.

It was left to the midwife to comfort Ellen as she attended to her post-delivery needs.

"Have you and your husband chosen a name for your newly born, Mrs Bryan?"

"We're calling her Ethel May: Ethel after my own grandmother and May after my husband's favourite aunt."

Ellen was drowsy but the look of concern and compassion in the midwife's eyes snapped her out of her stupor.

"What's wrong with her? Is she alright? Can I hold her now, please?"

As an alarmed Ellen began to sob, the midwife, gently explained.

"Your daughter has just gone through the trauma of an early birth, my dear. She had to push and squeeze her way into this world and now needs complete rest. She's tiny and extremely weak and I'm so sorry to have to tell you that you must prepare yourself for the likelihood that she may not survive the night. The doctor believes she might have the strength to fight for her life, but we shall all have to wait and see."

Ellen's cries could be heard across the maternity unit as she absorbed the warning. The midwife turned to her junior and ordered her to take the baby into an adjoining room. Ethel May was immediately wheeled away from the anguished cries of her heartbroken mother.

Ellen was moved into a post-delivery ward, where she was visited by the workhouse almoner and asked what her wishes were should her child not survive. She was advised that, if needed, a chaplain would arrive the following day to christen her daughter and she would then be taken to the chosen undertaker's Chapel of Rest. Ellen was not shown or given the opportunity to hold her child as it as was believed the sooner a stillborn baby was removed, the sooner the distressed mother would come to terms with the loss and recover her health. Arthur's thoughts and feelings were not considered; he was not of high-rank or influentially rich. Ellen was allowed no post-delivery visitors and spent the night among several other new mothers who had their babies sleeping in cots beside them which made the absence of her child a stark reality. All Ellen could do was mourn the anticipated loss of her child.

However, when the young nurse entered the anti-room some hours later, fully expecting to prepare Ethel May for her pre-burial christening, she discovered the baby's tiny hands grasping for life outside her swaddling wrap and heard faint mewing sounds. The baby was desperately clinging to life and hungry! The elated nurse immediately returned Ethel May to her mother to be comforted, fed, bathed and dressed, but a physically overwhelmed and emotionally drained Ellen, who had endured the entire night coming to terms with her loss, was stunned. She refused to accept that it could be her daughter and would have nothing to do with her.

Ethel May was cuddled and fed by the young nurse with warm, watered milk and honey, then tactically placed beside Ellen's bed. Eventually, as Ethel May's cries became more demanding, Ellen felt obliged, even if only to appease the other new mothers in the ward, to pick her up and take her into her own bed. But, there was to be no instant love, no delightful union; Ellen was too traumatised for that. She held her new arrival, fed, washed and dressed her, but felt no instinctive bond.

When Arthur arrived for his first visit, with brown hair slicked down and his six foot two, muscular frame, looking dapper in an Elliston and Cavell suit, he was comforted and utterly delighted to see his lovely wife's post-birth radiance. This reassured him that yesterday's fears were unfounded and he thanked the Lord Ruby would soon have her mother back and with a little sister.

****

Ellen and Arthur were not overly poor. Even though they never had two halfpennies to rub together at the end of each week, they were frugal and managed. Ellen's husband of three years was gainfully employed as a grocer's porter in the indoor market off Cornmarket Street. They shared a rented, terraced house in the area of Summertown, two miles north of Oxford City centre. Arthur, a sensitive and caring man with a maturity well above his tender years, was not shy of hard work. He toiled long hours, humping heavy sacks of fruit and vegetables, which built an enviable, muscular physique. He also did extra evening and odd weekend work, lifting heavy barrels to and from the basement at the Prince's Castle Inn in Barton Village. He was proud that his work ethic enabled him to provide a decent standard of living for his growing family.

Arthur loved life and his beautiful wife; God knows he didn't want to leave them, but early on in Ellen's pregnancy, Arthur had begun to suffer from periodic and ever-more severe headaches. He endured what everyone thought was migraine for some time, but as the headaches became more debilitating, often accompanied by profuse vomiting; his doctor decided that he should attend the Radcliffe Hospital for X-rays. A few days before Ellen went into labour, they were called in to see the Neurosurgeon and given devastating news. Arthur had an inoperable abscess on his brain and there was nothing the doctors could do to save him. He was twenty-two years old and had just a few months to live! It was deemed that the shock of hearing this diagnosis triggered the premature arrival of their second child.

When he learned he was to die within a few months, Arthur's first thoughts were not for himself, he held a deep and comforting belief that his God would look after him, he would be at peace. He was far more concerned about Ellen and his children and what was to become of them. He was determined to stay strong for his wife and managed to contain and control his grief as he tenderly told Ellen that she must not allow his death to drag her into a pit of despair, because their children would need their mother more than ever. He reassured her of his unending love for her and gave his sacred blessing for her to live life to the full and find love again.

****

Ellen's spirits lifted and she managed to put on a broad smile when she saw her handsome husband, flowers in hand, coyly walking towards her sporting that shy smile she knew so well. However, although she returned his smile, she certainly didn't feel joyful inside. Arthur should never know of last night's drama, he was simply not well enough for news like that and must be able to rejoice that his second daughter, although tiny, was alive, feeding well and safely held in her mother's arms.

The following day, Ellen's mother visited and Ellen revealed, between sobs, that she did not know how she was going to cope with the imminent loss of her supportive and gentle husband, no money coming in and two little girls to house, feed and clothe. Her mother desperately tried to reassure her that she was not alone and the whole family would pull together and things would be alright, although her mother knew, only too well, that life would not be easy as Arthur's health began to deteriorate.

During her convalescence, Ellen, a rational and no-nonsense young woman, considered her predicament. There was no such thing as state aid and she had no insurance policies to soften the blow of the loss of a husband at such a young age. She came to the conclusion that it would be impossible to care for both of her girls and the best thing to do was put her new born child up for adoption and find her a good home with someone who could love her and give her the things she needed. There would be no shame attached to her decision, it was not unusual or thought of as immoral for widowed mothers to offer unwanted babies for adoption, or even sale: there was no shortage of desperate takers. Children were universally advertised in local newspapers, both wanted and for sale and as there were no coherent adoption laws, parents could more or less do whatever they wanted with their children.

After Ellen's compulsory two week convalescence, Ethel May had gone from strength to strength and they were able to return home where Ellen's family were happy to provide the physical help she needed. Ellen surprised herself by settling into her new life with two children and as Ethel May grew stronger and less demanding, she began to rethink her decision to have her youngest daughter adopted. She did not touch alcohol and ate moderately, so quickly recovered her slender figure. She was considered by many to be a beauty and a great catch for Arthur. She had long, thick brown hair, which she wore in a loose bun piled on the top or her head, a clear complexion and all of her own, well-cared-for teeth. She and Arthur made a very attractive couple.

Arthur continued to work and was helping with additional house duties. Their respective families also honoured their promise to assist with caring for the girls and to help with their finances. However, this was to be a false dawn. Within weeks Arthur grew weaker. He found lifting and handling fully laden sacks impossible and all too soon he had to give up both jobs. Because the headaches had become unbearable and his vision dramatically impaired, he was prescribed ever increasing amounts of morphine which made him sleep for most of the time. As he needed day and night care, Arthur was moved into his parents' home. The intolerable pain could only be eased by ever-more opiates. He quickly became bed-fast, incontinent and eventually blind. Ellen moved to his parents home too, sleeping on the floor next to her husband. She devoted herself to his care; refusing to leave his bedside, tending to all his personal needs. She remained beside him until his passing, during the early hours of June 1st 1909.

Ellen Bryan and Ruby Florence 1909

2

TOTAL COLLAPSE

Ellen managed to hold herself together whilst she was busy dealing with unavoidable family and legal matters, along with the part-time care of Ruby and Ethel May. It was only after the funeral service, when Arthur was laid to rest next to family members in Dunstan Road Cemetery in Headington that she succumbed to the overwhelming sadness which engulfed her. Although Arthur's death was anticipated, when it finally happened it was such a shock to Ellen that she was totally crushed and had no will to live. The loving diligence with which she looked after Arthur had severely taken its toll. She suffered a total collapse, could not will herself to get out of bed and found it impossible to eat. Her mother spent many days beside her and worried that she might lose her daughter too, having heard her as she prayed to God.

"Please allow me to die too Lord. Give me cancer or a heart attack; I just can't stand this pain any longer."

Ellen's mother eventually managed to coax her daughter into a recovery and made her accept that one day love would find her again, she also reminded her of the deathbed promise she made to her dying husband. Her life must go on and she had to pull through for the sake of their two daughters, who were being looked after by Arthur's older brother, Thomas and his wife.

With her mother's encouragement, Ellen recovered enough to have Ruby home again and cared for her as best she could. However, as there was not the same loving bond with her younger child, it was some weeks before Ethel May was invited to return home. However, Ellen soon realised that she did not want to continue caring for her youngest daughter. Unable to cope she reverted to her earlier decision to have Ethel May re-homed and without telling members of either family, placed an advertisement in the Oxford Times for a couple to adopt the child.

Thomas, who had been caring for both girls, spotted the advertisement. He was very angry and confronted Ellen.

"You can't possibly mean to part with 'our' beautiful Ethel May it's a wicked immoral thing to even think of doing it. Arthur would turn in his bloody grave if he knew you were giving his daughter away to complete strangers. We love her, she is safe and secure with us, let us adopt the child and bring her up within our own loving family as our daughter."

Ellen snapped back.

"Ethel May is my daughter and it is up to me to decide what is best for her. To have her with you is much too close to home. Now, stop interfering!"

Following advice from his solicitor, Thomas knew he was powerless to intervene; Ellen's parental control over her child, now that Arthur was gone, was absolute. His deep distaste for Ellen and the course she was taking lasted for the rest of his life. Thomas never, spoke to Ellen again.

The advertisement was answered by both unscrupulous 'baby-dealers' and legitimate couples who had either lost a child themselves, or the wife was barren. It was never a consideration that it could possibly be the husband's fault a wife could not conceive.

Baby-dealers were rife and absolutely unscrupulous. Children were bought for cash and the older ones sold into slave labour as early as five years old, either for farm work or down the mines. Most of them simply disappeared and were forgotten.

However, there were childless couples who were genuine and desperately wanted a baby to fulfil their lives. One such young couple came to see Ethel May and very nearly adopted her, but on their second visit the husband, during a coughing fit, unintentionally revealed that he had recently recovered from tuberculosis. At that time TB was most certainly a killer disease to which could wipe-out whole families. Ellen immediately put a stop to their negotiations.

An American couple were refused immediately because they wanted fully legal, adoption papers drawn up to allow them to take Ethel May back to America with them.

A Welsh couple arrived and spent a day with Ellen and her girls; Ellen liked them very much and thought that they would meet her criteria, until they revealed it was their intention to return to Wales within a few years. So, they too were sent packing.

When questioned about her motives for not allowing anyone to lawfully and fully adopt Ethel May, Ellen said she did not want to give her up completely and wished to retain ultimate control over what happened to her as she grew up.

Eventually, Ethel May was taken by Mr and Mrs Meads, a local couple in their early thirties, Harry Meads, a tall willowy man with a calm, thoughtful manner, was a house painter in the building business. Ethel, his petite, fair-haired wife, had left her job as a seamstress when they married in 1904. They were comfortably off, owning their own home in the respected area of Littlehay Road, Cowley, a few miles east of Summertown. Mrs Meads had almost died from septicaemia, after the birth of their stillborn daughter, and was warned against attempting to have another child. They were desperate to have Ethel May and the coincidence of having a child with the same forename as the mother was of no consequence as they would always call her Ethel May.

The Meads visited several times, with Mrs Meads coming alone for a couple of evenings to put both girls to bed. This elegant couple were chosen by Ellen to be Ethel May's parents for her child and they took her into their care when she was just seven months old.

None of Ellen's or Arthur's family were ever told where Ethel May had gone and their agreement was never sought. The only 'problem', to manifest itself later, was that Mr and Mrs Meads were both stone deaf and could not speak.

Mr and Mrs Meads certainly loved and cared for their new baby and because Ethel May was so well nurtured with Benger's Food and honey, she rapidly grew strong and healthy. The baby slept in a rocker-cot which touched her new mum's side of the bed. This enabled Ethel May's doting 'mother' to rock her baby to sleep and soothingly stroke her if she was fretful. She could also dangle her leg over her daughter's cradle so she could feel any movement indicating her attentions were being demanded during the night. She always ensured that there was a small nightlight lit in her bedroom, so Ethel May was never left alone in the dark. Ethel May was raised as their own daughter in a kind and loving home.

However as Ethel May grew, she remained cocooned in their silent, isolated world. She was taught sign language, with her mother's hands gently placed over hers, and learned the ways of the deaf. One such aid was a pull-bell on the front door that was attached to a long string with a white ball on the end. When the bell was pulled, the small white ball would swing down into the middle of the parlour making the family aware that someone was there. Regular visitors knew they would most likely have to wait at the door until the hanging ball was noticed.

The Meads were lucky enough to have not only a good sized back garden, but an allotment. Ethel May often accompanied her father there and developed an early hands-in-the-earth appreciation of growing things and eating what they grew. Mr Meads attended local gardening clubs and would exhibit his produce. He won many awards, either small cups or colourful rosettes, which took pride of place in a glass-fronted cabinet in their front parlour.

Cowley inhabitants enjoyed being surrounded by three rivers and miles of undeveloped grassland and water meadows. The Meads were the proud owners of an Enfield motorbike and sidecar, the mode of transport commonly used by mid-income families. It meant Ethel May and her parents could reap the benefits of frequent trips around the Oxfordshire countryside, with long walks beside the River Thames, Isis or Cherwell.

As a full-time housewife with an abundance of home-grown fruit and vegetables, Mrs Meads made all her own preserves, cakes and biscuits. During summer weekends they delighted in home-made picnics, setting off on the motorbike, with mother and daughter tucked into the sidecar; their wicker basket full of delicious goodies. They spent many hours touring the area in search of great walks and places, such as Iffley Weir, Boars Hill and Woodstock, to linger and enjoy their food. Mrs Meads and Ethel May were never happier than when they were in the meadows picking wild flowers and making daisy chains or posies of wild buttercups, holding them under each other's chins to see if they liked butter.

Both parents were keen wild-water swimmers and taught their girl to swim before she was four years old. Ethel May, a bright and intuitive child, was schooled by her mother at home. Even at five years of age, as their circle of friends included several blind people, she was taught to read Braille through touch and was able to write a few words. She also loved to draw and paint alongside her mother who was an accomplished artist. Their life was blissfully happy, but extremely isolated. Due to their profound deafness, the family were sometimes mistakenly taken as being aloof or unfriendly and often avoided, even shunned, which only served to insulate their child even more. When Ethel May ran to greet other children she could only mumble a few words before her parents protectively motioned her away.

The family attended a local club for the hard of hearing and most of the Meads friends were either deaf or mute and spoke little, if at all. There were no other children in their social circle, so there was not much opportunity, or need, for Ethel May to talk. As she approached school age, she was an intelligent, good-natured, happy child with cascading brown hair and trusting pale-blue eyes, who could not speak properly.

The Meads were regularly visited by an affable officer from the Oxford Deaf and Dumb Welfare Society. When Ethel May was small his visits were not seen as a threat; they were something to look forward to and he often played with the child saying how bright and contented she seemed. The Meads had no way of knowing what lay ahead!

On Ethel May's fifth birthday, 1st of February 1914, a few close relations were invited to join in with her celebration lunch. As they arrived and 'rang' the ball bell, Ethel ran excitedly to the door and couldn't wait to see what they were carrying in their arms. The last entrants were so engrossed in their warm welcome they failed to notice that they had not fully closed the front door.

As a much cherished child she was bought the loveliest of presents by her 'adoptive' family. Her aged 'grandmother' bought her a baby doll and, being an accomplished seamstress, like her daughter, made the doll a beautiful, fur-trimmed, red, outdoor coat, leggings and bonnet. Tiny woolly mittens, threaded through the sleeves, dangled down ready for Ethel May to put on her doll's hands. An aunt had brought a pushchair for the doll to sit in with an intricately crocheted blanket as a cover. When Ethel May saw her new 'friend' she instantly fell in love. The doll was kissed and cuddled tight to Ethel's chest and given the name, Rosebud. Ethel May tucked her up in the push chair and chatting to her, wheeling her up and down the long narrow hallway. After a while she noticed the front door was slightly ajar, opened it and took her new found friend for a walk.

It was some time before the adults noticed that Ethel May was no longer playing in the hallway. A frantic search of the small house, garden and greenhouse ensued but it quickly became evident that Ethel May was missing and the front door was open. The police were alerted and everyone joined in the search. Nearby river banks and railway tracks were a priority and all neighbours within a quarter of a mile radius were asked to search their gardens and sheds.

Luckily it was a sunny day and Ethel May was warmly dressed in long, suede bootees: a full-length, red velvet dress: woollen leggings and a thick, knitted cardigan. She had wandered, totally unnoticed by anyone, along the main road and down a country lane which took her into an open meadow. The five year old felt quite at home in that environment and happily picked early sweet violets and placed them in Rosebud's hair and around her neck. As dusk was closing in she was found, unharmed, by a local policeman and quickly reunited with her shocked parents.

The Meads were issued with a stern warning to ensure their front door was kept locked and shut, next time they might not be so lucky. It was later assumed Ethel May had tried to recreate the picnic trips she had so enjoyed with her 'parents' and was unafraid because she was well used to being within a meadow environment and of course, she had her new best friend to keep her company.

Unfortunately however, the incident brought Ethel May to the attention of the authorities. Police inquiries were initiated as to how she managed to wander off on her own and this led to questions as to why this 'normal' child was living with a 'handicapped' couple and not with her birth mother.

Unbeknown to the Meads, it was also revealed by the constabulary to the Executive of the Deaf Society that this vulnerable little girl had never been legally adopted. The police were of the opinion that living within a deaf and dumb household was depriving the child of acceptable standards of learning. She was therefore deemed as disadvantaged and in their view, urgently needed to be reunited with her birth mother or rehoused within more appropriate surroundings, where she would learn to talk and develop acceptable social skills.

The inspector from the Deaf Society, who had been calling on the family for nearly five years and had seen Ethel May grow from a small baby into a happy, confident five year old was allocated the grim task of breaking the bad news. He had grown fond of the family, even perhaps being considered a friend, but, he was well aware of the child's inability to communicate with other children and the problems this might create as she grew older. He was torn between allowing her to stay in the home she loved or risk removing her to an orphanage. So with much trepidation he pulled the ball cord and waited for Mr Meads to open the door.

The Meads were horrified to hear his news and protested that Ethel May was safe and would be attending a 'normal' junior, state school when the new term started in the following September. Not wishing to stamp on any hope they had, he assured them that everything would turn out for the best and told them not to worry. He would be returning soon with news of the outcome of their investigations.

The inspector then visited Ellen Bryan and pleaded with her to take Ethel May back to save her from having to go into an institution. Ellen turned him away, refused to have a dialogue and told him it was impossible as she was about to re-marry and her fiancée was unaware of Ethel's existence. As the inspector was shown the door, he warned Ellen that she may have to attend a court hearing and state her case.

"You will also be asked to sign a consent form for your daughter to be taken into an institution, Mrs Bryan, are you really prepared to do that?"

Ellen merely shrugged, "If it comes to that, I will just have to do it then, won't I?" She firmly shut the door behind him.

The inquiry took a month and the Meads were informed, by letter, that Ethel May could not remain with them. Her birth mother had confirmed that she was not in a position to take her in, she would shortly be removed from their care and placed within a state orphanage and this placement would, quite lawfully, be chosen by local welfare officers.

When the officer returned to ensure that the Letter of Notice had been received and would be obeyed, the Meads told him they refused to accept this decision and would be fighting it in court. They both wept as they reminded the officer that he knew Ethel May was well cared for through his regular visits and was being well educated at home. He told them he was truly sorry, but there was nothing he could do; it was now in the hands of the Social Welfare and their decision was lawful and binding. He quickly let himself out and never returned.

As the front door closed, the Meads were too shocked to move. Mrs Meads recovered first and ran to Ethel May who was in the garden and sobbed and sobbed as she held onto her as if both their lives depended on it. Mr Meads grabbed his coat and left the house to seek an appointment with their solicitor to begin proceedings to stop them taking their child away.

They desperately fought the decision through the Oxford City Court in a vain attempt to retain custodianship of their cherished 'daughter', but as she was not lawfully theirs, Ethel May could be removed from them at any time. After a few weeks their solicitor, who had known the family for many years, was informed of the Courts final ruling and had the difficult task of passing the dire news to them. They had lost their case and Ethel May was to be taken by the authorities and placed in an industrial school for girls.

An overwhelming sense of bewilderment and betrayal overcame them. They had lost their first daughter at birth and were now about to lose their second, just because they were deaf. It was too much to bear and they asked if it was too late for them to legally adopt Ethel May, but their solicitor had to tell them that Ellen Bryan would never agree to it. She had never meant to fully give up her rights to her daughter, but she didn't want her back either. She was about to marry another man, William Couldry and would not 'impose' another child upon him, especially one he didn't even know existed. The Meads had to accept that they had lost their legal struggle and were eventually ordered under the Industrial School Act: 58 (1) B as 'Having a parent that does not exercise proper guidance' – the 'parent' in this case being Ellen Bryan and not the Meads, who were informed that they had to ensure a lawful and peaceful handover of the child within four weeks.

Mrs Meads fought to keep her emotions under control as she tried to prepare Ethel May for what was to come. She explained that she would soon need to go to a residential school to learn to speak properly, but she would have lots of new friends to play with. She reassured her that it would only be for a short time; they would visit her often and would still be able to take her on the beloved picnics.

Ethel May really believed that she was about to go to find new playmates and enjoy other children's company for the first time, so she was excited and, trusting her parents, accepted what she was told. Had the Meads known where Ethel May was actually being taken and how long for, they would have been mortified.

So it was, on a Saturday afternoon in the late summer of 1914 the Meads tearfully packed a small, brown leather suitcase with everything they felt their daughter would need until they were able to visit. They then unwillingly slipped Ethel May, clutching Rosebud and dressed in her Sunday best outfit of warm, blue velvet coat, matching bonnet and leggings, into their sidecar, with no inkling it was to be for the very last time.

They drove to the offices of the Oxford Deaf and Dumb Society, where they had been summoned by Court Order to deliver Ethel May and hand her over to bureaucrats from the Welfare Department. As they took their seats on the hard, wooden bench within the bleak reception office, Ethel May, unafraid and blissfully unaware of what was to come, climbed onto her 'mother's' lap and pulled Rosebud up to join them. Knowing this might be the last time she was able to hold her daughter for some weeks, Ethel Meads buried her face into the nape of her daughter's warm, sweet smelling neck. Feeling the plump softness of her skin on her lips, she drank in her essence to capture and memorise it until they were together again.

When two, stern faced, male welfare officers entered, seemingly unconcerned by what they were about to do, Mrs Meads lost her inner battle to remain calm. She panicked and clung on grimly to her 'daughter'. The officers tried to drag the now terrified child from her 'mother's' arms. Mr Meads stepped in and with the utmost poise and dignity, carefully but firmly made the officers release his daughter and motioned his insistence that they step back and away from his panic-stricken wife. As his soothing but unspoken gestures calmed his beloved family, he was able to gently lift Ethel May from her mother's arms and hand her to the two men. He could then only watch and try to comfort his sobbing wife as they took Ethel May kicking and screaming out through the door and into a waiting cab.

Ethel May was immediately taken to Oxford Railway Station to begin a long and frightening train journey. Ethel and Harry Meads would not see Ethel May again for nine years.

ENTRANCE GATES TO PRINCESS MARYS

3

INCARCERATION

Ethel May was taken by train from Oxford to Addlestone, near Weybridge, Surrey, where she was deposited, shocked, subdued and withdrawn, into the bleak reception area of the *'Princess Marys Home and Industrial School for Girls'*. Clinging desperately to her doll, the bewildered child was taken into the Matron's office to have her arrival registered.

From there she was collected by one of the strict carers and entered a trance-like state as, with no kind or reassuring words of explanation, Rosebud was pulled away from her and stuffed into her suitcase. Hair-ribbons were removed and tucked into the carer's' pocket and her long, curly hair, roughly cropped short. The severed hair was carefully tied into bunches, ready to be sold to wig-makers. Her own colourful clothes were stripped away and replaced with grey flannel knickers, vest and petticoat: she was made to don a black school dress with a white apron, a black cloak, then black stockings and shoes: A white scarf was tied around her young neck and finally a black beret was placed on her clipped head. The suitcase, still full of all her precious possessions and Rosebud, was confiscated.

The middle-aged Housemother, Miss Fitzhugh, who wore a black dress which covered her from neck to floor, topped by a black lace bonnet, took Ethel to her house and up to the dormitory. Ethel May was allotted a small metal-framed bed with a urine stained, horsehair mattress, a sheet, thin grey blanket and one small, stained pillow. A wicker basket, to hold any items supplied by the school, was tucked under the bed. Timid and frightened she joined the other girls within the house and so began her life as an inmate of Princess Marys.

The effect on the five year old child was absolutely devastating. She thought her mother and father no longer wanted her because of something she had done and whatever that awful misdemeanour was, it had brought this dark fate upon her. She was to learn that Princess Mary's had been founded, in 1872, by two wealthy supporters of orphaned children, Caroline

Cavendish and Susan Meredith. They felt that several cottages surrounding an open green were better for their purpose than a solid, monolithic block. It initially opened to house the children of prisoners and was to be called 'Mrs Meredith's Prison School'. But this was changed after a kind, timely comment by Princess Mary Adelaide, granddaughter of King George the third, who remarked that the school name would inevitably stigmatize the children as having come from a 'prison school'. This resulted in the name being changed to Princess Marys Industrial School, but, it failed to stop it becoming universally recognised as one of the cruellest orphanages in Britain.

Ethel May joined 200 girls who were all housed in the separate cottages, with most of the staff located in a house of their own. There was also a school hall, chapel and a small infirmary. The cottages were sparsely furnished with essential and practical items only. There was a kitchen, dining room, toilet, locker room and three bedrooms, each with six beds. So, every cottage housed eighteen girls and one house mistress. There was no mains water or electricity, so water had to be fetched from stand pipes in the grounds and a strict weekly ration of a pound and a half of candles was supplied for light. Once the candle ration was exhausted, the cottage remained in darkness from dusk till dawn.

Ethel May's House Mistress, Miss Gilbarta Fitzhugh, was a peevish Scottish woman who suffered from a crumbling spine which endowed her with a small, bent, stature. She wore metal rimmed spectacles and possessed a craving for gin. Her teeth hadn't seen a dentist's drill for many a year and so most were just brown stumps or missing altogether, which made her breath foul and her smile demonic. She frightened the living daylights out of most of her charges. However, she enjoyed the luxury of her own carpeted staircase, bedroom and comfortable sitting room, with an open fire. Miss Fitzhugh was a Methodist disciplinarian and ruled over 'her' girls with a rod of bamboo. She was a bully and delighted in the intimidation of her charges; especially after indulging in 'mothers-ruin'. The girls always knew when she had partaken as she would totter sideways and slur her words. They soon learned that they had to be careful what they got up to. Her stair carpet semi-muffled her approach, but as she could only take one step at a time, it mostly gave them ample time to scurry back to their own beds.

If passages of the Bible were not read and fully-understood by an 'inmate', as Miss Fitzhugh referred to them, a girl would have nothing to eat or drink unless she wrote out the passage over and over and over again or until she developed a clearer understanding and could describe the *accepted* meaning. If their fingers got sore and bled whilst doing this, it was, "God's will" and "Divine punishment" not hers.

Ethel May cried a lot during her early incarceration, but, due to taking of the 'clear nectar', it went unheard by Miss Fitzhugh. Had she heard Ethel May she would have severely punished her. As she was wont to say in her broad Scottish accent, "Weakness will na be tolerated here gels and one day yer will thank me for instilling the strength of our Lord within yer."

If she caught one of the girls glaring back at her, she would call her out in the middle of the room and say, "Eh gel, yer look is as black as the Earl of

Hells waistcoat. I'll gie ye a skelpit lug." Having given the unfortunate girl a clip around the ear, she would be locked in the cupboard.

When they heard the house mother's loud snoring, the girls often crept into each other's beds to try and salvage some scrap of comfort. Ethel May who had been a sheltered child from birth, made one particular friend. Hannah, a six year old with an exotically dark complexion, was the pole opposite of Ethel. She was bold and brimming with confidence, extremely thin and her head was topped off by an unruly mass of dark brown curls. Her swarthy, Barbadian father, a sailor, absconded long before she was born. She was placed in Princess Mary's because her mother, who had been a housemaid to a wealthy family 'up-north', was confined to a prison workhouse for stealing leftover food and some worn-out children's clothing which her employer had asked her to dispose of. It was mostly Hannah who encouraged and taught Ethel May to talk. This evolving friendship made their lives tolerable and they soon became inseparable, more like sisters. They shared everything, much relished past-life memories, the drudgery and grind of chores and the relentless punishment.

Every morning, come rain, snow or shine, the whole school had to line up and drill around the quadrangle in full school uniform. Only death or serious disease would allow them to miss it without grim consequences. Once she got used to this discipline, Ethel didn't mind the drills at all, it allowed her to see the garden and hear the birds' early morning chorus. It also reminded her there was an outside world and that one day she might be part of it.

Princess Mary's was always short of money and had to take in public washing to help make ends meet. Over 2,500 items of filthy linen were collected every week, which earned the school in the region of £750 a year. A donated donkey and cart became a recognised sight locally as it collected regular loads of dirty laundry from private estates and well-to-do houses of the area. It was, however, the pupils who had to do all the washing and ironing, by hand. Delicate, more personal items were washed by the youngest girls, such as Ethel May and Hannah, in stone sinks filled with warm water and harsh soap flakes. Their soft hands soon became red-raw and needed Vaseline rubbed into them every night, or they couldn't carry out their work. When they were older, Ethel and Hannah had to help with the main laundry. As they went into the vast sheds in which this was done for the first time, they were hit by clammy, hot air and found the noise and smell of bleach, smoke and sweat, so overpowering, it made them both vomit. No one ever got used to that stench.

There were dozens of girls working in the main laundry sheds deployed in teams to sort through heaps of smelly, dirty linen and clothes, spread all over the stone floor. The washing had to be separated into three piles; whites first, coloureds next and industrial, which meant filthy or infected with excrement or pus, last.

To get all the boiling hot water needed to cope with such vast amounts of washing, huge cast-iron pots were set up on bricks in the back yard and at 5am every morning the groundsmen built fires under them to heat the water ready for the day. Soapy water was prepared in smaller tubs and clear rinse water in others. A 'rub board' was slid into the washing tub and, after a five minute soak, clothes were scrubbed on it. Then a 'dolly', a stout broomstick with three pointed prongs attached to the end, was used to manually rotate the washing. The other end of the broom was used to lift the washing from one tub to the other and both Ethel May and Hannah got scalded many times carrying out that operation.

After rinsing, the clothes were fed through a giant mangle to squeeze out much of the water, which was a two girl task. They were then hung out with clothes-pins on rope clotheslines slung across the yards until hoisted high by pulleys. Hopefully the sun and wind would dry the clothes enough to be brought inside before dark. On winter days, the girl's wet hands turned purple with cold before all the clothes were hung up to dry. Sometimes the clothes would freeze as they were pinned to the line, becoming as stiff as boards. In that state they never dried, so frozen fingers had to take them down and shake off the ice before they could be taken inside to dry.

The next part of the process was ironing. The dry clothes were mostly dipped in starch, a white stiffening agent extracted from potatoes and grain to give a stiffer, smarter finish, but as this cost a halfpenny extra per article, few clients bothered. However, starched or not, all washing had to be sprinkled with water, rolled-up tightly in a sheet or pillow case to get slightly damp through and through before ironing. The flat irons were solid, extremely heavy and heated on a stove with the handles wrapped in cloth to prevent hand burns. The clothes had to be ironed to perfection. Some girls never got the hang of this and were punished. Their wet hands caned for not achieving the demanded finish. Caning wet hands increased the pain! Finally items were weighed, then, either hung on hangers or folded neatly, ready to be placed into baskets with a handwritten bill-note and returned to the owners with a request for prompt and full payment. This work all needed to be achieved alongside the girls' regular lessons and chores.

The girls were also taught basic cookery, with this finer food going to the governors, not the girls, and to clean; the idea being that they would be ready to go 'into service' when they left Princess Marys at fourteen.

They also had to make their own clothes and stockings or socks. A much welcomed sewing room, complete with a prized Singer sewing machine, was donated by Queen Mary who was the mother of the school's namesake, Princess Mary.

Rich benefactors were encouraged to support individual girls for one shilling a week, although neither Ethel May or Hannah was ever one of those. Another property, Homelands, lay within the site. There were twenty six girls housed in there having been 'rescued' from brothels, prostitution or sexual abuse. As there was no government support or supervision, special 'benefactors' were also found to support those girls, but for *two* shillings a week. But within that house, paid and unconscionable carers allowed benefactors private visits with their chosen girls.

The daily routine for five year old Ethel began at 7am, when she washed, dressed and performed in-household chores. Breakfast, which consisted of bread, one knob of sugar and watered milk, was served in the austere dining room and followed by morning parade and drill. Lessons were in the hall from 9am till noon.

They went back to their own cottages for a meagre lunch of thin, tasteless cabbage and rice soup. Afternoon lessons were from 1.30pm till 4pm, followed by more chores. Ethel May helped as the girls prepared their own very basic evening meal of bread and cheese or fish paste, which was eaten at 5.30pm. They were then free to read assigned books, sew or to say their prayers till bed and total silence.

When Ethel was eight she became an an 'older girl' and her daily regime changed. She was up by 5.30am to start dealing with the never ending piles of laundry. Then a porridge breakfast followed by morning drill and lessons until 11.30am. After this it was the tasteless rice and cabbage soup, followed by more washing. This work went on until 7 pm, then, after a meagre supper of bread, margarine and black treacle, it was time for prayers and bed. The only treat Ethel or Hannah received was being allowed home-made marmalade on their bread on Christmas Day.

A 'cat-o-nine-tails', a whip with nine leather straps attached, was used to humble and punish girls caught after running away or stealing food. If anyone wet the bed they were made to stand outside on the roof until their sheets dried in the wind, and then taken back in, wash them and hang them out to dry again. If they remained damp in the evening, they still had to sleep in them. Many girls, as a direct result of this treatment and a lack of decent food, died from chest infections such as consumption (TB), bronchitis or pneumonia. Illness was rife. Ringworm (a fungal disease transmitted through infected bedding) and scabies (a highly contagious skin disease marked by intense itching, inflammation, and red lumps). Fleas were rife and easily spread. During her time there, Ethel suffered from ringworm, chicken pox, bronchitis and many flea infestations.

The Sunday Collect, a prayer, had to be learned and memorised every week by all girls over seven years. Failure to do so resulted in not being allowed to eat. Girls were habitually punished with thrashings or solitary confinement, where they were locked into small cupboards and given only bread and water. This could be for the most trivial of misdemeanours, such as picking a garden flower, singing, talking in bed, looking out of the windows during lessons and many more. Ethel's 'crimes' were: being caught, twice, in Hannah's bed, passing some of her food to other girls, making daisy chains and grinning in chapel. On each count she was dragged or marched to the small cubbyhole and locked in for 24 hours. Initially, these punishments would make her scream out loud, bang on the door until her hands bled and pinch and scratch herself. But after a year or so, she became hardened and unfazed by the penance. She learned to transport herself far away from all the hatefulness and in her mind she would return to the water meadow walks she had loved so much with her mother and father. She remembered her mother's delicious food, the smell of her father's leather jacket, the sound of his motorbike engine as they sat in the sidecar: her Mum's favoured Bluebell perfume and the scent of damp grass as they put down rugs and laid out their picnics. She fondly remembered picking wild flowers with her Mum and swimming in the cool waters of the river. What wonderful days they were and how she ached to be back home with them and in her pretty bedroom in Oxford.

There was one art teacher of whom Ethel became very fond. Miss Childs joined the school in 1917, when Ethel was in her third year. Miss Mavis Childs, Mivie as she asked to be called when they were alone, was quite a catch for the institution. She was a school friend of Princess Mary and had only agreed to teach at the school after a visit where she was deeply saddened to note that none of the inmates were allowed the opportunity to develop any artistic talents they might have. She was provided with her own small apartment and allowed to invite any girls, showing artistic promise, to visit her there.

Miss Childs was a highly respected artist. She was kind, patient and inspired confidence in her students. She soon encouraged Ethel to take more interest in drawing and painting, the best of which were regularly displayed on the art room walls for all to see. Ethel May blossomed under her encouragement and spent many contented hours with her tutor over the next three years. They were even allowed to escape into the nearby fields now and then, to draw or paint whatever took their fancy. Ethel's existence began to revolve around her times with Miss Childs and her art lessons. She was always early for their days out and had her drawing paraphernalia and easel ready long before her teacher or any of the other girls appeared.

Towards the autumn of 1920, Miss Childs insisted on getting out into the fresh air more and more, even on damp, cold days. Ethel didn't mind this; in fact she relished being outside and enjoyed her periods of freedom from the oppressive atmosphere of the institution, even if they did have to shorten later outings due to an incessant cough Miss Childs had developed.

One morning, Ethel was disappointed to find that Miss Childs was not well enough to hold her usual teaching session due to ill health and before long her lessons stopped altogether. Ethel asked for and obtained special permission to visit her teacher in her private apartment. She could hear her coughing even before she knocked on her bedroom door.

"Come in," rasped Miss Childs.

Ethel was completely taken aback to see how frail her adored tutor had become. Her skin had taken on a yellowish hue and her eyes, which used to be so bright and a vivid blue, were now sunken, red-edged and lifeless. Ethel faltered as she moved towards the bed, desperately trying to hide the alarm she felt. The skeletal figure lying within the bed recognised and understood her visitor's shock.

"Ethel, please do not come any closer", she whispered. "It is wonderful to see you my dear, but, as you can see, my health will not allow me to join you for our cherished lessons. Not for the moment".

Even saying these few words seemed to take her breath way and she began to cough uncontrollably. She lifted a blood-stained, cotton handkerchief to her mouth and, as a nurse entered the room, they both frantically waved Ethel away. Ethel couldn't take her eyes off her teacher as she backed out of the room. The nurse's soothing words and that dreadful cough followed her as she ran down the stairs and out from the building.

No amount of crying would erase the fright of seeing her idol in such a state of despair. She prayed that she would soon recover and they could resume their painting together, but, it was not to be. Ethel never saw Miss Childs again. She was taken to a London hospital that night and passed away within a few days. She died of tuberculosis.

The loss of Miss Childs left a hollow gap in Ethel's life, compounded a few weeks later by losing the company of her close friend, Hannah. Hannah's mother had a new man in her life who issued a written guarantee to put a roof over their heads and support them all, once she and her daughter were released.

Hannah and Ethel were granted one last walk in the countryside together. They held hands as they wandered along the now familiar lanes and out into the open fields above the school. As they sat on the damp grass they gazed down at the grey complex of the school and talked of what they would do one day when they were both free. Hannah mused that it would be wonderful if they could simply run away, there and then. Ethel agreed, but imagined the beating they would get and the possibility of five years in prison if they were tracked down and caught. They both knew that they had to return and face whatever the future held for them. Hannah had no idea where she would be living, but promised to write and let Ethel know and to visit her when she too found freedom.

The next day Ethel accompanied her friend out of the house and up to the gates where her mother and her new man were waiting. After discharge paperwork was exchanged, Hannah had a small suitcase given to her. She had not seen it since her entry into the School some years before. Her mother was asked to inspect the meagre contents and confirm that everything her daughter had arrived with was there. As soon as this was done, the girls sobbed as they embraced each other and said their final goodbyes.

As she walked away to her new life, Hannah turned and called, "Pray for me Ethel. I will write as soon as we get settled and you will know where to come when you are free."

"I will. Don't forget me Hannah" Ethel shouted, "I will come and see you very soon, I hope".

Ethel never knew what happened to her dearest friend because she was never allowed to receive any letters from anyone. So she never knew if Hannah had tried to keep her promise. However, as a senior girl, she had to turn her attention to helping newly arrived young girls settle in and avoid her own innocent pitfalls. This helped to ease her pain at the loss of her friend and the teacher she so admired.

Walking back from the laundry, a few months after the death of Miss Child, Ethel saw girls and teachers running towards her cottage. She joined the throng gathering outside the front door and saw Miss Fitzhugh lying in a mangled heap at the foot of the stairs. She was being attended by the school physician and both nurses from the sickbay. Apparently, the poor wretch had fallen down the stairs and broken her neck. Miss Fitzhugh was dead, but it was impossible for the girls not to feel anything other than relief at her passing. Perhaps, subject to her replacement, there would be no more bullying. No more daily recitals, bleeding hands or beatings. Her replacement turned out to be one of the most senior girls from the school. She had been recruited on the day she was given her freedom and to the relief of all, the cottage became a better and happier place to live. Later the news filtered through to the inhabitants of Miss Fitzhugh's house that she had once been married and had born two daughters, but her husband and both girls had died of Tuberculosis long before she became a house mother at Princess Mary's. It was thought this is what turned her heart to stone and initiated her dependence on gin.

Excitement was hard to contain in 1921 when the girls were informed that Queen Mary, wife of King George V, was to visit the School. This meant that the houses, common parts and grounds had to be made immaculate and on the day, all girls were up at dawn and made to wash and don a clean uniform. Their white aprons were starched so much that they stood up on their own. Ethel lined up, with the whole school, in front of the flag pole. With a huge Union Jack flapping above their heads they gave a rapturous rendition of '*Jerusalem*' as Her Majesty and full entourage of Lords, Ladies and officials, drove into the school grounds. They would never have guessed that some of the girls had been severely punished to ensure they were word perfect and sang in key.

However all that was forgotten in awe of the grace and beauty of the Queen and her followers, the clothes, beautifully crafted hats and shoes, their fragrance and the way they seemed to effortlessly glide across the courtyard. Not one girl would ever forget her first meeting with her Queen. After an accompanied walk over to the main house and through one of the cottages, Queen Mary generously shook most of the girls' hands, not knowing that half of them had fleas and the other half ringworm. At that time, Ethel had both!

Later that year, not long after the Queen's visit, several reports filtered out about the number of girls dying or running away and the school was reported to the Home Office. The police were ordered to mount an investigation and it was only then that the abuse and neglect of the girls was finally uncovered. The result was that a high proportion of the staff were sacked, many ledgers and records redacted and a whole new regime took over the running of the School.

There was a notable change and the girls were, at long last, treated in a more humane manner, even if most of the new staff were also cold and aloof. They were finally given a smidgen of education, but still made to do the town's laundry, clean the kitchens, scrub the wooden floors, tables and black-lead the huge stoves. Their diet, although still meagre, was improved and more attention was paid to the quality and preparation of the food. Although abusive treatment, even cruelty, was still metered out by some house mistresses and teachers, it was not as intolerably life-threatening as before.

Ethel May was well aware that something had happened, but the pupils were never told why everything had changed and their lives made a little easier. Ethel's internment at the Home became more tolerable and in her final years she began to learn how to prepare and cook high quality food for the new Board of Directors. She was also taught to serve them properly in their special dining room.

With her honesty and guidance, Ethel gained the trust of the young, new inmates and she did all she could to help teach and protect them. She discovered that she had been blessed, perhaps through her early life with the Meads, with an aptitude to instinctively understand and respond to the needs of others.

****

Ethel, my mum, told me that this period of her life was to provide her with the qualities she would need to get her through some of her most gruelling times to come; it equipped her with the inner strength to cope, without which she would surely not have survived. Ellen, my grandmother, asked that I not judge her. She told me that she never regretted her decision to give mum away. She always held it was in very different times and in very difficult circumstances.

St Marys Morning Parade

4

WALK TO FREEDOM

In 1923, well past the middle of her fourteenth year, Ethel was told to wash her hair, clean her teeth and dress in her Sunday best. She had been summoned to appear before the school governors. As she entered the room, no attempt was made to put her at her ease. She was told to sit in front of a table of four very stern looking men and two self-righteous looking women.

The Chairman opened proceedings.

"Ethel, now that you are fourteen years of age, you can no longer remain at Princess Marys. You are to be released on licence to live with a trustworthy and respectable parent."

The woman on his right interjected. "Do you feel able to return to your family and live an honest and industrious life, young lady?"

Ethel was caught off-guard and simply stared at them. Had she heard correctly? Was she really being told she could go home?

"Well?" said the woman "Speak up girl or we shall think you are not ready."

"Yes ma-am," she stammered, "I'm more than ready to return home."

"Do you understand what 'Released on Licence' means Ethel?" asked the Chairman. "It means," he continued pompously, without waiting for her answer, "that you must remain within the designated family home until you are fifteen and one half years old. There will be three-monthly reviews as to your behaviour. If you are lawless or try to abscond, you will face a workhouse prison sentence of up to five years."

Questions followed as to her suitability to live within the community again. Ethel gave her considered responses, hoping they would convince them that she was indeed ready to go home.

The Chairman gave no indication as to whether or not she had been successful and told her that she was now free to leave the room and would receive their decision later that day.

As Ethel turned to leave, she couldn't help but wonder why the committee felt the need to issue her with such dire warnings and perplexed by their line of questioning. Why on earth would they think she would ever want to escape from Ethel and Harry Meads' home? She was about to close the heavy, mahogany door, when one of the board members asked if he could speak with her on another matter. He showed her into a small office and indicated towards a chair.

"Please sit down, Ethel."

She was surprised to hear a board member say 'please' as no one there ever felt the need to say please or thank you to the inmates. He then asked her if she would consider staying on and working at the school as a cook or teacher, he did not seem to mind which, so long as she stayed there.

Although terrified as to what his reaction might be, she thanked him for his kind offer, but, she wanted to get home to her parents. He was obviously disappointed. He told her she had impressed 'The Board' and if she changed her mind there would always be a place for her at Princess Marys. He also told her that she would be free to leave the school in a few days' time.

Ethel was beside herself with joy as she walked away from that room. After nine long, harrowing and often painful years she was finally free and on her way back to her parents. She immediately wrote to the Meads with the good news. They were equally thrilled, but surprised that the school had not informed them directly that Ethel was to be released into their care. However, delighted to be getting their daughter back they sent her fashionable new clothes and money for the train fare back to Oxford.

A few days later, Ethel, dressed in her new finery, was escorted out of the cottage that had been her home for so long and into the reception hall she had first seen as a five year old.

The recently appointed headmistress, Miss Cooper, was at her desk and actually smiled at Ethel as she beckoned her into her office and indicated that she should sit in the armchair opposite her. She offered her a cup of tea which made Ethel begin to feel extremely nervous and she wondered what on earth did the headmistress have to say, that prompted the need for tea?

As a school girl maid poured the tea and plated up some biscuits, the headmistress looked at the well-spoken, bright young lady in front of her, who was clearly brimming-over with hope and anticipation. She felt sickened at the news she was about to impart to the poor thing.

"Ethel, I have been delving into your background and I feel that there are things you need to know before you leave here today."

Ethel shifted to the edge of her seat, sensing that this was not going to be something she wanted to hear.

Miss Cooper continued in a soothing voice.

"There is no kind or easy way to say this my dear, but Mr and Mrs Meads are not in fact your birth parents. You were fostered by them at the age of seven months, until you were forcibly removed from their care at five years of age."

She hesitated, allowing the unwanted revelation to land on those young shoulders before continuing.

"It seems that your birth mother faced insurmountable difficulties when your father died, only six months after your premature birth. She wanted you to have a loving home, with both a mother and father, so she allowed the Meads to become your guardians. But, as no legal adoption papers were ever signed, you remain the responsibility of your birth mother, Ellen Bryan. Your mother, who remarried a few years ago, is now called Ellen Couldry." Her voice began to falter as she continued. "You also have an older sister, fifteen year old Ruby Flo………," her voice trailed off as Ethel jumped up and threw herself over the front of the large, mahogany desk.

"I'm Ethel Meads, Miss Cooper; you're mistaking me for someone else. I'm going home to my mother and father, Harry and Ethel Meads today. The train leaves in an hour and it's taking me to Oxford, where they live. It's my home!"

A disconcerted Miss Cooper came from behind her desk to take the frantic girl in her arms. She had yet another hammer-blow to deliver.

"Ethel, there is no mistake. You will still be catching the Oxford train my dear, but you will be going to your real mother's home, she also lives in Oxford. As cruel and shocking as it may seem Ethel, in order to comply with the law, you have to go and live with Ellen and William Couldry, at least until you are fifteen and a half. If you don't, you face going to prison for a very long time. Once you are of age, you can live wherever you please, but for now ……."

Ethel pushed Miss Cooper away and collapsed back into her seat. To numb for tears, she sat there in disbelief, bewilderment and isolation.

Desperate to bring the uncomfortable meeting to a close, Miss Cooper handed Ethel the small, brown leather suitcase, which had originally been so carefully packed for her by Mrs Meads nine years before. She asked Ethel to open it and check that everything was there. As a stunned Ethel, still reeling with shock, tried to get up and do as she was bid, her legs buckled, her world went black and she collapsed.

As the smelling salts under her nose did their work and jerked her back to consciousness, she coughed and vomited across the thickly carpeted floor. Miss Cooper was well used to dealing with girls in these situations, but it was usually because their parents had died or been sent back into prison. It was never quite as complicated as it was for this poor girl.

When Ethel recovered, she was grateful to accept the proffered tea and begin to take stock of what she had been told. She recognised that the headmistress was being very sympathetic and unusually kind. She had a million questions in her head, but asked only a few and the head answered her as thoroughly and patiently as she could, before reminding Ethel of the small, somewhat over-stuffed, suitcase which remained unopened in front of her and asking her to open it and check the contents.

As Ethel slowly unclipped the two clasps, it sprang open and the first thing she saw, embedded on the top of all her childhood clothes, was Rosebud! As she gently lifted her beloved friend out from the case, she began to weep, not ordinary tears, but struggling for breath sobbing which engulfed her whole body and being. She was inconsolable. Slumping back into the chair she felt betrayed and totally alone. But, after a while, she noticed that Rosebud had slipped to the floor and was looking up at her with a smile on her beautiful, familiar face. It reminded her of her 'mum and dad' and their days spent all together in the meadows of her beloved Cowley. She had their recent letter in her pocket and was wearing the new clothes her 'mother' had chosen for her. She remembered that they still loved her and were also waiting for her; for now that was enough!

Ethel scooped up Rosebud and, getting to her feet, closed her case. She recognised and accepted that she had suffered an irrecoverable loss, but now it was time to leave the school behind and find out what lay ahead. She thanked Miss Cooper and told her it was time for her to go. Collecting her larger case, which contained the rest of her lovely new clothes, she walked out from Princess Marys and never looked back.

'Princess Marys Cottages'

Oxford Railway

5

THE HOMECOMING

When Ellen Couldry, formally Bryan, awoke early on the morning of December 20th 1923, it took a moment to remember why a cloud of doom was about to envelop her. It was a day she had always known would arrive. Ethel May was coming back into her life.

She never wanted to tell her second husband and her older daughter, Ruby, of Ethel's existence, it was her own guilty secret, but the visit from the solicitor changed all that. She kept putting it off but eventually, with only two weeks to go, she summed up the courage to tell them. It gave them little time as a family, to plan and get used to the idea.

William Couldry loved his wife deeply and didn't want to upset her. He was taken aback by the revelation, but managed to conceal his disappointment and convinced Ellen that he understood and accepted her reasons. His experience in The Great War had instilled a sense of what was important in life and his new family was paramount.

But, for Ruby, the news was devastating and not something she was prepared to come to terms with.

"Surely you don't expect me to accept a complete stranger into my home," she ranted. "Well, I won't! You've already made me accept a new father, now you're expecting me to welcome a long lost sister. Well, I won't! I won't!"

Ellen tried to reason with her, explaining that it was only for a short time, to comply with the law, but Ruby was still reeling from the news and fiercely antagonistic, especially on that day. Her unwanted sister was due to arrive by train at Oxford Station at 8pm. Her step father was going to the station to meet her, but she would not go with him. Appearing keen to welcome the interloper was the last thing she wanted.

However, due to a fortunate connection at Reading, Ethel had arrived two hours early and not wishing to while away the time outside the cold, dark station, used the money she had received from the Meads to take a taxi to Summertown for the last few miles of her journey. So her arrival outside Ellen's door was, as her birth, premature.

When someone knocked on the door, Ruby refused to go, so Ellen went to the door and peered out into the darkness. George Street was dimly lit with few gas lamps but she could make out the silhouette of a young, slim woman on the doorstep.

"Can I help you?" She asked the question abruptly, without making a connection with the expected arrival of her daughter, but gasped in amazement when the caller stepped forward into the light from the hall way. It was an impeccably dressed young lady, carrying two suitcases. High cheek boned and slim she was a mirror image of her younger self and spoke in a pleasant, educated voice.

"Hello. I'm looking for Ellen Bryan."

Ellen quickly regained her composure.

"Oh, it's you Ethel. You're early. My name's Ellen Couldry now. You might as well come in and meet your sister."

From what Miss Cooper had told her about her situation and birth mother, Ethel was not expecting a warm welcome, but she was taken aback by the cold abruptness. It was obvious she was not welcome and even more so when Ellen introduced her to Ruby, who joined them in the hallway.

"So, you're here then, little orphan girl. You might as well know I won't be treating you as a sister. As far as I'm concerned, you don't exist. It wouldn't worry me if you had to go to prison. Anything would be better than having you here."

Ellen stepped between them.

"That's enough of that, Ruby. It's inconvenient for all of us, but we'll just have to get along and stay within the law. It won't be for long; Ethel will be old enough to leave us in eighteen months' time."

"That's forever!" wailed Ruby. "She will have destroyed my life by then!"

"As I say, Ruby, we'll just have to rub along. Now, go and make a pot of tea while I show Ethel her bedroom."

"I'm expected to be a servant now, am I? Well, just this once! Don't expect me to make it a habit!"

Ruby flounced into the kitchen as Ellen moved to the foot of the stairs.

"The stairs are very steep. You'll have to carry your cases up one at a time."

Ethel chose the small brown case and followed Ellen up the narrow staircase, where she led her to a door at the end of the landing.

"This will be your bedroom."

Ellen closed the door behind them.

"Ethel, I consider the past to be a closed book. I never want to discuss your fostering or the reasons behind it. It was a long time ago when things were very different. I'm sure you would agree that we all have new lives now and it can do no good to dwell on the past."

Ethel said nothing, merely nodding her acceptance. The situation may seem intolerable for Ruby, but for her it was a stepping stone to the future. However, she could not help but wonder how Ruby would have coped with the deprivations and hardships of Princess Marys.

To give her her due, Ruby made a good pot of tea and did proffer a large plate of nicely arranged biscuits towards her. Ethel took one and thanked her politely, but, apart from that exchange there was little in the way of conversation until William, Ellen's second husband, arrived home. He had been attending a local club's Christmas Luncheon and, being in a jovial mood, he made a more concerted effort to put his new step-daughter at her ease. He put his arms around her.

"So you're the prodigal daughter. Well, welcome home lass. I'm back early t'meet you from railway station, but as you've saved me t'walk, least I can do is carry yon suitcase up t'stairs."

Ethel's step-father, William Couldrey, had married Ellen in May 1915. He was thirty five and very tall. He had a kind face and still had lots of dark hair above his heavy spectacles. He proudly told Ethel that he was from Yorkshire and a Mechanical Driver in the Army Service Corp. He seemed kind and accepting of her and her unexpected arrival in their home.

Ellen and William's house in George Street, Summertown was a flat-fronted, Victorian three up and two down, terraced house. It was very clean and well furnished. The scullery was at the rear of the house and the privy at the bottom of the long, narrow garden. There was, of course, no bathroom, no heating other than coal fires and only the one cold water tap over a stone sink in the kitchen. Because no one, other than William and Ruby, had been told that Ellen had another child, no one else was aware of Ethel's existence and Ellen wanted to keep it that way. Ethel was only to be with them until her School Licence expired. She could then go and live with the Meads. She was warned to maintain the secrecy of her background and would have to remain upstairs when visitors called. Should she be questioned, she was a visiting relative.

Ruby was much larger and more robust than her sibling and initially extremely jealous of her younger, prettier sister, a sister suddenly thrust upon her. She had grown up with her mother all to herself and had not the slightest intention of sharing her affections with this unfamiliar interloper. She had her own life and circle of friends and the last thing she would want was for them to find out about Ethel. Consequently she treated Ethel as if she was not there.

Receiving such treatment could have been upsetting, but Ethel quickly put it into perspective and at the first opportunity went to see Mr and Mrs Meads. Their reunion could not have been more different. As they opened their front door they instantly recognised the elegant, young woman as the five year old they had had to part with. So when Ethel mouthed. "Hello mum, hello dad" they were overjoyed that their girl had finally come home. She was immediately scooped up into Harry's arms and carried into the house: the home she had dreamed of for so many years. There were so many things that needed to be explained to Ethel: why they had 'adopted' her in the first place: why she had been taken to Princess Marys: why their gifts had never arrived and their pleas for visits refused. But, all this could wait and be explained in time, for now, it was Christmas!

Together again, they would celebrate her return. For Ethel, it was as if nine Christmases had come all at once when she celebrated Christmas 1923 with the Meads. There were no presents bought for her in the Couldry household, Ellen said they did not have the money to fritter away on such luxuries. In the Meads household it was a very different matter. All the remaining members of their family trooped round to welcome her back into the fold and Ethel was showered with the most wonderful gifts.

Never in her wildest dreams during her internment, did she envisage that one day she would be shown so much love and affection. Ethel remained with the Meads until after the New Year celebrations, but had to return to her designated home with the intention of escaping as frequently as she could, which suited Ellen. It gave her the ideal opportunity to suggest to the Meads that it would be best if they bought all the clothes Ethel required. The Meads jumped at the chance, as it meant they could be stored in Ethel's own room, awaiting her permanent return to them. They met her in Oxford's finest department stores to buy coats, shoes and dresses. Ethel, who had never worn such lovely clothes, adored trying on the latest modern designs and as she looked at herself in full length
mirrors, she became aware that she was changing from a girl to a young woman. She possessed an alluring and shapely figure.

From that point, Ethel rapidly grew accustomed to normal life and relished her new-found freedom and independence.

Sister Helen Irene at St Johns Convent

6

INTO THINE ARMS

The Meads were lifelong enthusiasts and active supporters of their local commune of nuns, The Society of All Saints Sisters of the Poor, who inhabit and manage St. Johns Convent in St. Marys Road, Cowley.

During Ethel's early childhood she always accompanied them to their various charitable events. The nuns, cloistered within their walls, had taken great delight in entertaining baby Ethel May and were more than happy to amuse her whilst her diligent 'parents' presided over fund-raising tasks. Once again, Ethel joined her 'parents' in supporting the Convent and spent much of her time in companionship with the older nuns in 'God's waiting room'. She enjoyed being there so much she arranged to take full-time employment there when she reached fifteen and a half. So it was that on the first of April 1924, Ethel tied back her hair, donned her brand new grey and white striped dress, complete with highly starched collar, cuffs and white apron and began work as a junior nursing auxiliary at St. Johns Home. As was customary for a mother of a student nurse, Mrs Meads bought her a black petersham belt with an individually designed, silver 'nurses' buckle which fastened the belt around the waist; this clasp was highly prized and would be the one worn throughout the nurse's entire career. She would also have to get used to being called 'Bryan', as all nurses were called by their surnames, never their forenames.

Ethel was welcomed with open arms by the Reverend Sisters, especially Sisters Verena, Elizabeth Noel and Helen Irene. These gentle and caring nuns treated her as if she were their own, long-lost daughter and taught her how to give compassionate and practised care to the more fragile patients, mostly nuns and clergy, in the last days of their lives.

Ethel attended chapel with Sister Verena and learned the ritualistic ways of religion in convent life. She loved her work in St. John's. It was the beginning of a rewarding lifetime and life-saving relationship with the Sisters of All Saints at St. Johns. It was also the foundation for Ethel May's life-long vocation in nursing and caring.

Mary, one of her first patients was 105 years old. She was not a nun, but a trained nurse, who was revered within the Home because in 1854 she had sailed with Florence Nightingale to Constantinople and served in the Crimean War. She then joined 'The Lady with the Lamp' in setting up St. Thomas' Hospital,

London in 1860 and the Nightingale Training School established within it.

Mary was totally deaf by the time Ethel was caring for her, but being well practised in communicating with the deaf she soon became the only nurse Mary would allow to carry out her more personal care. She always referred to Ethel, not by her surname but as 'Martha' and her voice would boom down the corridor as she called for 'Martha' to wash her feet'.

Religious and devout, Mary had her coffin made, 'ready to meet her Lord', when she was 90. When she finally passed away, peacefully in her sleep at 105, the Irish night nurse, who had dozed off in her chair, nearly died of shock when she awoke to find that her illustrious patient had expired.

Later, in her lilting Irish accent, she told Ethel,

"Sweet Mary, Mother of Jesus, Bryan. I nearly died me-sel when I found her highness stone-dead and as cold as marble." The Irish night nurse was a mere 82 years old!

When she had turned 16, Ethel was on night duty with a fully-trained nurse, when she was told to sit beside the bed of a 90 year old nun, whilst the nurse went off to do her rounds in another ward.

"You watch her Bryan and ring that bell if you notice any change in her, any change at all."

The old nun was very large and in a coma. The small, stone walled 'cell', which she had inhabited for many years, was dimly lit with just as a small night candle on her bedside table. Faint moonlight coming through a small, gothic window, cast an unnerving ghostly light over the old lady's pillow-propped body.

Ethel sat beside her patient, hour after hour, but

as the dying nun's previously laboured breathing became softer, it lulled Ethel to sleep, only to be jolted awake when it stopped altogether. Ethel leant forward to grab the bell, but before she could ring it, the nun sat bolt upright and bellowed out, "It's too cold for sixpence" and fell back, dead! Ethel was almost frightened to death by the eerie experience and when the trained nurse arrived she found Ethel frantically ringing the bell over the dead nun and had to prise it away to make her stop.

As frightening as that was, Ethel's most harrowing experience at St. John's was when she was standing in the entrance hall, talking to a tramp who was begging for food. A wildly distraught mother ran into the Home carrying her child, screaming for someone to save her child. The child, a three year old girl, had been playing in the road outside when she was hit by a passing motor cyclist. Clearly she had suffered severe head and chest wounds. The mother begged Ethel, "Help, help me. She's hurt. For God's sake help us. Don't let her die!"

The limp, unconscious child was placed into Ethel's outstretched arms by the panic-stricken mother. Hearing the agonised screams, Sisters flooded into the hallway. Sister Superior had the child rushed to the Radcliffe Hospital, but there was nothing they could do to resuscitate her. The little girl had died in Ethel's arms.

Although deeply shocked and shaken by the experience, Ethel refused the leave offered to her, she preferred to keep herself occupied rather than sit at home reliving the tragedy. The Sister's held a special service in their beautiful chapel for the little girl, which was attended by everyone from the Home and the child's family and friends. The parents later told Ethel that they felt their daughter had been taken into God's hands at his calling. The fact she had passed away in St. Johns seemed to bring them some vestige of comfort, but Ethel never forgot that horrific incident and it played in her mind every time she walked up the stone stairway into St. Johns.

Captivated by the otherwise gentle life within the convent, Ethel found the yearned for love and companionship which had eluded her for so much of her young life and came to the conclusion that she wanted to become a nun, a fully-fledged member of the religious order. By forsaking the real world and serving God and the local community, she could help the sick and remain within her beloved, cosseted world of St. Johns. It would mean starting a two year postulate programme to become a novice, then taking her initial vows before going on for a further three years to become an Ordained Nun in the 'Taking of the Vows Ceremony'.

At the same time, Ethel got out into the community and found life in the burgeoning city of Oxford exciting. The gift of a bicycle from Harry Meads meant she had the freedom to get about as she pleased and being a good-looking, happy girl she made friends easily, joining in the local young person's life of parties, pubs and boating. Her independent streak and new-found zest for life came to the fore and within the year it fell to Sister Verena to diplomatically explain to her protégée that Reverend Mother and some senior sisters felt that being such a free-spirit, she needed to find her wings outside the convent. Ethel was crestfallen when told the news. She offered to give up her friends and vowed to prove that she was humble enough to join their Order and abide by their beliefs and disciplines. But Sister Verena told her that to give up her friends was not the answer. She needed to enjoy being with her own age group, especially after the years spent cooped-up in Princess Marys. She advised her to give it another couple of years and then see how she felt.

Her wise words were true and Ethel, who was still only seventeen, found the tight disciplines within St. John's conflicted with her burgeoning life outside. So, after further discussions with her mentor and accepting that St. Johns could not in fact give her accredited nurse training, she agreed to leave and seek training as a professional nurse elsewhere. However, she soon discovered she could not begin nurse training at the Radcliff Hospital until she was twenty one and decided to begin her nursing career caring for the elderly within the medical wing of the Cowley Road Workhouse. The place was dismal, the work hard and hours long. Initially she loathed the place. It housed over two hundred elderly poor people and had a fifteen bed maternity unit, there was never enough staff and the governors were reluctant to spend money on the fabric of the building or the workers that toiled within it. Physicians, who preferred fee-paying clients, had little, if any, respect for the nurses and none at all for anyone below the rank of 'State Registered Nurse'. Basic hygiene was mostly ignored and it was felt by the hierarchy that the inhabitants were going to die anyway. Life expectancy for a poor person at that time was about sixty, if they were lucky.

Ethel soon wanted to return to her safe-place, St. Johns. But the workhouse Matron, whom she greatly admired because she cared so much for her patients, persuaded her to stay. She encouraged her to, toughen up and continue with her much appreciated work and promised that if Ethel did this, within a year she would have her transferred to a more tranquil and much coveted post at the children's hospital on Hayling Island. Ethel agreed to stay on and soon found that she was actually enjoying the work and making a much welcomed difference to the lives of the diseased and dying. She also found the support and companionship she sought and eventually stayed for over three years. It was during her third year that her colleague and friend, the Matron, was diagnosed with pancreatic cancer. She died at Cowley Road with Ethel at her side.

The replacement Matron was a cold-hearted woman, indifferent to the patients within her care and Ethel, along with several of her colleagues, soon left the Cowley Road and went to work as auxiliary nurses at the Radcliffe Hospital in St. Giles.

With her open and honest manner, Ethel quickly made new friends and joined in with the trendy social North Oxonian scene. Medical students wined and dined the pretty student nurses, taking them to dances, parties and introducing them to some of the most popular watering holes in Oxfordshire.

A new door opened for Ethel when she attended a friend's party at the Lamb and Flag Inn in St. Giles. A local band was playing and a girl of about her own age came up and asked if she wanted to join her for a drink, A stranger to Oxford she felt isolated from the main gathering. She added, in a strong Welsh accent that she felt daft drinking alone.

The pair hit it off immediately and remained together for the rest of the evening. It was the beginning of a lifelong friendship. Katie was married to a tough Welsh miner called Ifan, Ivan in English. They lived in the Rhondda Valley and had a two year old daughter, Betrys (Welsh for Beatrice). Katie had been seconded to the Radcliffe for specialist experience and was staying with a nurse friend in a bedsit close to the Radcliffe, but was due to return home.

Katie extolled the many virtues of her friendly, beautiful country and told Ethel they were crying out for nurses at her local hospital in Wales. It would be tough work compared to the Radcliffe, but they offered a two year, State Enrolled Nurse training scheme, which would gain Ethel the accreditation she needed and would be accepted anywhere in the UK. As it happened, Katie was returning to Wales the following week, so would Ethel like to accompany her and take a look at what Wales had to offer? Also, if she liked the idea, she would be able to lodge with her and her family for the two years.

Ethel, who liked the idea of remaining close to her new-found friend, eagerly agreed and they caught the train to Wales the following weekend. On the long train journey, Katie took the opportunity to expand more fully on her love for her Country and the allure of the Welsh Valleys. She talked of the genuine warmth of its people and the unbreakable inborn spirit of community. A spirit which had been forged in homes, chapels and on the rugby playing fields, over centuries. Her husband, Ifan, was a member of the local Male

Voice Choir, as were most of the men from their mining village. Not anyone was accepted into those ancient choirs. They had to have clear, beautiful voices, such as her Ifan's and be local miners or sons of local miners.

Within her own area, fanning out above the Welsh capital of Cardiff, 'The Valleys' were the heart of the coalfields of South Wales. They stretched from the Bristol Channel toward the Brecon Beacons and every few miles up and down the valleys, you would see the stark spectacle of tall pit head gear and shaft heads. Katie did, however, warn Ethel that she would have to get used to the black slag heaps, which loomed menacingly over all the mining villages. Colliers, like her husband, had been extracting high quality coal by cutting it directly from the rich seams, from several feet down, to more than a quarter-mile under the surface. During the winter Ifan never saw the sun except on Sundays, going into the pits before daybreak and emerging again after dark. If they had a son, his father would automatically expect him to follow him underground from as early as thirteen years of age. At that point Katie, becoming emotional and began to weep.

"I have no intention of letting any son of mine go down the mines, Ethel. I'll fight to see that he has a decent education to keep him out of that hell-hole." She paused. "But, in my heart, I know I'll have little say in the matter."

"Why not?" asked Ethel, "surely it should be a joint decision?"

"It would go against the spirit of community which exists in the valleys. Miners' wives are expected to make a decent home, often for very large families. They clean, cook and care for the kids all day, every day. As a nurse I'm an exception, but I'm still expected to follow the unwritten rules of our society. All I can do is pray-to-God that our children will all be girls." She then gave Ethel a rueful grin. "So far, it's worked."

Ethel laughed. "It almost sounds as if you're trying to put me off, Katie."

"That's the last thing I want, Ethel. I'm just telling you how it is. Mining's a dangerous business. In the UK a mining death happens every six hours and a serious injury every twelve minutes. Mining communities in The Rhondda Valley suffer as much if not more than most, so in that respect Aberdare General Hospital is a grim place to work. We often feel the underground gas explosions before the siren at the pit-head alerts the community. Wives, mothers and daughters rush there, not knowing if husbands, sons or boyfriends have been killed or maimed. In the hospital all we can do is prepare, wait and pray."

There was a long silence and Ethel felt relieved that their mood lifted when the train slowed as it neared its destination.

"Cardiff, this is Cardiff," said Katie.

Ethel smiled at her friend. "Thanks for telling me as it is, Katie. At least I know what to expect."

When Ethel alighted from the train, her excitement was mixed with a healthy dose of trepidation, at the thought of a new life in Wales. Ifan was at the station to meet them with their young daughter. He was indeed a strapping, very fit young man. He wore a wide smile and had a flirtatious twinkle in his deeply set, brown eyes. He was still in his twenties, but had the soot ingrained face of a coal miner, which made him appear older. He greeted Ethel with a tad more gusto than seemed appropriate, actually kissing her on the mouth. She glanced at her friend, but Katie, busy greeting little Betrys, showed no concern, so Ethel thought it must be the aforementioned, 'warm Welsh welcome'.

Ifan carried the cases, following Katie and Ethel, each holding onto one of Betrys's hands, swinging her back and forth as they made their way to the bus stop. The journey to Aberdare took ages as the valley was shrouded in a dense, cold fog. By the time they arrived it was getting dark and they had to pick their way through puddled gullies in the back lanes of miners' terraced houses. They were crunching over layers of sodden clinkers which had been swept from the coal-fire hearths and tipped there on a daily basis. By the time they reached the house, tired, wet and blackened with soot, Ethel couldn't help but joke that maybe it wasn't such a perfect place to train after all.

In the morning the fog had cleared and the sun shone, which made things seem much brighter. Ethel dressed and went down to the warm, tidy kitchen. It was Sunday, a day reserved for religious worship and rest from toil. Katie was up at daylight and prepared a full Welsh breakfast. She saw Ifan off to a meeting at his local club, knowing he would be back in time to escort them to church. She asked Ethel if she wanted to stay or catch the next train back Oxford. Ethel told her friend she had already unpacked and was looking forward to her interview at Aberdare General the following day.

In her interview, Ethel learned that the hospital provided eighty four beds, which included an accident and emergency ward with two operating theatres attached. The beds were divided by Male and Female wards and a Children's Ward. There was also an Out-Patients Department. The hospital served the local community and regularly dealt with the aftermath of mining accidents within the valley. She was offered a position as a trainee nurse on a State Enrolled Nurse two year course, which meant less technical training and a more practical, hands-on nursing. It was a course which appealed to Ethel, but she was warned that her job would take her straight into the deep end of the Accident and Emergency Unit. She would then work her way through each department until completion of her training, after which, if she wanted to stay, she could elect the department for her permanent post.

Ethel eagerly accepted the job and arranged to return to Wales within a couple of weeks. She had to return to Oxford to tell the Meads of her plans. On learning her news, they told her that although they were sad to see her leave, it was only for two years and they thought it would be good for her, it would certainly expand her horizons, so she would leave with their blessing.

Within weeks Ethel joined her friend and lodged in a bedroom of their small home. On her first day at Aberdare General she was assigned to shadow a bi-lingual nurse. It was difficult as Ethel was the only English girl working within the hospital and with Welsh being the main language, she encountered problems communicating. But with encouragement from Nurse Jenkins and Katie's help to learn a few pertinent words to get by, she eventually became fluent in a mixture of her mother tongue and Welsh.

Ethel found life tough. It was a steep learning curve and she was only on £2 a week. Obviously, as a trained nurse, Katie earned more and Ivor was on £26. Miners also had a generous allowance of free coal, which was dumped on the front door step to be shovelled into a wheelbarrow and hauled through the house into the 'coal-hole'. The house was small, but they adapted to living together. Ethel played her part in helping to look after Betrys and Ifan and it was not long before she was well integrated into the local community.

The work was new and quite frightening. Ethel was used to caring for elderly patients at their natural life's end, not strapping young men rushed into hospital with limbs blown off, or crushed under runaway coal carts. They arrived in an urgent life or death situation. She also had to learn how to respond to the families of the injured as they pleaded for news of their loved ones and wanting to know if their injuries would stop them from further work in the mines. Outside the mines, there was little chance of earning a living in the Rhondda Valley.

Ethel quickly acclimatised and become a reliable, competent member of the Accident and emergency team. With their guidance and support she was soon providing badly injured, highly traumatised miners and their families with compassionate, professional care, both during and after tending to their injuries.

The most damaged patient she ever saw was Ifan's uncle. It was during one of the worst disasters she witnessed whilst in Wales. Everyone in the A&E team felt the unmistakable tremor of an underground explosion. It was a big one, quickly followed by warning sirens from the local Abernant pit. They immediately began to prepare for a panicked influx of miners and their families. Ethel shared their fear, Abernant was the pit Ifan worked in!

As injured and traumatised miners began to arrive, Katie ran into A&E, calling her husband's name. She questioned anyone stumbling in from the mine, pleading to know if Ifan was still underground? He was, but she was assured that he was part of the rescue party, not one of the injured or dead. Then, his uncle was wheeled in. He was unconscious and as black as the coal dust which had engulfed him. His wounds were horrific and they all knew that if his injuries didn't kill him, the infections to follow, certainly would. They fought hard to keep what was left of him alive, but he died when his heart simply gave up the fight and no amount of pummelling would get it going again. He was wheeled away, as were others, to be cleansed in the hospital mortuary.

The A&E team were augmented by other nurses and doctors within the hospital, Katie included and support was requested from other hospitals and district nurses were called in. They worked together tirelessly as a well-practised unit, saving many lives, but four miners died in the disaster and several others sustained life-limiting injuries, such that they would never find work in the mines again.

Eventually, Ifan arrived, coughing, choking and rasping. His throat and lungs were coated with coal dust and smoke, but otherwise unharmed. He was soon followed by his uncle's family, who were desperate for news. Each family was allowed access to their loved ones before they were either taken home, retained for further care, transferred to larger hospitals, or laid-out in the mortuary.

There were over 800 men working in the Abernant Pit and every week, at least one would be killed. Ethel soon realised that the mining communities in Wales lived with tragedy. Death and danger, woven into their fabric of life, bred a particular fatalism in their attitudes. They considered themselves lucky if they got through each passing year in one piece, let alone alive.

Recognition for her compassionate and diligent work came when Nurse Bryan, as a semi-Welsh speaking, English student nurse, was singled out to be presented to Queen Elizabeth, wife of King George V1. It was only two months after their Coronation she and the King visited sick and injured miners, during their Welsh Tour in July 1937. An immensely proud Ethel showed her Queen around the hospital, providing interpretation where necessary. The Queen insisted on saying a few words to every patient so Ethel spent much longer in the Queen's company than anticipated. Afterwards they enjoyed a cup of tea together and Her Majesty thanked Ethel for her diligent and dedicated work, concluding.

"I am delighted that you have exemplified English nursing so well, Nurse Bryan. I am sure you have a long and happy career ahead of you."

Ethel was thrilled and never forgot a single moment of that first meeting with her much revered Queen.

At the age of 21, Ethel developed severe pain in her mouth. Pyorrhoea, an incurable disease of the ligaments and bones that support the teeth was diagnosed and she had to undergo an operation in Aberdare General to have all her teeth out. It was considered the gum disorder was due to the poor diet and lack of care she had whilst in the orphanage.

The agony which followed was almost unbearable and she became critically ill as a raging mouth infection spread through her throat, oesophagus and into her upper intestine. It was thought that she might not survive. She remained in hospital for a month before being allowed 'home' into the care of Katie. Her friend stayed by her side and cared for her throughout her illness, eventually helping her to eat, exercise and recover.

The day came when Ethel had to put in her new dentures for the first time and take a look in the mirror. She was horrified at first and immediately removed them and cried her heart out. But the effect on her face of having no teeth, especially after all the weight she had lost, was far worse. So she put them back in and tolerated the pain of new dentures for several weeks and finally became used to them and after a couple of refits, forgot she had them in.

Following two months convalescence, Ethel resumed her role within the hospital and attained her State Enrolled Nurse registration. She was now fully qualified to work as a nurse anywhere in the UK, but chose to stay at Aberdare General for a third year. She loved her work there and felt she was making a difference.

Welsh Mining Town

Rhondda Valley miners 1935

7

MANY A SLIP

At the end of her third year, Ethel received an urgent phone call from Mr Meads. His wife had suffered a sudden, severe stroke. He begged her to come home to help look after her. Ethel immediately resigned her position at Aberdare and went back to Oxford, where she found Mrs Meads paralysed down her right side and could do nothing for herself. She needed day and night care. Ethel put her own life on hold and nursed her sick 'mother' for some months. As she began to recover and respond to intense physiotherapy, Ethel was able to consider her own situation. She was eager to return to work, even if only part-time.

Her initial job was at a private maternity home, The Willows, in High Wycombe It was run by two spinsters, who obviously had no personal experience of childbirth. The staff were intolerant and without compassion for the mostly unmarried girls within their care, who were denied any pain relief whatsoever. Midwives told them to stop shouting.

"You made your own bed, now you must lie in it!"

Ethel was horrified. She gave her notice and left after the first week.

She then nursed a doctor in High Wycombe until his death, before finding a job at the London Road Hospital in Headington. Ironically, this was the old workhouse where she had to fight so hard for her own life, following her premature birth. However, she had only been there for a few months when she collapsed on the ward from dizziness which led to profuse vomiting and acute pain from the top of her head down into her shoulder. She was rushed into the Radcliffe Infirmary. Ethel knew her father had died from an abscess on the brain when he was only twenty two, she feared she was going to die of the same thing and at a similar age.

However, she was told that was not the case, but would have to undergo an emergency operation for the removal of Mastoiditis, a serious bacterial infection in her middle-ear. It was thought this could be linked to the Pyorrhoea she had suffered in Wales.

A Mastectomy was a very precarious procedure which entailed cutting through the mastoid bone behind the ear and removing the ear drum to enable complete clearance of any infected tissue. Ethel knew from her medical training that the operation could lead to an abscess forming on the brain and that was in her mind as the nurse placed the chloroform mask over her mouth and she drifted off into blissful, unaware sleep.

During the operation, which satisfactorily removed all infected tissue, the surgeon accidentally damaged a nerve within her ear canal. When she woke up, she remained in intense pain and on trying to stand fell down, her world spinning around her. She had completely lost her sense of balance and the post-operative pain was so overwhelming, she was helped back into bed and received firm instructions to stay there. She was given morphine to help relieve the pain, but it was many weeks before she could come off it and was unable to walk unaided for several weeks after that. She eventually recovered after a long stay in a convalescent home in Hastings, but the hearing in her left ear never returned.

Following that debilitating episode in her life, Ethel accepted a nursing post in the Amersham General Hospital and lived between the hospital nurse's wing and the Meads' home in Oxford. She quickly fitted in and one of her nursing friends asked if she would like to go to a local Amersham pub for a meal and would she mind if her older brother joined them. Ethel did not mind at all, in fact they got on rather well and so began her first serious relationship with a boyfriend, Stanley (Stan) Cooper. Ethel, as with most young ladies of that time, did not even consider having sex before marriage and no decent man would ever expect it either. However, Ethel and Stan became very close and enjoyed life together as a couple. He asked her to marry him, but Ethel refused as she felt it was too soon and she was too young for marriage. He pledged to wait and ask her again in a year's time.

Mrs Meads had recovered to a point where Mr Meads could care for her, so Ethel was able to make the most of her young life. She enjoyed the best of both worlds: the hectic social scene of Oxford with friends and the quieter, more countrified life, in and around the picturesque villages of Amersham and Chesham Bois, with Stan.

This period of bliss was rudely interrupted when she was urgently called to the phone in the hospital. It was a distraught sobbing Ifan. Katie was in an infirmary suffering from TB. She had suffered from a chronic cough for some weeks, but they had put it down to a continuance of a bronchial infection she had a few weeks before. However tests revealed she had Tuberculosis and had had it for some months. There was not much they could do for her as it was too far advanced, so she was transferred from Aberdare General to a specialist isolation sanatorium, not too far from home.

Ethel immediately dropped everything and travelled to Wales to take care of her friend. Having suffered a period of intensive and most unpleasant experimental treatments, Katie was diagnosed as terminally ill and discharged home into Ethel's care. She was much weakened and weighing only six stone, had just a few weeks to live. Ethel ignored the risks posed by nursing someone with TB and cared for her friend. Ethel knew TB to be a highly infectious disease of the lungs. Which during the 30's and 40's ravaged through many coal mining towns and villages. The local village shop owner had already lost his wife, his mother and three of their five children to it, all within the space of three years.

Katie's terminal home care involved rest, fresh air and lots of high protein food, especially full fat cow's milk which was provided free by the government to any family with a member suffering from TB. Ethel would read to her friend for most of the day. They both loved books which transported them into a different world, far away from the problems of their everyday lives. Katie and Ethel both knew that entire families were being wiped out by the galloping consumption. Treating TB was an occupational hazard for medical staff and one local physician was notorious for instructing his patients to turn their heads and 'cough towards the nurse' when he examined them.

As Katie was obviously too weak to do anything, Ethel also cared for Ifan and Betrys. She cooked, cleaned and took over the mantle of work for family life. Ifan seemed appreciative as he often came home from choral practice or rugby meetings with a box of chocolates or a bottle of milk-stout for her.

Katie died, peacefully, with her family and Ethel around her, just six weeks later. She had planned her funeral and left instructions as to what was to happen to Betrys, her effects and where she was to be buried. Her chosen undertakers duly arrived and Ifan cried like a child on Ethel's shoulder as his wife's body was removed and taken to the Chapel of Rest.

When the door had closed, he was still obviously delirious with sadness as he hadn't noticed that his hand had slipped down over Ethel's bosom and she had to gently, but firmly, remove it! The funeral was not large, just members of the family and a few friends. Katie was quietly laid to rest in St John the Baptist's Churchyard in Aberdare.

Afterwards the mourners gathered in one of the many pubs in the town. Ifan drank too much and became aggressively morose as the evening wore on. Ethel was asked if she would escort him home. She struggled under the weight of her friend's widower, but managed to get him home and find the key. As they entered the cottage, Ifan who had been in a drunken stupor, began to talk.

"You don't know how lonely I have been over these last few months, Ethel. It's has been so good to have you back here, it's where you belong. I've become very fond of you Ethel. I've come to love you as much as Katie did. Why don't you stay and make a new life, here in Wales, with us?"

Ethel replied soothingly, having dealt with many drunken patients in her nursing career.

"No, I can't stay Ifan; I have my own life and family in Oxford. But I could remain here for a few days, just until you find your feet."

"No!" He responded angrily. "I mean, marry me and become a mother to Betrys."

Ethel, glared at him, "What? You want me to take over where Katie left off! Is that what you're saying?"

"WELL, WHY NOT?" he shouted as he glowered back at her. He had shed his sad demeanour and was clearly developing a drunken rage.

Ethel spoke softly in an effort to placate him. "It's best not to say any more, Ifan. We'll have a chat in the morning when the drink has worn off."

"WHY NOT NOW?" He grabbed hold of her and tried to carry her upstairs, but, because he was so very drunk, Ethel managed to push him off balance and he fell into the small sofa and passed out.

Ethel had no intention of hanging around to see what would happen in the morning. She packed her case, walked to the bus station and caught the first bus to Cardiff. She never saw or heard from Ifan again.

Upon her return to Cowley, Ethel was completely shocked and taken off guard to learn that during her absence, Mrs Meads had suffered a fatal heart attack and died. No one, not even Mr Meads, had thought to let her know. Her 'mother' had been buried; and laid to rest in the churchyard of St. Mary and St. John in Cowley.

Without stopping to change from her travel attire, Ethel wept as she ran from the house, only stopping to buy fresh flowers to place on her beloved 'mother's' grave. She found the recently mounded grave, with funeral flowers still laid on top, and remained there for some time. She took some comfort from being able to tell Ethel Meads just how much she had meant to her and how she wished they had been able to spend her younger years together.

When she returned to the house, she found a letter from Stan. It had been sitting there for two weeks. He wrote that he had met someone else and although he still cared very much for her, he had decided it was best if he moved on with his life. Strangely enough, Ethel found this a huge relief. She had enough to cope with now she had Mr Meads to care for. She considered him to be her father, as much as she thought of Mrs Meads as her mother. Stan had probably made the right decision.

As she came to terms with the loss of her beloved friend and her 'mother', Ethel also had to help her 'father' with his overwhelming grief. She remained at home more and more, seeking solace in their gardens and the normal day to day activates of just living. She was now twenty four years old and had big decisions to make as to where her life was going.

One day, as she was collecting fresh fruit and vegetables from their back garden she heard a startled cry from next door. Peering over the low fence, she saw a young man lying in next door's vegetable patch. He was swearing and trying to get up having slipped on the wet path. Ethel's offer of help was agitatedly accepted, so she hopped over the fence and went to his aid. On helping him to his feet, it became clear that, although not injured by his fall, he suffered from some form of disablement in his legs. He needed to hold onto her hands to get up and then use two sticks to walk. He thanked her for her prompt assistance, she gave the customary response.

"I'm just glad I was there and able to help". She looked at his face as he replied.

"So am I, thank you."

She could not help but notice how unnervingly good-looking he was. He was of slim build and around 5ft 10" tall. As he nonchalantly swept his hand through Brylcreemed, dark hair and pushed it back from his eyes to look at her, his face broke into an easy smile which revealed perfectly well cared for teeth under a slim, pencil moustache. She fleetingly thought he resembled a young matinee film idol, such as Douglas

Fairbanks Jnr. When he looked at her, his unwavering gaze seemed so intense, she had to look away so that he would not spot the overwhelming sense of giddiness that had engulfed her. She loved him at first sight. He seemed not to notice her coyness as he explained he was lodging with his friend, whilst looking for work in Oxford. She detected a light northern accent which was confirmed when he told her that he was from Redcar in the north Riding of Yorkshire. He was a carpenter by trade and was hoping to find a job in one of Oxford's motor factories.

After assisting him back into his friend's house, she cleaned and dressed a wound on his arm and it was not long before they were on first name terms. His name was Thomas Williams, but most people called him Tom. As they sat in the friend's kitchen, drinking tea, neither of them seemed to want to break away from the moment. Tom asked Ethel about herself and what her intentions were. He also talked more of his plans to move to Oxford, find a home and settle down. As Ethel left Tom that evening, she couldn't help but feel the delicious excitement that comes with knowing she had just met the man she wanted to marry.

The next day Mr. Meads, wanting to meet this young man his daughter seemed in such awe of, invited Tom to join them for supper. As the evening progressed Ethel's 'father' could clearly see the already strong connection between his daughter and this man and selfishly feared he might lose her before too long and that scared him.

Ethel couldn't wait to see Tom again and hoped she had made a good impression. She need not have worried, as later that week Tom invited her to join him when he went to watch his sister, Ada, play tennis at Magdalen College. Ada had recently moved from the family home of Redcar to Oxford with her new husband, Ted. They both worked at Morris Motors.

So began their courtship. Tom, who was a highly accomplished upholsterer as well as carpenter, quickly moved to Oxford when he secured a Line Manager position at Morris Motors. He was put in charge of the design, cutting and sewing of the leathers used for the upholstery in the newly built cars. After renting a house in Cowley, he joined Ethel in her enjoyment of Oxford's vibrant pre-war social scene. There were so many great eating and drinking haunts, which Ethel was well acquainted with from her earlier days. They either took a punt or rowing boat for trips on the River Thames from Foley Bridge. They swam in a murky River Cherwell at Cutteslowe, but someone always had to remove the green, weedy slime and hoick out the dead fish before they could jump in. They had many outings to the riverside Trout Inn at Godstow, a small village south-east of Oxford, where they were offered free pint glasses of Pimms No.1 with their meal during the summer months. Picnics on the Trust land at Boars Hill which overlooked Oxford's Dreaming Spires and where they could walk for miles were a special treat that reminded her of her young days out with the Meads. The whole of the Thames Valley was at their disposal.

They joined the Magdalen Tennis Club with Ada and Ted, and enjoyed private dinners, concerts and balls. Then as Oxford with its magnificent rivers was a world-renowned rowing centre, they joined the Oxford Pleasure Rowing Club, the only one to allow women members. They were a well matched couple, enjoying the same interests and having a similar optimistic and cheerful outlook on life. Being very much in love and blissfully happy, they revelled in those golden days. Friends began to tease them for going everywhere together and nicknamed them 'the twins'.

The 17th century, Lamb and Flag Inn, The Eagle and Child in St. Giles and the New Inn in St. Aldates were their favourite haunts and the people they met within those pubs were destined to play a big part in their lives. Situated in St. Giles, the Lamb & Flag had always held an important place in Oxford's history and was the go-to stomping ground for students and masters alike. When Ethel and Tom were there the landlord, Stan Richards, welcomed writers such as Tolkien who lived in nearby Northmoor Road and CS Lewis who lived at The Kilns, not far from where Ethel was born in Headington. The Lamb and Flag enjoyed an intellectual buzz which 'the twins' relished. The ceilings and walls were covered with oars and rowing shields from Oxford University rowing achievements. It had a clock that went backwards displaying 'Theakston's Old Peculiar time' and a comforting fireplace in the back of the bar that dated from the 18th century.

Although they made the most of all of those stimulating places, Ethel had her responsibilities. She was still living between her home with Mr. Meads and the Amersham General. Mr Meads had, up to this point, been a most kind and generous father figure, never failing to support her. However, he was incapable of coming to terms with the loss of his cherished wife and gradually sank into a state of hopeless despair. He was recently retired, on a decent pension, from his latest position at the local Institute for the Deaf and Dumb. Not an unattractive man, he had forever taken great pride in his appearance, always wearing suits with a waistcoat, a clean shirt every day, bow tie and highly polished shoes. Still only in his early sixties, tall and slim, Ethel felt that he had a full life to live, once he got over his grief. She cared for and supported him as best she could. However, from once being more or less teetotal, he began drinking more and more. He started to travel by train to London every weekend and began to blow his savings and his pension in the bars, clubs and brothels of the shadier parts of the city.

He started bringing some of his lady friends' home and after spending a bawdy night in the bedroom next to Ethel's, saw them back onto the train to London the following day, with ticket paid and ample funds for their journey.

Eventually he returned home with Mrs Cornwall, a new lady friend from one of his pleasure houses. He introduced her as Nancy. She was also deaf and dumb, brazen, extremely shrewd and had her own agenda for Mr Meads. She must have found him a pathetic easy target and insisted on staying for a few days. She obviously saw Ethel as a threat to her well laid plans and was openly hostile to her on sight, demanding to know who she was and why she was living with her boyfriend. She quickly became a regular visitor, staying for longer and longer periods of time until she eventually moved in and assumed the position of mistress of the house and of the man. She was a muscular and overly-tall woman, who smoked like a chimney and dominated Harry Meads. She insisted on trips to London every weekend and encouraged Harry out to local pubs during the week; always coming home very late and the worse for drink.

Nancy soon made it her business to cause trouble between Ethel and Harry. She began to point out to Harry that Ethel preferred Tom to him. She complained that Ethel was spying on them and spending extravagantly on the electric and gas and, eventually demanded that he choose between her and Ethel. Ethel had to go or she would.

A ferocious argument broke out between Harry and Nancy which became quite physical, as with a deaf and dumb couple there could be violent hand waving and splaying of arms. Then Nancy began to cry and gestured to Harry that he didn't love her any more. That he preferred to take his daughter's side rather than support her. Ethel could see that her dear 'father' was being cruelly manipulated and placed in the awful position of having to choose one over the other. Taking Harry's arm, Ethel led him into another room and sat him down. Sitting beside him, she took his hands in hers, kissed his tear stained cheek and calmly explained to him that this really could not continue. It was simply too distressing for all three of them. She signed that although she loved him dearly and certainly did not want to leave, it was time for her to strike out on her own. She had a good friend she could stay with and would leave in the morning. She clearly saw relief on his face when he realised that his 'daughter' had made the extremely difficult choice for him. Harry embraced Ethel and thanked her for understanding his position. He smiled and turning to leave the room, grabbed the decanter of dry sherry from the sideboard. As he walked through the door neither of them knew it would be the last time they would see each other.

Ethel packed up all she could carry and, not wanting any further confrontation with Nancy, left the following morning before anyone was up. She moved in with a nursing friend from her hospital days in the Cowley Workhouse.

With Ethel gone, Mrs Cornwall's husband, James, moved in to join them. Ethel later heard that the police were called there on several occasions because of the two men fighting, but felt it best not to return. It was many years later she discovered, by chance, that, by fair means or foul, Mr Meads had died. No one had informed her and none of his friends were invited to attend his funeral. Mr and Mrs Cornwall got the house which Mr and Mrs Meads had promised Ethel. Purportedly, his Last Will and Testament had been changed and she received nothing.

ETHEL AND TOM'S WEDDING

8

HAPPY DAYS

Following the death of Harry Meads, Ethel reconnected with Ellen, her birth mother and her sister, Ruby. It was not perfect, but they began to mend bridges and settle into a mutually respectful relationship. They were introduced to Tom but Ellen never took to him. She always thought he was a bit of a fly-by-night and warned Ethel that he was a philanderer and would let her down one day. Despite that, Ruby and Ethel although not exactly friends, managed to rub along together and formed a comfortable rapport.

Ethel and Tom attended Ruby's wedding when she married a publican, William Parker. They had been sweethearts for some time and were very happy. They set up home together managing and living in their first pub, The Red Lion in Britwell Salome; they had three sons and a daughter together.

On May 1st 1939, Ethel and Tom walked to Magdalen Bridge after celebrating the night away during the Magdalen May Day all-night Ball at the College. They knew they needed to be on the bridge over the River Cherwell by 6am. They hurried to join the hundreds of revellers waiting to hear the Magdalen College Choir sing their usual, 'Hymn-us Eucharistic-us', from the top of Magdalen Tower. During the singing of the hymn, Tom turned Ethel towards him and took a small, black box from his inner pocket. As he handed it to a stunned, but thrilled Ethel, he asked her to marry him. Ethel beamed with delight and said, 'yes'. Tom removed the diamond solitaire ring from the box and placed it on her finger as the hymn came to an end.

Plans were made for their wedding, which was to be in August of that year. The church was reserved and a lavish reception for all their family and friends at The Old Parsonage Hotel on the Woodstock Road was booked and deposits paid. Invitations were posted out and with so many guests having to travel quite a distance several rooms were reserved in the hotel. The hotel offered Ethel and Tom a free Bridle Suite for the night of the wedding and a popular big-band was booked for dancing until dawn.

When Ethel's mother was told of the forthcoming wedding, she was furious. She had never liked Tom although a lot of friends thought she was treacherously jealous of Ethel's loving relationship with him. Without the couple's knowledge she cancelled the wedding reception, the bedrooms and the band. She also told the cake maker the cake was no longer required. When Ethel found out what Ellen has done, she was heartbroken, but it was too late to reinstate anything, the hotel had booked another wedding on that date and all guest rooms had been reassigned. There was nothing the hotel could do, they kept the deposit and because it was so late in the day, neither she nor Tom could find an alternative venue. The wedding cake had not been started and the baker had accepted other assignments.

Ethel asked her mother why she had done such a terrible thing and Ellen's answer was that he was not the man for her. She should not marry him and the cancellation would provide time for her to come to her senses. Ethel was beside herself with rage and telling her mother that she would never forgive her, walked out of her life. Ruby took her sister's part and told Ellen it was a truly wicked thing to do and did she not think that Ethel had suffered enough from her habitual maltreatment of her. Ruby offered her pub but it was too small and had no letting rooms, but said if it helped, they could use it for the day. Ethel was grateful for the offer, but it was not, as Ruby had said, big enough and it was a long way out of town.

When the landlord at The Lamb and Flag heard what had happened, he stepped in and offered his pub for the wedding reception. A friend made a replacement cake and rooms were booked in other hotels. They married, as arranged, in August 1939; Ethel was thirty and Tom was twenty six. The Wedding Service was at St. Mary and St. John Church in Cowley.

In spite of Ellen's attempts to cancel their day, it was perfect. Ethel wore an elegant, white silk gown, with flowing lace veil, a coronet of white rosebuds and she carried a bouquet of white roses. The groom wore a black, immaculately tailored, double breasted suit. They made a radiant and supremely happy couple. Her pageboy and bridesmaid were two of Ruby's children, Jeffrey and Joan. The celebration was well attended by many friends and family, with a large contingent from Yorkshire. Neither Ellen nor William attended, but Ruby did and several of the Reverend Sisters from St. Johns managed to obtain the obligatory, special permission from the Bishop of Oxford and that helped make up for the missing parents. The reception at the Lamb and Flag was a huge success and many of the regulars joined in the celebrations before waving the newly-weds off on a short honeymoon in Cornwall and a new life together.

On their return they listened, as everyone else did, to the Declaration of War, made at 11.15am on September 3rd 1939 by the Prime Minister, Neville Chamberlin. All places of entertainment were closed, crowding was forbidden, except for church services and the BBC TV Service was shut down.

Then, on October 1st Winston Churchill gave his first wartime radio broadcast and they heard that Morris Motors was to cease car production in Oxford and all Cowley workers were to report either to the Army Recruitment Office or the Labour Exchange.

Tom was not accepted into the army due to his hip. He had broken it when he was ten years old and it developed into what was called a TB Hip. He was hospitalised for six months with hips and legs plastered and fixed in traction. However the procedure was not successful and his hip joint became disfigured, resulting in one leg being shorter than the other. He walked with a pronounced gait and needed a stick, sometimes two.

Ethel also attended an interview, but when she told them she was working at the Amersham hospital they suggested she remain in her post, or relocate to the Cowley Road Hospital which was to become a hospital for war wounded. So she was not 'called-up' either.

The newly-weds moved into a small, rented house in Phipps Road at £2 a week. Although there was never much money about, they were young, in love and happy. Ethel continued her job as a nurse working in the local hospital and Tom found other work as a carpenter/upholsterer, but he wanted more. He was besotted by the cars he helped to produce at Morris Motors and his attention was drawn to the American cars which were being imported from the States. He desperately wanted to become his own boss and, despite the war, was determined to open his own business. He was adamant it must involve prestigious motor cars in some way and talked of his plans to friends in the pubs of St. Giles to garner their advice and support. The Lamb and Flag became a popular watering hole for local wartime politicians and Tom developed binding friendships with them. He needed to find investors for his new project and with Ethel's blessing he spent more and more time socialising with these wealthy, influential men and one in particular, Robert Boothby. A Conservative Member of

Parliament, Boothby agreed to invest, if Tom could find an irresistible project he could not say no to.

Ethel needed no convincing, she knew Tom had what it took to start up his own taxi business and they both realised that with the onset of war, it was imperative they obtained only the highest quality motors to attract the wealthier clients. Tom rightly reasoned that only the wealthy few would have any money until the war was over.

They found the perfect premises in a disused car showroom in Long Wall, close to the centre of Oxford's university area. It had garages and a shop front, perfect for use as their reception area and offices. Ethel reduced her hours at the hospital and joined Tom in the administration of the new business. As well as using all their savings and obtaining a bank loan, Tom borrowed £2,000 from Robert Boothby. Considered a tad raffish, Bob Boothby was Personal Private Secretary to Churchill for a time and known to be having a long standing affair with Harold MacMillan's wife, Dorothy, although she was never seen in the pub. He would eventually become The Right Honourable, Lord Boothby KBE. Over the following year Tom bought three cars and employed ten drivers, who were all smartly dressed in full liveried chauffeur uniforms. All their plans were coming to fruition and they were also delighted when they discovered that their first child was on its way and should arrive in time for Christmas. They had developed a highly successful Private Chauffeur business with two prestigious, British engineered Armstrong Siddeley 5-litre, six- cylinder cars for a whopping £600 each and an American, five-passenger sedan: a black Packard with white-walled-tyres, for about the same money. Ethel really enjoyed her work, but as her pregnancy progressed, she had to begrudgingly hand over the burden of organisation. Tom employed an administrator, so Ethel no longer played any part in the day-to-day running of the business.

Ethel went into labour on 17 th December 1940. Her three day confinement, at home, was painful and very bloody. Bryan Thomas Williams was born healthy and hungry, on 20th December 1940, weighing in at a colossal 10lbs 10ozs. As he was delivered, the doctor was heard to say, "Good Lord, look, it's the great white hope."

Ethel was much weakened afterwards and Tom summoned his mother and sister from Yorkshire to spend Christmas with them and look after her. He was hardly at home over the festive period which earned them mega bucks. Ethel recovered enough for the Williams family to leave shortly after the New Year.

Bryan's baptism was attended by dotting parents, family and friends, in the Chapel at St. Johns Convent in February of 1940 and life settled into a new routine for Ethel and with her baby son to care for she greatly enjoyed not having to work. Tom spent more time at home and adored his baby son. They once again began to go out and about for drives in the country and riverside walks with Bryan in his shiny black, coach built pram. They enjoyed exclusive, ration-free suppers at reputable, no questions asked restaurants, courtesy of the many wealthy clients they drove.

Ethel felt safe, loved and fulfilled in her world, she could not have wished for anything more. Tom came home one day saying that he had a surprise for her and from under his coat he produced a small puppy. It was a black and white mongrel terrier with a black spot over its right ear. Named 'Spot', he was immediately adored as a member of their family. Tom was generous with money and ensured that she had enough to buy whatever she wanted. Not that there was much to buy in the shops as war continued to rage throughout Britain, Europe and beyond.

Ethel maintained her connection with St. Johns and often took Bryan and Spot to visit the nuns. It wasn't long before Ellen got in touch to ask if she could call in to meet her new grandson. Because she was so content with her new life and not wanting to allow old grudges to cast dark shadows over her life, Ethel agreed and they tentatively picked up their relationship.

****

Ruby and William Parker were also in a favourable position. In 1939 they left the Red Lion and took over the lease of a new, much larger pub, the London Road Inn, in Benson. RAF Benson would be right on their doorstep. It was to be deployed as the home of a new Photographic Recognisance Unit, which meant that many well-paid officers and airmen would be drafted in to help in the war effort. They were jovial, hospitable landlords and knew their trade, inside, out. They had the knack of making everyone feel welcome and the London Road Inn became a 'home from home' for many of the airmen. Serving good beer and providing excellent food, they quickly became very popular. The Inn had a large, immaculately maintained beer garden and held many musical evenings with local groups and singers performing there. Ruby was charismatic, buxom and had fabulous legs. One regular even made a model of them and with the name 'Ruby's Legs', this fine piece of sculpture was placed in a prominent position behind the snug bar. Ruby would ask for a donation into their local charity box when a new 'punter' asked to see or put a hand on 'Ruby's Legs': the ornament, not her own!

William kept a register to keep track of old and new clients and ensured they all received Christmas cards as a reminder of their visit to the London Road Inn. Running the pub was hard work but they were well used to it and the place made a very comfortable living for them and their four children. The living was supplemented by buying and selling valuable black-market goods: cigarettes, cigars, spirits, nylons, and chocolate, anything that it was difficult for people to get hold of during rationing. All of these precious items were stored in an enormous attic under a much admired, thick thatched roof, which kept the merchandise at an ambient temperature. It was an ideal cover for their illicit trade, until a hot, sunny day on the 18th of August 1942.

Ruby and William were heavy smokers. Ruby smoked forty cigarettes a day and William had a passion for large expensive cigars. After spending a busy lunchtime chatting and drinking with his regulars, William told Ruby he was off to take a long, cool bath. As he sank into the cool water, William casually flicked the butt of the Churchillian cigar he had been smoking out through the bathroom window. Within a few minutes, he noticed smoke drifting into the bathroom. Instead of falling to earth, as hundreds of others had done, the cigar had somehow lodged and set light to the ultra-dry thatch! He leapt from the bath and grabbing a robe ran down stairs and rushed outside to see how far the smouldering had gone, only to see that part of the roof was fully ablaze. As soon as he saw the speed with which the fire was spreading he ran back inside shouting "Fire! Fire! Everybody out! Get out! Now!"

He screamed at Ruby, "Call the bloody Fire Brigade and get the kids out! Now!"

He ran upstairs to try and save some of the more precious items from their private rooms, but it was a fool's errand. The fire was erupting all over the roof and down into the attic where exploding spirits were fuelling the inferno. It was only a matter of minutes before the roof was ablaze from end to end. He heard the fire engines as they raced up from the airbase and saw dozens of airmen running towards him. But it was too late to save the pub, his home and all the contraband which was to secure their family's future after the war. Everything they had was going up in smoke.

The firemen and helpers did their best, but the pub burned down with only a few ground floor walls surviving. Ruby, William and their four children were homeless and had to seek shelter with family until they could hopefully find another pub to manage.

London Road Inn
before the fire

After the fire

****

In the meantime the demand for Tom's glamorous, chauffeur driven cars had grown incredibly quickly. All the drivers were happy to work around the clock, receiving huge tips and many perks from pet clients for their elite service. They became 'first call' for affluent British and American Airmen and the occasional politician. Singers, musicians and actors, from Oxford's New Theatre and the Playhouse, were eager to be seen alighting from Tom's luxury limousines.

It was not all doom and gloom at this stage of the war. The fashionable and wealthy classes continued their soirées and dinner parties as if there were no conflict which kept the lucrative taxi business very healthy. It was also fortunate that Oxford City, with its historic college buildings, was protected from bombing raids by Hitler. He wanted Oxford City, as his Command Headquarters and Blenheim Palace as his official English home following the invasion!

Fate also dealt Ethel and Tom a lucky hand when America entered the war after Pearl Harbour was attacked by the Japanese in December 1941. One and a half million American Servicemen landed on Britain's shores in 1942, bringing with them candy, cola, cigarettes, nylons and salaries more than five times higher than those of British airmen. With no living expenses, they had huge amounts of disposable income and their generous nature made them a big hit with British women who had never experienced such generosity. The money flowed and there were exuberant and abundant parties, which meant a burgeoning need for stylish taxis with Tom's the most sought after.

Tom and Ethel quickly found themselves in a position where they could afford their own home and bought a terraced house in Crescent Road, Cowley for £1,400. Business was good, but inevitably, more time had to be dedicated to it. Tom worked all hours to manage the chauffeuring and began driving himself to help keep up with demand.

A bizarre detachment from reality became the norm for the team of drivers. Through their clients, they were experiencing a gaiety and abandon they had never known before. Their customers had money to blow, time to enjoy it and they were driving them to wild parties and watching as inhibitions were cast aside, morals abandoned and carefree times had by all. The knock-on effect destroyed several of the drivers' marriages.

As Ethel was no longer involved in the day-to-day running of the business, she was unaware of these problems and taken by surprised when an angry wife came knocking on her door to say that her husband had been getting home later and later and even staying out all night. Other drivers were not coming home for days on end. Ethel was disturbed by this and reassured her that she would speak to Tom about the drivers' hours.

When questioned, Tom put his arms around her and told her there was nothing to be concerned about. It was one sad wife's delusional paranoia. He explained that the drivers were simply under extreme pressure to get the job done and bring in the money. He insisted that she should ignore their domestic trivia and, anyway, she had her own problems to deal with. Ethel did indeed have enough to think about with her demanding baby son, so with complete trust in her husband, she was content to leave matters for him to sort out.

However, within two years, even though Tom was working every hour God gave, the business seemed to be showing less profit. She floated the idea of caring for one elderly paying guest within their home to bolster their finances. Tom happily agreed and it was not long before Ethel had found and installed an elderly female guest in their spare bedroom.

Once this paying guest, who needed help with her personal care, meals and laundry, arrived, more money did come into the family coffers. Ethel's time was now split between caring for her son and the tenant; she had little time to think of herself and certainly none to worry about why their business was not making the profits it used to. But, as Tom appeared unconcerned and repeatedly reassured her that all was fine and he hoped to buy two more cars to grow the Company, she assumed he had everything in-hand.

Life slipped into a regular pattern with Ethel looking after home affairs and Tom, working long hours, to maintain the taxi business. However it was not long before Ethel found, to her delight, that she was pregnant with their second child. She was hoping for a girl, in which case the baby would be christened, Betty Ann. Her wish was granted and I arrived in January 1945, shortly before the end of WW2 in Europe.

PACKARD LIMOUSINE

9

BETRAYAL

Family money was getting very tight. Tom could no longer hide the fact that although he was working day and night, money was not ending up in my mother's purse and she thanked the lord that she still had the tenant and her four guineas (£4.20p)) a week. However, she soon discovered that bills remained unpaid and the business was falling into debt. Interest on loans was not being paid and Robert Boothby, who had always been a friend and mentor to my father, was spurning face to face meetings and demanding his money back, with accruing interest. The bank withdrew credit, cancelled the overdraft facility and demanded full repayment of all loans, with interest trebled and default fees added. Tom would have to try and sell up.

No buyers for the business came forward and customers dwindled as US airmen returned home. Tom told Ethel that he was going to sell all three cars, but although mum was not a business woman, it did not make sense. Even if he could find a buyer in the post-war depression, it would be at a greatly reduced price and not clear the unfathomable debts my father had somehow accrued. She proposed they sell the family home, clear off all debts and move into a rented house, with more bedrooms so that she could take in three more residential patients, each paying four guineas a week. Then, when the post war economy had recovered, they would start all over again. Tom enthusiastically agreed. He would keep on running the three cars to ensure some income was coming in, but would immediately put the house on the market with an estate agent friend.

The banks and Boothby backed off as soon as they knew their home was to be sold, but placed a charge on it so that as and when it was sold, the Bank got first dibs and Boothby the second.

Mum eventually found a suitable property to rent in Chieveley, a few miles outside Oxford. She secured a reduced rent by promising to redecorate the house at her own cost and moved us all there before the family home was sold. My father was away a lot, but when he was there mum felt things would improve once the country recovered from the war.

It was 1946 and she was pregnant with my sister. Bryan caught measles, then whooping cough which he passed onto my mother during her last month of pregnancy. Somehow she managed to care for four ambulant residents, with the help of one carer employed on five mornings a week.

A beautifully angelic and adored by all, Rosemary Margaret, was born, mum always said "coughed out", on January 5th 1947. Because mum suffered a prolapsed womb after the birth and from the after effects of the whooping cough, she had to remain in the nursing home for another two weeks. The Yorkshire family came and looked after us all, with Ada and Ted paying the nursing home fees.

The house in Cowley had been on the market for nearly two years, but astonishingly it had not sold. Tom was working away from home for several days at a time. He apparently had lucrative, long weekend trips to Scotland and Wales with remaining post-war American airmen. When the Williams family went back to Yorkshire, mum still needed help as she now had three small children and four elderly clients needing her attention.

Aware of this, Colin, one of Tom's former drivers came to see my mother. His wife, Anne, was the woman who knocked on mum's door years before to complain about the wayward lives of Tom's drivers. Colin had stopped working for Tom at the time, as he did not like what he saw happening to the families of other drivers. Colin and his wife, Anne, offered to help mum cope and turned out to be a gift from heaven. As mum was to say later, "the quiet hand of God was on my shoulder the day they arrived." Colin could odd-job, tend the garden and do any running around, while his considerate, caring wife would cook and help with the household chores. They worked for very little, only what mum could afford.

One day in the early-winter of 1948, Tom told Mum that he would be away for a couple of weeks, but it was good money as he was taking an actress up to London and she had asked him to be her chauffeur for the duration of her trip. He excitedly added that he hoped to be introduced to a new bank manager in the City by the actress. A new banker might be able to solve all their financial problems and open doors that had up until then been firmly closed. He kissed her as he said, "Don't give up on me Ethel, I feel like another door really is opening for us; I just need a bit more time to get us all through it."

This was music to mum's ears as she knew that if anyone could sweet-talk a bank into taking on new business it was her husband. He had done it before, so why not again. Re-energised and having complete faith in him, she wished him luck and they hugged and kissed again, before she waved him goodbye as he drove away in one of the Armstrongs. When he had gone Colin approached mum. He spoke quietly.

"Ethel, could I talk to you for a moment? I know you may think it's none of my business, but I simply can't standby and not say something,"

"Of course we can talk, Colin. You're looking very serious, what's the problem?"

"Not here," he said. "Can we talk in private; perhaps in the back garden?"

Mum began to feel apprehensive. Was he about to tell her that he had found a job and was leaving? She followed him through the house into the garden, where he asked her to take a seat beside him on a bench and gently laid his hand over hers.

"Ethel, I am so sorry, but there is something I feel you really do need to know and now!"

By this time, mum was convinced they were both about to leave and was resigned to hear the bad news. He looked at her with a 'Sunday face' as he continued.

"Ethel, I'm so desperately sorry to have to be the one to tell you this, but Tom is living a double life. He's living-in-sin with this actress, Hilary Kilby and it's in your old home, Ethel. Also, they have a baby daughter!"

Mum's world imploded. She could not believe what she had just heard. Tom couldn't be that cruel; that deceitful? Colin had got it wrong! Only a short while before, when she was so very ill after haemorrhaging and suffering a prolapsed womb, Tom had sobbed as he knelt beside her bed, telling her how much he loved her and begging her not to die, not to leave him.

"You've got it all wrong, Colin. Tom has just left to go to London to refinance the business, he's taking……….." her voice trailed off as she slowly grasped that what Colin had said was true. Her throat closed up. Numb with shock she could not speak.

Seeing her utter distress, Colin put an arm around her and Anne, who had been watching from the house, rushed out into the garden to help bring some comfort to my mother. But mum pushed them both away and with a mixed sense of disbelief, bewilderment and betrayal, stumbled indoors and up to her bedroom.

Only then did the images of how Tom's irrational behaviour had developed over the last three years, flood into her mind. The times he had said he had been somewhere, only for her to find out he hadn't been there at all. The times he was somewhere when he wasn't supposed to be; the times he had inexplicably bathed before coming into their bed. The hotel and restaurant receipts she had questioned, only to be reassured that they were bookings made for clients, not for him, he had forgotten to give them to the accountant. She had stupidly believed him. What a bloody fool! What a fool he had made of her! Tom was living with another woman, in their old home and with a love child; it seemed everyone knew, except her. The thoughts swirled around in her ravaged brain until they burst forth in agonised sobs of a pain. Pain she had not experienced before, not even in her darkest days at Princess Marys. She couldn't bear it. She couldn't go through all that again. She wanted, even prayed, to die and sank into a deep abyss from which she could not escape, not eat or sleep properly for weeks.

The affair with the actress had been going on for over three years. Her heart was broken, the life had been sucked out of her and it was as if nothing was left, but her shell. Colin and his wife were phenomenally supportive and took over the full care of all of us during this wretched period. They moved Bryan, Rosemary and me into the same bedroom so that they could have a bedroom and be there day and night.

Tom was nowhere to be found. He had driven away knowing that he had no intention of going to London, no plans to meet any bank managers and certainly no 'opening doors for us'. He had left us to be with his actress and their illegitimate child. Mum could not understand why he had come to the house that day, full of empty promises. He kissed and hugged her that day. In God's name, why?

My mother emerged from her bottomless pit to finally accept that Tom was no longer her Tom, the man she had loved for so long. Their life had been an absolute lie for years. She resolved to do whatever it took to keep us altogether with a roof over our heads, but first she needed to find out exactly what had been going on, behind her back.

She discovered that Tom had indeed been living with Hilary Kilby and their child, for over two years, in our old family home at Crescent Road, but that Tom had sold it weeks before and the money had all gone. Two of the cars had been taken as debt repayment; most of which had built up due to the lavishly expensive, Thespian way of life Tom and Hilary Kilby had been leading.

Tom was eventually traced and, at mum's request, he arranged to come to see us. Colin, who had often witnessed Tom's tendency to cut up rough if he felt thwarted, offered to stay and ensure that my father remained civil, but mum asked him to leave her to it, as it was between them alone and she was sure Tom would not react in that way.

Tom, to mum's surprise, did not use his key; he rang the bell, stepped back and waited. After ushering us three into the front sitting room, mum opened the door. When she saw his ashen face, she thought she was going to crumple. Instead, she held tightly onto the door and with great control, indicated that he should come in. Only when they were seated inthe kitchen with the door firmly closed did she speak.

"Why have you deserted us Tom? Were we not enough for you?"

He put his head in his hands and cried. Ethel was unmoved; she had witnessed the act before, in the hospital. He sobbed his answer.

"I am so sorry Ethel; things just seemed to spiral out of control and before I knew it, there was a child on the way and I was in too deep to back out."

"What about us, Tom? You, me, our children, does our marriage mean nothing to you? Are you coming back to us?"

"Of course our marriage means something to me. I still love you all," he spewed.

Mum repeated the question. "Are you coming home Tom?"

"Oh Christ Ethel, I can't. I won't give her up. I can't walk away from them, they're my family now and they need me."

It was clear he no longer loved or cared about us and anyway, as far as mum was concerned, it was too late. After three years or more of betrayal, there was no way back.

"So, what happens to us then Tom? How will you provide for both families?"

His voice stiffened as he replied. "The bank and Bob Boothby have taken all the proceeds from the sale of the house and they're suing me for more. The last car's gone and there's no way I can afford to keep two bloody homes going. I'm bankrupt Ethel, so it's no good you expecting any support from me. You've got your own business that will have to see you through."

A deep silence fell between them as they both stared into thin air. They were completely drained and overcome by differing emotions.

Eventually he stood to leave.

"Can I see the children before I go? They know I'm here Ethel, its only right I say goodbye to them."

Ethel merely nodded, but remained in her chair, her legs felt numb. There was no screaming. No shouting. It was not my mother's way of dealing with things, but as Tom kissed us goodbye and began to walk towards the front door, mum stiffly rose from her chair and followed him.

"Can I have the house keys Tom? You won't need them any more, will you?"

Tom looked startled at her question. It hung in the invisible chasm that had opened up between them and silently signified the end of their marriage. It shocked them both as they could plainly see there was no turning back.

Later, Bryan, who had silently crept out of the sitting room and stood, watching this, told me it was the first time he had witnessed the cruel side of his father, who removed his door keys from several he had on a chain and slapped them into mum's hand.

"There you are Ethel. I could give you the other keys. The spare keys to our old home, but as it's been sold you won't be in need of those, will you?"

Without looking back he walked out through the door, slamming it shut with a loud bang. Mum's calm demeanour evaporated and she slowly and deliberately allowed herself to slide to the floor.

Bryan and I quietly watched our father leave through the sitting room window. We did not cry or call after him; I suppose we had got used to not having him around. We were far too young to recognise the awful situation he had left us in.

Without telling Mum, Tom quickly and quietly moved out of the area with his new family and it would be many years before we saw him again. My mother eventually managed to locate him through the Labour Office and applied to the Court for a Maintenance Order. Both of them had to attend the court hearing.

The judge told Tom he was a dishonourable man and should do the decent thing and return to his lawful wife and three children. As he awarded mum £2.10 shillings a week, Tom shook his head in mock disappointment. He ignored Mum throughout the whole hearing and didn't acknowledge her as he stormed out from the courtroom.

Over the next few months, one by one, mum's residents passed away or left. Finding no replacements we were soon destitute. Tom never paid one penny. As mum couldn't pay the rent she soon received a court order to quit the premises within four weeks and a 'To Rent' board was placed in the front garden of our home. Everything my parents had planned, everything they had strived so hard for, had perished in front of my mother's eyes.

Bryan was eight, I was four, and Rosemary was two. Rosemary and I did not know any of this at the time of course, we merely knew that we no longer saw our father. For us it meant that the gay, unburdened mother we had known was gone, to be replaced by a woman who bore the weight of the world on her slim shoulders.

"The Lord will open another door for us; we have to be ready and willing to step through it."

That was our mother's true belief, but none of us could ever have envisaged the years of relentless hardship which lay ahead.

Betty 2 Bryan 6 at Crescent Road 1947

The Holy Chapel at St. Johns Convent

10

DOWNWARD SPIRAL

My destitute mother wrote a pleading, desperate letter to her great friends, Sister Elizabeth Noel and Sister Helen Irene at St. Johns Convent. Sister Verena, my Godmother, had become the very Reverend Mother. Mum asked them if they could possibly offer the four of us and Spot, our dog, shelter within their convent for three months. Sister Elizabeth Noel spoke with the Reverend Mother who, although she loved us dearly, could not countenance seeing us cooped-up in one small room, even for a short time.

As luck would have it, mum spotted an advertisement for a night nurse at St. Johns in a local newspaper. She dressed us all in our Sunday best and got a friend to drive us to St. Johns where she saw Reverend Mother and pleaded to be given the job and the room that went with it. The Reverend Mother took pity on us, relented, and gave her consent for us to take temporary refuge within the serene sanctuary of the Convent.

We moved out from our rented house and into St. Johns Home in March 1949. After selling or donating most of what we had, we were left with enough clothes and possessions to get by. Spot was able to have the freedom of the convent and became a much loved and very spoilt community pet. It was cramped and our room had just one gas ring and a kettle, but we could survive there and still be all together. After all, it was only going to be for three months, wasn't it?

Mum worked four nights a week caring for the Sisters and Clergy, who were mostly awaiting the call from St. Peter at the Pearly Gates. The strict weekday regime saw her get Bryan and me to school at 8.45am and Rosemary to the nursery for 9. She would then grab a few hours' sleep, before getting us back from school and nursery at 3.30pm. 6 pm was supper and bed. Before she disappeared on night duty at 8pm, she would tell Bryan to look after us; although she popped back to check on us at 10pm and 2am, during her tea breaks. She was scheduled to come off duty at 7am but sometimes it was extended to 8am.

To give her a break, the sisters would take us to play in the day rooms and gardens. We felt wanted, content and comfortably secure amongst the elderly sisters and they seemed to enjoy entertaining us.

If we behaved and were quiet, Bryan and I were allowed into their beautiful chapel. Even though we were so young, we would sit and watch what went on and listen to the prayers, psalms and hymns.

Easter arrived and started with Holy Week. The Christian Church, and therefore St. Johns, celebrates Easter even more than Christmas. It began in earnest on Shrove Tuesday, which meant pancakes with oodles of sugar and lemon juice for breakfast, pudding and, by our demands, supper. I found out later that Lent means 40 days of fasting and begins the following day. It was traditionally a way of using any over-supply of rich food, such as flour, jam, sugar and eggs.

As St Johns needed to be suitably adorned a few days before Easter, we were delighted to accompany the Sisters into the gardens to find lots of moss, small sticky-buds and early flowers to help make 'Easter Gardens', which would bring the essence of Easter to everyone. The mini-gardens would be liberally placed around the Convent together with arrangements of spring foliage and flowers. Our Easter Gardens consisted of large deep trays, with small glass fish paste jars hidden in a thick lining of damp moss. Small posies of primrose, crocus and violets were arranged in the jars. A tomb was made from heaped stones with a large flat stone rolled across the front and a crucifix was placed at the opposite side of the garden. A small mirror was placed in front of the cave to reflect like a pond. Great care was taken as they brought so much pleasure to everyone who saw them. It also helped teach very young visitors the story behind Easter. After the festival, the gardens were placed around the

Convent to create a feeling of spring and new beginnings within the Home.

At communal breakfast on Palm Sunday, a week before Easter, the Sisters gave us crosses made from dried Palm leaves, symbolic of the ones laid at Jesus's feet during his triumphal return to Jerusalem riding a donkey. Later we joined a long procession of local children, one leading a small donkey, to the local Church for their pre-Easter service. On Easter Sunday everyone in the Home received a chocolate egg as part of the Easter Feast, including us!

As three months turned into eight and spring became summer, then winter, we remained in St. Johns and life took on a regular pattern of us attending the local school, mum working and us spending time with the sisters and staff at the Home.

Christmas time at St Johns was very special. A buzz of excitement took hold as soon as the donated tree was erected at the top of the main entrance and stone staircase. The tree brought festive cheer to the cavernous grey brick and stone hallway, especially when the candles and lanterns were placed around it.

A much prized convent heirloom, with an ornately carved, wooden nativity scene was carefully unwrapped. This consisted of an empty crib, beautifully painted statues of the baby Jesus, Joseph, Mary, the three Wise Men, the three Kings, a shepherd and a boy with a lamb on his shoulders. These things were placed within a large wooden stable with the floor covered in clean straw and above all this hung a bright, silver star. Baby Jesus was not placed in the crib until early on Christmas morning.

We attended the local church and St. John's chapel many times over the festive season and we were happily immersed in the sounds and scents of a truly holy, Christian Christmas.

The sisters were adept seamstresses and made Rosemary and me red velvet dresses with white lace collars and attached velvet belts that tied in big bows at the back. They collected money from the staff and bought us black, shiny patent leather slippers and long white socks. Bryan was given his very first pair of long, grey flannel trousers, a striped blue and white shirt and a fawn V-neck jumper.

We proudly wore our new outfits on Christmas day and received presents of sweets, fruit, a small toy and ate our Christmas lunch with the Sisters in their dining room.

As mum was allowed Christmas night off, we were able to spend both nights with her. Life within St. Johns felt safe and secure for us children, sheltered from the ravages of life on the outside. We had not a jot of understanding for mum's problems. Of her trying to come to terms with her losses and juggle life between us and her job in the Home. She appreciated, and often thanked God in her prayers, for the Sisters and their unstinting support of us all.

The anticipated three months had turned into over a year and mum was almost on her knees with exhaustion. Clearly, she could not carry on like this. and the crunch came in the spring of 1950 when an influenza epidemic took hold of the Country. It was rife and especially so within the aged community of Sisters and mum had to work extra shifts as more and more of the Sisters succumbed and died. In a state of total exhaustion, she eventually caught the flu which led to a complete collapse.

Bryan overheard the Home doctor sternly telling the Sisters that our mother could not carry on like this and they had to do something to help. This helpful advice turned out to be a double edged sword because mum, who was living with us in what was supposed to be working nurses' accommodation, wasn't able to work. So it wasn't long before Sister Elizabeth Noel came to our room and sitting on Mum's bed, sensitively told her what the doctor had said. She explained that she had discussed this with Reverend Mother and they both felt it was time we left St. Johns and found more suitable accommodation, perhaps a housekeeping post with appropriate family accommodation but in the meantime, she should allow her three children to go into an orphanage.

"Only for a short time my dear," she said soothingly, "whilst you find somewhere else for you all to live. We have an affiliated home for children. It's St. Ediths in Clevedon, Somerset. Although I have never been there myself, it could be an appropriate placement for Bryan, Betty and Rosemary. Perhaps you should just go and take a look."

Our mother was horrified at the very thought of having to put us into an orphanage. It was her childhood all over again!

"No! I can't possibly do that to them Sister. I'll search for a post with accommodation."

She struggled to get out of bed and Sister Elizabeth Noel was concerned for her.

"Not now, Ethel. We'll give you more time."

But when mum was well enough to begin her search, it soon became apparent that she was not going to find anywhere. It was post-war Britain, thousands had nowhere to live and were begging for work.

Eventually Reverend Mother had no option but to ask my mother to accept that we had to go somewhere and our frantic mother unwillingly accepted that as a temporary measure we could possibly go to St. Ediths. Just for a few weeks while she found us a home.

Mum sat us all on the bed and managed to hide her pain as she told us that we would be going to a new home for a while, but it would only be for a short time. She reassured us that she loved us and would come and see us regularly to make sure we were alright. We could take Spot too, so we would all be together and our big brother would make sure we were okay. At the thought of having other kids to play with, Rosemary and I were quite excited, but being older, Bryan, recognised mum's distress and putting his arms around her neck, promised he would take good care of us and Spot too.

This must have been her tipping point. It was only then that I was frightened to see tears streaming down her demoralised face. She twisted round and lay on our bed with her face in our pillows and sobbed and we all began to cry at her distress. Until that moment, I had happily and innocently accepted our fate, but mum knew what was waiting around our corner.

The unmarried, childless nuns lived within a very cloistered, somewhat insulated world, more to do with what was in heaven, than here on earth. Most of them had little notion of the indifference, even pitilessness, which was heaped upon children in the orphanages of the mid-1900's, but my mother, did!

St Ediths confirmed they could immediately take all three of us and Spot. So once Reverend Mother had been informed that it was indeed possible for us all to go to the Home, the dye was cast. We had no option other than to go and soon. Sister Elizabeth Noel made the arrangements and it was confirmed that we would arrive there in a weeks time. So that was that, we were on our way, but mum firmly reassured us.

"Remember, it's only for a few weeks. I will soon find us a home and we will all be back together again."

Oh, bless her hopeful heart. If only!

SISTER ELIZABETH NOEL

St. Ediths Orphanage Clevedon

11

HISTORY REPEATS

It wasn't long before mum secured a night nurse post in a nursing home eight miles from St. Ediths. Although there was no family accommodation, it was only a one bed-sit room, it would have to do until she could save enough to rent somewhere for us all. While she was close to Clevedon she used the opportunity to check out the orphanage. The Sister in Charge must have done a very good job of convincing her all was well, because on the 1st of June 1950, we were all packed and on a bus to St. Ediths. Even I could tell her heart was

130

breaking and although she tried desperately, she could not hide her tears as we stepped onto that bus. She had no other choice but to take us there and just pray to God that we would be alright and she would soon be picking us up again.

St. Ediths was established as an orphanage for children of the poor in 1890 and housed forty two children. It was a large, late Victorian, four storey, grey stone mansion, built in the Gothic Style. Being very well positioned on Clevedon's highest point, Dial Hill, it had views across the town and out over the Bristol Channel. The foreboding front façade had an ornate central, turreted tower with two sets of balustraded stone steps leading to the double-front door and countless gabled windows. Even on a sunny day it would have sent shivers down an adult spine, let alone small children on a miserably wet day. As we walked towards the Home, Bryan was holding Spot's lead and two small suitcases, I was clutching my doll and Rosemary was holding on tight to her Teddy in one hand and mum in the other. My brother was nine, I was five and my little sister was three. We were apprehensive but thinking we were going into a caring Home for a short stay with some kindly nuns, like the wonderful sisters from St. Johns. We anticipated lots of new playmates of a similar age who, like us, were temporarily impoverished and in need of a kindly harbour during a stormy time in their lives. Mum coaxed us in with the promise that our much loved Spot was going with us and it would only be a short time before we were reunited.

We were met in the entrance hall of St. Ediths by a very tall, rather stern looking Senior Sister. She said hello and shook mum's hand as Rosemary and I cowered behind her. Bryan was braver and dutifully stepped forward to shake the Sister's proffered hand. Spot was tethered to our small amount of luggage in the spacious hallway, as the Sister ushered us into her stark office. She made an effort to make us feel more at ease by organising tea and biscuits and told us about the history of the Home and the philosophy behind the provision of shelter for children who had lost both parents. We, of course, had one parent, but as our mother, through no fault of her own, had fallen on hard times, giving all three of us shelter was the Christian thing to do.

We were then handed over to the house mistress who escorted us up the wide wooden, carpet-less staircase to the dormitories. Ours was on the first floor; Bryan was on an upper floor. The boys were separated from the girls and as an older boy was summoned to escort my brother up to his dormitory, we were told to say our goodbyes and had the first inkling that everything was not going to be as our loving mother had been led to believe. I was startled when mum grasped my brother and clung on to him. The tears began to flow as we all hugged Bryan, mum was weeping too. Bryan turned deathly pale as he hovered in the doorway, his bravado swept aside by the reality of our dire situation. I thought he was going to be sick. The older boy tugged his arm and whisked him away.

After that, we only saw Bryan across the dining room at supper time and we were not allowed to speak to him. Essentially, he was lost to us.

Our dormitory was a large room with bare wooden floorboards and tall, high windows. There were a dozen small, tidily-made beds in lines. Each bed had a small bedside chair. The Housemother asked mum to unpack our few things and put them on a chair.

"Just one toy on each bed Mrs. Williams and then kindly leave the girls to settle in and please take the dog to the kitchen on the way out."

That was that! Mum had to leave but we did not make it easy, clinging to her as if our young lives depended upon it. We hugged and kissed her. She had to take us with her and away from this soulless place. She had to change her mind. She must. She must. But it was to no avail, sadly, our mother had no choice and as she walked down the stairs to Spot, she looked over her shoulder and sobbed, "Be good girls, never forget I love you all very much. Remember to say your prayers every night and I'll be back for you, very, very soon."

She disappeared from view as she crossed the hallway, her footsteps dying away as they went into the kitchen. We heard the heavy door slam shut behind them and immediately rushed to the window and stood on a bed hoping to see her just one more time. But it wasn't to be, the window looked out onto the side of the house and we did not see our mother again for many months.

****

After she left us, mum had to make a lonely seven mile hike to her job in the nursing home. God alone knows how she must have suffered when she left us with only the clothes she stood up in and a small suitcase. She had not a penny to her name, nothing left in the world, other than the three of us and Spot. She wandered onto a deserted beach and that was the nearest she came to being totally destroyed. She sat in the most unutterable pain, staring into the waves, questioning her God as to why he had abandoned us. It was a warm afternoon so she removed her coat, rolled it up and, using it as a pillow, lay back to think about the path ahead. In her exhausted state she slipped into the sweet oblivion of sleep.

Fortunately, mum strongly believed that suicide is a holy sin and that the irreparable damage her death, by her own hand, would impose on us children would impact on us for the rest of our lives. When she awoke she somehow accepted that the action she had taken was the only way out of her situation and vowed that come what may, she could and would cope.

With her unshakable faith and with her Lord's hand on her shoulder again, she found the physical and mental strength to continue her trek to the nursing home and begin to work on making a new start for us all.

When she finally arrived at the Home a young carer, clearly seeing her distress, summoned the Matron. Mercifully, this astute and compassionate woman understood the trauma mum was going through and was very kind. She gave her a decent meal and two pre-owned uniforms, a fob watch, cap and flat, black utility shoes. She insisted that my mother take a couple of quiet days to rest and settle-in.

That supportive woman must have been sent by my mother's holy being to help her. However, once rested and calmed, mum knew that she was there to work and that's just what she did. She threw herself into the job working by night and sleeping by day. In fact it was the only thing she could do and work proved to be her salvation.

****

How we sobbed after mum left, curling up on one bed together, we cried ourselves to sleep clutching each other and our beloved toys, my doll and her teddy. It seemed like ages later when one of the older girls came and told us to get up, wash our hands and go down for supper. We followed her down the stairs and into the dining room, which was scarily silent as we entered. Although it seated all the children, there was no sound. Without a word we were shown to a wooden bench where there were two places laid up with margarine spread bread and honey, also a glass of tepid milk. We looked around to see that Bryan was already seated at the boys only table, he smiled at us, but I could clearly see that he had been crying a lot. We duly took our places and after the recital of grace by one of the Sisters, we were motioned to eat our supper.

After the meal we were allowed some free time to do as we wished so Rosemary and I returned to her bed and stayed there playing with dolly and teddy. Later we younger girls were summoned into the hall, given permission to get ready for bed and warned not to wet the bed. We soon learned that his warning was delivered every evening. This was something we found very odd, as neither of us had done that for a long time. On returning to our bed, a care assistant accosted me.

"This is not your dormitory Betty, you're in here."

My few things were gathered up and I was marched to a separate dormitory. I started kicking up a fuss and was pushed into this second room and onto one of the beds. Rosemary followed me; then, throwing herself next to me she refused to leave. I sat beside her and we both screamed that we would not be separated; mum had promised we would be together. But it was all to no avail, my baby sister was dragged out screaming.

Apparently, separating siblings of the same sex was another of the rules which the Sister had not told mum about. Indeed she had misled her into believing we would have adjacent beds.

However, we were on the same floor so saw each other on a regular basis, but Bryan had completely disappeared. What we did not know was that the Sisters from St. Ediths wrote to mum to say they could not keep Bryan. He was pining for her all day, would not eat and caused disruption amongst the other children. He had to be removed and quickly.

Mum arranged for him to go to a Home for Boys in Broadstairs. But, within a matter of days, they too asked him to leave. She had no option but to take him back with her to the Nursing Home. At least they were reunited and she had one of her children close to her. Her bedsit was too small for the two of them, but the cook at the Nursing Home kindly let him stay with her family until mum could find a home for us all.

Bryan was happy in the cook's house. There were several other children so he was able to be with them and attend their local school. He visited mum every week and spent the odd night sleeping alongside her on her bedroom floor. It seemed like an adventure to him, so he was more than happy with his situation.

It was definitely not so happy for us, but we managed to avoid some of the barbarism as we never wet our beds. The traumatised children who did were severely punished. The carers seemed to think it was done deliberately, so the 'sinners' were not allowed any supper the following evening. Repeat offenders were often made to take cold baths, or to stand in the attic with their soiled sheet over their heads. Offenders would also be hit with heavy rulers and referred to as "dirty bed-bedwetters."

However, although I was young, I did stand up for myself and the smaller kids, so received my fair share of punishment. Rosemary was never punished, because she was only three years old, very placid, content to comply and, as ever, always more sweet natured than her elder sister.

We were schooled at a small school down the hill and attended church every Sunday. We walked in a long line to both destinations every day, except Saturday. This was quite a challenge for such young children so by the time we reached our destination we were worn out and some fell asleep during the droning sermons.

Two or three of the older girls were dispatched to a local cake shop late on a Saturday afternoon where

they scavenged any left-over cake that was available. The baker would box any unsold goodies and the girls carried them back to the Home. Heaven help any girl who was found to have eaten any of them on the way. We never saw any of the cakes, so assumed the 'carers' claimed them.

The Sisters kept chickens and tended a vegetable and soft fruit garden, but I don't recall ever eating a fresh whole egg, or receiving any fresh fruit. Breakfast was porridge or bread and margarine, sometimes accompanied by golden syrup or honey. There was soup or stew and bread for lunch followed by a hot pudding. Tea/supper was bread with spam, cheese or fish paste.

Life at St. Ediths was very much about going without and silence. Both Rosemary and I suffered from Chickenpox and had to remain in isolation with calamine lotion applied to stop us scratching. We also caught the flu, as did most of the children. For this we were treated with vapour chest rubs, steaming tin bowls of hot water in the room and Aspirin. Head-lice were a constant menace, for which the treatment was a stinking lotion, and painful nit-combing, in an attempt to get rid of the eggs.

We were at St. Ediths twice. The first time was from 1st June 1950 until 17th June1951. We were then transferred to another orphanage in Weston-Super-Mare.

ST. MARGARETS WESTON -SUPER-MARE

12

ST. MARGARETS

We never knew why we were moved from Clevedon to Weston-Super-Mare; we were simply told to pack our belongings and be ready to leave by ten o'clock that day. I packed up our few things, but couldn't find my doll. Rosemary clutched her Teddy, but had not seen Rosie. It was time to go and I was desperately looking in and under all the beds, but someone had taken her! I yelled blue murder and refused to leave until she was found, but I was roughly frogmarched out to the waiting car. We knew we were leaving Spot behind, he had become a welcome pet for all the orphans at St. Ediths and it would not have been fair to take him away. We

139

simply had to make the best of it, leave our friends behind and start all over again in St. Margarets, but at least we knew the disciplines of an orphanage, so it should be easier.

We were welcomed by the Sister Superior, a gentle, kind and very holy being who I honestly believed was connected directly to God. We were to discover that all the girls loved her and moments in her company were prized and precious. Unfortunately, she was not directly involved in the day to day activities of the Home. That was left to Miss Bird, the House Mistress. Miss Bird was not one of the Sisters. She was a 'twin-set, pearls and tweed skirt' type of lady; a comely woman with naturally white hair and a long, overly stern and unsmiling face. She ruled with an indifferent aloofness and nothing seemed to please her more than making life difficult for her charges.

We were very quickly absorbed into the monotonous, regimented life of the new Home. Rosemary, who was four, adapted easily. She was small for her age, with straight blonde hair, huge blue eyes and an angelic face. She made friends and with her quiet accepting manner could get away with anything. She was always on the hunt for creatures to mother. A stray cat would be top of her list, but she would find all sorts of insects, except spiders, we were both terrified of spiders. Slugs, snails, butterflies, beetles, ladybirds, anything she could lay her little hands on would go into a jar and have pride of place beside her bed. If they died, they had to have a funeral. As tiny as she was, she would say a prayer to send them to Jesus in the hope they would be accepted into heaven. She confided in her, more or less hairless, Teddy, chatting to him and telling him all her secrets.

The dormitories had several, smaller than normal beds, in lines, spread across the large rooms. They were graded into the ages of the girls and as at St. Ediths, we were allowed one soft toy each, which we could leave on the top of the bed during the day. I no longer had my treasured doll so my bed remained vacant.

About two months after the move, mum came to visit and we were amazed when she arrived by taxi. How could she possibly afford one? Our question was answered when the driver got out and opened her door; it was her old friend Colin. He and his wife Anne had started a taxi business which was going well and bringing mum to see us was their way of helping out.

On that first visit to St. Margarets, mum offered to buy me another doll as soon as she could afford it; but as Rosebud could never be replaced, I told her I did not want one. Anyway, mum managed to bring us something, although we knew from our St. Ediths experience, that anything too ostentatious would be confiscated and sweets eaten by the staff or handed out to their favourite children. We became well versed in keeping them hidden from view. It was remarkable that mum could come by such luxuries, let alone afford them; sweets were still rationed in the early 1950's. On that first visit to St. Margarets, I was able to tell mum that Rosemary had settled in very well and there was no need to worry. I was always there for her anyway, and enjoyed looking after her. I was teaching her to read and there was an abiding bond of love between us which no one could break and that helped us to cope.

What I did not tell her was that I was finding the adjustment to the new home very difficult. I was of slim build with fine, mousy fair hair and being much taller than other six year old girls, taken for being older. Consequently I was expected to behave in a more grown-up manner and accept adult responsibilities.

This is where a clearer memory of my early life begins and the unburdened innocence of my own childhood ends. I was a loner and had little inclination to mix with the other girls or make friends. I would constantly drift off into my own small world and wonder what mum and Bryan were doing each day and if they missed us as much as we missed them. Mum was never far from my thoughts. It was obvious, every time we had to say goodbye, following an all too brief visit that left all three of us devastated, I did not want to add to mum's distress by burdening her with my problems. Instead, I told her how enjoyable it was to have summer walks and swims at weekends, or early evenings, along the glorious Weston Sea Front. With two miles of golden, sandy beach and views out towards Wales and Exmoor, it provided everything anyone could possibly want for the quintessential trip to the English seaside.

On busy, summer weekends, our two-by-two line of girls walked just that little bit faster once we could hear the high pitched squeals and laughter of excited children on the beach.

Evenings and early mornings were the best times to see race horses train on the Weston sands. They enjoyed training on the soft sand waterline because it was easier on their legs and the salt water good for their hooves. We sometimes watched as a dozen horses galloped along the beach, a truly magnificent sight as they splashed through the waves with the sea glistening off their muscled, wet flanks.

Those happy walks reassured me that we were not totally abandoned and still belonged to a larger world outside the Home.

We went on an outing to the circus, my first time ever, and it was mesmerising. During the show we were all given the rare treat of a fig roll biscuit and a small Aero chocolate bar. I had never seen one before and thought mine was stale because it was full of small holes! However, once I saw the others munching and obviously relishing theirs, I could see my mistake. I found out later that mum had brought the box of Aero bars on her last visit and gave them directly to the Sister Superior for our outing.

We enjoyed a Christmas party with a visit from a magician who produced a sixpence from behind my ear. He gave it to me to keep and I was enthralled, thinking he was for real and wishing he was my dad and could magic up loads of money for my family.

The other girls at St. Margarets were aged from 4 to 14 years. They were either orphans, or the unfortunates of parents who had hit upon tough times, not always of their own making, or in prison for debt or some other misdemeanour. We were banned from talking about why we were there or our family situation. There was never any bullying between the girls. We were all too dependent on each other for that. We had a mutually frightening aggressor to worry about: the staff!

I was never a mild mannered or quietly accepting child and often rebelled against the authoritative and hard discipline of the institutes we lived sometimes in. If I saw another girl being unfairly disciplined, I couldn't help but go to her aid. I suppose I didn't make things easy for myself, or for them. I hated being there and made sure everyone was aware of it. On the many occasions when I misbehaved or questioned authority, I would be marginalised and isolated from my sister and the rest of the girls. The amount of time I spent in the chapel or sitting on my bed must have accounted for half of my time there, but at least I was too young to be forced to clean toilets or scrub and polish the kitchen, floors and windows. When I misbehaved I was often banished to the dormitory and made to stay there, alone, except for the Bible, until I was allowed out and down into the dining room for supper. This would be after all the other children had finished and the house cat had been allowed to eat my fish paste, or sliced luncheon meat. By the time I arrived it was just bread and 'cat licked' margarine for supper!

There was a ridged, strictly adhered to time schedule within the Home, with repetitive routines for praying, washing, bathing, toilet and more praying. A drink before bedtime was strictly forbidden as it led to bed wetting and although bedwetters were not dealt with in the barbaric St. Ediths way, it was still frowned upon. If we were desperately thirsty we had to secretly dip our flannels into the dirty, dusty water of the fire buckets on the way to the bathroom for the last pee of the day and suck on the flannel. If caught we would be hauled up before one of the carers, given a smack round the legs, and made to stand, late into the evening in the dark corridor. It was 'ungodly' to have committed a sin and for some minor misdemeanour, long prayers would have to be written out, or an apologetic note written to the Sister Superior. I don't think she ever saw them or even knew a lot of what was going on within the Home. But, even so, woe betide us if the spelling or grammar was not correct.

Every night we knelt beside our beds on the hard wooden floor in our cream flannel night dresses, to pray. If we had misbehaved, we had to kneel a bit longer to gain God's understanding and forgiveness which made my knees sore and legs numb. My own private prayers were always said once I was in bed and alone. That was where I made my repetitive, secret requests for help and attention.

Few relatives ever visited the Home, as most of them lived too far away and could never have afforded to make the journey anyway. When visitors were expected, we would be told to be quiet, not to speak to or interact in any way with the other children's visitors and, if we really had to be seen, make sure we were not heard. An appointment to visit the orphanage had to be sanctioned well in advance. This was to ensure that we would be pristinely presented to the rarely incoming outside world, with hard-soap scrubbed teeth and face, tidy hair and a clean frock, in the summer, or blouse, cardigan and skirt in the winter. Underneath, summer or winter, we wore thick navy knickers, a vest and rubber-buttoned liberty bodice. They were rubber buttoned so they could go through the mangle without the buttons breaking.

At long last it was our day! We knew the appointment had been made and sanctioned. We had not seen mum for months, but she was about to visit us!

We were up, dressed and downstairs long before the 'time to get up' bells rang out. After breakfast we were the only children left in the drab dining room, adorned only by stern images of long departed nuns and clergy. We had been peering through the huge windows for the first glimpse of mum's arrival for so long, Rosemary had wandered off into the hallway.

I recognised Colin's taxi as it drove into view. His wife Anne was sitting in the back with mum. She always accompanied mum on her visits and would go for a walk on the beach with Colin for an hour or so, but not on that day: it was teeming with rain.

"Mums here!" I shouted.

My little sister dashed back into the room and pushed her way in front of me. She was excitedly jumping up and down clapping her hands together.

"Let me see, Betty! Let me see!"

I lifted her up to peer over the white blind covering the bottom half of the window. I never did work out if it was there to stop us seeing out, or the outside world seeing in.

Rosemary squealed with delight as mum got out of the taxi with two big, brown-paper carrier bags and hurried up the steps towards the ornately carved stone portico in the heavy rain. She was wearing her one and only semi-fitted, light grey wool coat and on her head, a half-folded, floral silk headscarf, the points of which were tied in a double knot under her chin. We both charged out from the dining room with our brown leather sandals clattering over the bare wooden floor.

"Stop running and walk quietly, girls."

The gentle command came from the Sister Superior who was gracefully gliding through the dark,

146

wood panelled, entrance hall. With her long black gown brushing the floor.

Sister Superior always gave me the impression that she was gliding. She was most likely in her 40's, but seemed ancient to us. She was a short, plump lady, who wore National Health, clear framed specs. We never knew what colour her hair was, or even if she actually had any, because she never removed her tight fitting and face framing bandeau, or the fine white, heavily starched cotton veil, from her head. We always assumed that she must also sleep in her wimple and habit; we could never imagine her putting on a nightie like the rest of us. Her robes and habit were black and she wore a thick, rope-like belt, with a huge set of keys hanging from it. Around her neck, hanging on a silver chain and black-beaded necklace, was a black crucifix with a silver figure of Christ, nailed to the cross. She always looked immaculate, had a soapy clean, coal tar fragrance and a covering of fine fair hair over most of a very pale face. Her glide towards the front door put paid to our race to be first embraced by mum.

One of the senior girls was already at the door and demurely ushered our rain drenched mother in. Under her wet coat a thin cotton floral dress, draped slightly lower so the wet hem dripped onto her nurses black, practical and flat lace-up shoes. I thought she was so beautiful. She was slim, about 5' 5" tall with permed brown curly hair. She would often have to turn her head to one side to hear what people were saying because of her deaf ear.

Sister Superior welcomed mum. Had she come into the entrance hall to say hello, or did' she just happen to be passing? I prefer to believe that, through her connection with St. Johns, she had a genuine interest in mum and her well-being. Mum lowered her head, a kind of salute which inferred respect, but her kind eyes looked into those of Sister Superior as she quietly wished her good morning and asked how she was. They exchanged a few niceties as Sister Superior walked with us to the dining room and wished us an enjoyable reunion. She was on her way to the chapel. It seemed to us girls that the Sisters were always on their way to, or coming from, their precious chapel; their inner sanctum. They spent most of their lives in there, for Saints' Days, Holy Days, Evening Vespers, Daily Prayers and spiritual singing of psalms and hymns.

Rosemary and I could not care less about our mother's wet coat. We threw ourselves with cries of joy at her and snuggled into her arms.

"SILENCE"! What on earth is all this noise and fuss about?"

Miss Bird strode into the room. The House Mistress was a bully who revelled in lording it over the disadvantaged. She looked disapprovingly at mum.

"So Mrs Williams, what have you brought with you to spoil your girls today?"

Mum was still in the process of trying to free herself from a wet coat, head scarf and two clinging daughters. The precious moment as she hugged us after such a long absence had been abruptly destroyed, as intended. She was visibly upset but knowing Miss Bird was in a position of absolute authority and not wishing to make life any more difficult for us than it already was, she replied in a soft apologetic tone.

"Hello Miss Bird. Sorry about the noise." She let us go and picked-up the two brown paper carrier bags, which being waxed had weathered the rain remarkably well.

"I've brought thirty six ice creams for all the girls and four, fresh chickens for the Sisters."

"We can use the chickens, I'll take them to the kitchen," snapped Miss Bird, with not a hint of thanks in her voice, but it changed to triumphalism as she continued. "But the ice creams cannot be accepted: much too indulgent in these austere times. Please see that you take them away with you when you leave."

She gave mum a long stony stare to quell any thought of protest and when none came, took the chickens, turned on her heel and marched away.

It was much later that Colin told me that the other taxi drivers, knowing of my mother's visit had clubbed together with coupons and money and bought ice creams for her to give to us.

Mum had to put them, still in the bag, into the basket in the hallway, all thirty six of them, and we could only watch as they melted away to form a pool of soggy paper and creamy white sludge. I am sure the Sisters enjoyed their chicken, but it was the pointless denial of the ice cream treats and allowing them to go to waste as a sop to Miss Bird's vanity which struck home.

For the first time in my young life, I saw and understood my mum's absolute despair and I felt her misery. She tried desperately to hide it from us but there was no disguising her humiliation. I recognised, for the first time, how unkind some members of the human race can be, even the ones who should be the most intuitive and humble, placed as they are in a position of absolute authority. They are the ones who should be the most understanding, caring and compassionately concerned for their subordinates, but for many of them, the primary concern was their own personal betterment and gain. From that point I understood and fully accepted that I had to become more responsible for my little sister and help my mother as much as I could.

However, despite the dreadful start, we made the most of mum's visit. We joyously played ludo, snakes & ladders and she read to us from an album of girls' stories, which she brought with her on every visit. Always took it away with her, sure in the knowledge that it would be confiscated, as would the sweet treats hidden within mum's enchanted pockets. I had a secret place for our sweets, and rationed them between us but they never lasted until her next visit.

Much too soon the magical one and a half hour visit was over and mum had to leave.

The three of us were plunged, yet again into the despair of another tearful parting; perhaps a few more minutes together, maybe another loving hug? No, our time was up!

Mum looked crushed, but tried desperately to control her tears. Rosemary was yelling her head off whilst I did my best to comfort her. We watched as mum slipped out through the door, carrying the soggy bag of ice creams and walked through the gate to the waiting car. Suddenly she was being driven away to resume her night-time work. The taxi disappeared into the rain and in an instant she was gone and we were, once again, on our own.

But not quite. Sister Superior silently arrived in the hallway to give me an encouraging smile and tenderly take Rosemary by the hand. Talking to her gently, she coaxed her into another room to calm down. I took comfort from the love she showed us and quickly took refuge in the empty dormitory where I slumped onto my bed and cried myself into the welcome relief of sleep.

I suppose that was the reason relatives were not permitted to come very often. It was too upsetting for the children and their parents, but, just as likely, it was an annoyance to the staff and upset the Home regime of quiet reflection, prayer and the all important discipline.

We all needed, and longed for the reassurance and hope that one day our young lives would be better and this is what a visit by our parents could bring us.

Sometimes we would be allowed to share the sublime quiet of the inner sanctum, the small Chapel. Perhaps for a special service, like Easter or Christmas; this was always a most welcome and wonderful experience. If we misbehaved, as a penance, we could be sent to the chapel to reflect on our 'sin', which was no punishment for me as I loved it in there. It was so calm and peaceful and made me feel safe knowing God was watching over us all and would always care for us. I enjoyed an innocent and absolute faith in our Heavenly Father in those days. The perfume from the frankincense which wafted around the chapel, symbolised the ascension of our prayers to God in heaven and the holy water was sprinkled about to cleanse the soul. It was intoxicating stuff and I relished it. Small wonder the visiting Sisters were constantly in their chapel, then looked like they were floating when

151

they came out. They were serene, quiet and endowed with a peace of mind we mere mortals could never hope to attain. I much preferred it in there to visits to the local church, which always meant a long, silent walk, mostly in the rain or fog, and then a cold, long sit on hard wooden pews, listening to the vicar telling us we would burn in hell's fire if we didn't follow the faith.

I often used to stand alone outside the chapel window. Rosemary would never standstill or be quiet for long enough, so I would not allow her to interrupt my self-imposed solitude. I listened to and quietly joined in with their chanting and singing. I learned most of it off by heart. I was always surprised and delighted that no other girls came to my special place, so I did not have to share it with anyone else. The incense would drift out through the open window as I stood quietly taking it all in. It was so calming and comforting in an otherwise cold and harsh environment. I felt closer to God there and hoped he would see me and take the time to answer my prayers and get our family back together again. I also made up my mind that one day I would be a nun.

At 7am sharp every morning, we were brought back to the harsh reality of life at St. Margarets by the deafening sound of a hand bell, shaken with great vigour by an already washed and dressed nun. The bells would sound again at five mins past and yet again ten mins later. We had to be out of bed and dressed before the second bell, then make our beds before the third. We had to ensure the sheet and blanket were tucked in correctly, as we had been shown when we first arrived at the Home. Failure meant we would be made to strip the bed and re-make it, which for a small child was a huge and daunting chore. I never had a problem getting out of bed, so did not once have to strip and remake the bed, but a few little ones needed my help, especially Rosemary, who was in the room next door and just too small to carry out the task. I did enjoy looking after my sister and the smaller girls. It gave me a purpose and a reason to get up in the mornings.

We were not allowed a 'good-girls' prettily flowered frock if we misbehaved, so I always ended up with a plain, dull, mid-blue 'naughty girls' flannelette blouse and grey skirt. I hardly ever had the nice cotton dress like the other girls. I seemed to be one of just a few in the wretched blouse and skirt.

After a breakfast of tea, porridge, or toast and margarine, we were given a dessert spoon of sweet malt. That was lovely, but the cod liver oil which followed was horrid.

We were taken, en-masse, to the toilets every morning after breakfast and before school. Sitting on the smelly toilet in the freezing cold, was torture and you had to sit there until you produced something and called out, "nurse, I'm ready." The motion would be checked and we would be mopped up and sent on our way. Sometimes we had to sit so long our bottoms would stick to the toilet seat, or our legs went numb and we could not stand up.

Due to day-dreaming, I would often be one of the last out of the cubicle and have to run to catch-up the snaking line of girls as they walked to church or some odd outings. Sometimes, as we walked along, local children, especially boys, would fall-in beside us and jeer shouting that our parents were prisoners or our mums and dads did not want us any more. How I hated being mocked like that and when one boy got too close to my face I was so angry, I punched his face. I didn't get any supper that night, but it was worth it to hear him howl and I must admit it felt marvellous.

There was never any popular music played in the Home, no music at all, other than the lyrical singing in the chapel and that really summed-up the atmosphere of both Homes. It was all about abstinence, servitude, prayer, obedience and reverence.

As I have said, I was a loner, but one of the very few girls that I did befriend was, Susan, the daughter of an imprisoned mother who could not visit. Susan was not very strong. She had German measles as a baby which left her very deaf and with poor vision. We were the same age and shared the same birth month so were both Capricorns. She didn't have to attend lessons and the Sisters taught her stuff from her bible and an abacus with multi-coloured beads spread across wires on a frame. Susan became very ill and lay in her bed all day, for days on end. I was allowed to go and talk to her for a few moments every other day.

On the last day I ever saw her, I was flabbergasted to see she had a lovely, new, pale pink taffeta and lace dress on. I assumed that her mother must have brought it in for her as a surprise and, amazingly, she was actually allowed to wear it. And in bed too! She was so thrilled with her new dress and showed it off to me and to everybody who came in. As I watched her, proud as a peacock, lying back in her bed and eating a luxurious, freshly peeled orange; she looked so happy. I flew into a childish fit of jealousy, knocked the orange out of her hands and hit out at her, actually tearing her lovely dress in the process. She was startled and began to scream. She was not physically hurt, but shocked and frightened. She fainted and looked like she was dead. I was dragged off her, hauled out of the room and taken in front of the Sister Superior, the person who I admired so much and was so close to God. Surely she was going to be very angry with me, but she was very calm, her usual serene self and spoke quietly.

"Your friend, Susan, is seriously ill and might be about to enter heaven. You should have shown more compassion and love towards her, Betty and not be blinded by your own selfish envy."

I was shocked. "I'm so sorry. I didn't know. Can I go back to her room and tell her I'm so sorry and I love her?"

Sister Superior shook her head. "No it's too late for that, Betty. Susan is much too tired for more talk today, perhaps tomorrow. And, you should know that the dress Susan was wearing, the one you were so envious of, did not come from her mother. It was loaned to her by Irene, one of the carers, for a photograph which has been taken to send to her mother. Now, Betty, you are to go immediately to the Chapel and pray for God's forgiveness and guidance. Reflect on what you have done and do not come out until you are called."

I remained in the Chapel until late into the evening. Unbeknown to Sister, it was actually no punishment for me. I sat quietly contemplating my wickedness, through all their evensong singing and prayers. I was ordered to come out in time for a drink of water before I was sent to bed. My friend, who I never saw again, was taken away in an ambulance the next

155

day and a few days later I was told that she flown off to join the angels.

When I heard the bad news I was mortified and my own punishment kicked in, made worse because I did not have the chance to tell her how sorry I was for my dreadful behaviour.

Amazingly, whilst we were at St. Margarets, I was awarded a prize. It was for teaching my sister to read her first book which we always read together. It was 'Ned the Lonely Donkey' and she could read it perfectly from cover to cover by the time we left the Home. That book was to travel with us wherever we went for the next five years and always came out to be read during difficult times.

****

The last time I read that book to Rosemary was in August 2018 as my beautiful sister lay dying of cancer in a hospice in Oxford.

Adelaide House, Clevedon

13

YOU CAN'T EAT THE ROSES

Our mother saved her pay and promised that as soon as she had enough money she would rent a flat in Clevedon and get us back together again. It took over two years, but eventually she had enough to search through the agents for a suitable place. However, as a single parent, with three small children it was proving impossible to find a landlord prepared to take the risk. Then her doctor mentioned a patient who was looking for a suitable tenant for a large house on Clevedon seafront. Wasting no time, mum went to view the house from the outside. It was a handsome, detached property, sitting within its own grounds with six bedrooms.

Mum went to see the agent and although he already had a pile of letters and telegrams from interested parties, he accompanied her to the property and walked her around the house and grounds. It was a perfect fit for mum's needs. The agent advised that she should move fast and visit the lady who owned the property to explain what she wanted to do with it. Mum agreed and the agent made an appointment for her to see the lady, that afternoon.

The address the agent gave her turned out to be an even larger house situated in one of the smarter parts of Clevedon. The houses along the tree-lined avenue were very select and most sat within their own grounds. Undaunted and saying a silent prayer, mum walked up the drive and knocked on the front door. It was opened by a very pleasant housekeeper who showed her into a sitting room overlooking a beautifully tended garden. As she stood admiring the garden an elegantly attired, elderly lady came into the room, gave her a reassuring smile and invited her to take a seat next to a small table. She then turned to the housekeeper.

"Thank you, Mary. Will you bring us some tea please?"

The housekeeper returned her smile. "Of course. Would you like shortcake biscuits, Florence? I've just made a batch."

"That will be perfect, thank you."

As the housekeeper left the room, the elderly lady sat in the chair opposite mum.

"Thank you for coming to see me Mrs Williams. It was Mary who took the call from the agent. We are most intrigued by what the agent had to tell us."

"Thank you for seeing me at such short notice, Mrs Barnett."

"Not at all my dear; we couldn't wait to hear more about your exciting project. It's also a wonderful excuse to partake of my favourite biscuits."

Mum laughed at her little joke.

"Mary has been my housekeeper for over fifteen years and I have come to value her opinion. You will have noticed that we are on first name terms. I prefer it that way. I loathe being called Mrs Barnett, it makes me feel quite old, so please call me Florence. You are?"

"Ethel, Ethel Williams," mum was glad to confirm. She rather liked the old lady.

"Well, Ethel. Let me tell you about the property you're interested in."

Florence Barnett explained that the seafront house was once her family home. It was where she and her, now deceased, husband raised their children. It was a house full of fond memories which she had rented to a family friend for many years, but as her friend's children had flown the nest she and her husband found something smaller and more manageable.

Mary came in with the tea and the prized biscuits and placed the tray on the low table.

"Do you take your tea with milk, Mrs Williams?"

Florence interjected, "It's, Ethel, Mary. Mrs Williams has kindly agreed to first names."

"Good, that's so much easier," Mary agreed. "Lemon or a splash of milk, Ethel?"

"Err, milk please."

Mum could hardly believe her ears. There she was about to ask for an enormous favour, yet Mrs Barnett had managed to switch roles and make her feel completely at ease. It was the act of an extremely gracious and courteous lady.

Mary dutifully poured the fragrant tea into three delicate, bone china cups, adding a splash of milk to each. She placed a cup and saucer in front of Ethel and handed another to Florence, who grinned like a naughty schoolgirl as she helped herself to a biscuit before passing the plate to mum.

"Mary makes the most delightful shortcake biscuits, Ethel. You had better take two before I eat the lot!"

She smiled as mum took two and took a sip of tea before leaning forward.

"Now, down to business. What can we help you with Ethel?"

Mum following the example set by Florence Barnett, took a sip of tea then began to spell out why she was sitting there in front of the owner of that lovely house. She wanted to turn it into a registered Home for the Elderly. Florence and Mary listened in silence as she told them about her caring and nursing back ground and explained that due to Tom's desertion, which lead to destitution, her three children had been sent to St. Ediths, but the two girls were currently in St. Margarets, another orphanage in Weston Super-Mare. She was worried that making that admission might have damaged her chances, but Mary interjected.

"Oh, Florence is a great supporter of St. Ediths and has been for many years. She might have met your girls during one of her visits there."

"You could be right, Mary," said Florence, "I know things might not be perfect there, Ethel, but I think they provide a much needed service in very difficult circumstances, even so, it must have been dreadfully tough for you my dear, having to leave your girls there."

Mum knew not to harp on too much about her difficulties, so merely said "Yes, it was, but we coped."

"I'm very impressed with your experience and honesty, Ethel."

Florence paused to have a sip of tea and a nibble at one of her favourite biscuits. She dabbed her mouth with a serviette before continuing.

"It seems to me that you would put my property to much needed and mutually beneficial use, Ethel. My husband and I were in business together for many years, so I do realise the difficulties you might face in obtaining the required finance to start your new enterprise."

Rising from her chair, she walked over to the window where she looked out over the garden for some time before turning to return to her seat.

"Mary, could you kindly refresh the teapot whilst Ethel and I continue our discussions."

As Mary left the room, Florence retook her seat and lowered her voice, "I am amazed that you have survived such a perfectly terrible ordeal intact and I congratulate you on that, Ethel; I would like to help you my dear, if you would allow an old lady to offer you some assistance."

She went on to offer terms that were more than acceptable to mum's ears and she couldn't believe her luck when after a couple of hours of very pleasant conversation, many cups of tea and the complete demolition of the shortcake biscuits, she was not only offered the house, but all its contents. Florence promised to waive the need for any deposit, whether her solicitors liked it or not and, prior to the signing of an agreement, she would have unfettered access to the property to enable her to obtain the obligatory permissions from the Planning Authority, Social Services and The Fire Department.

As mum retraced her steps back down the avenue, she had a spring in her step. She had actually secured that perfect house, fully furnished too. She felt that sometimes magical things do happen and told us later she could not stop smiling all the way back to her room at the Nursing Home.

Florence Barnett was as good as her word and everything went through swimmingly, although her solicitor did baulk at the waiving of a deposit and a two year lease. He 'allowed' the lack of any deposit, but insisted on drawing up a one year lease. However, he accepted a verbal agreement that no unnecessary obstacles would be put in the way of renewing the lease after the first year.

Hospitals were advised of the imminent opening of the Home and mum soon had clients lined up to enter as soon as Registration was received.

Mum called the Home 'Adelaide House' after my Godmother, Sister Adelaide.

'Adelaide House' was registered for seven residents within eight weeks, but there was a downside.

Registration for seven meant that we could not live with her yet. My mother knew she would need all the income she could get to enable her to firmly establish the business and make our return permanent, but there was no doubt things were getting better.

Neither Rosemary or I were aware our mother had obtained a house and was opening a Home, so, we were confused when, at 7am on the morning of 26th of April 1952, we got up as usual only to be told not to make our beds, but collect and pack all our things and be ready to leave the Home by 10am. We were to be transferred back to St. Ediths!

After acclimatising to Weston Super Mare for over a year, we were not too keen on the idea, so when the taxi stopped outside St. Ediths, neither of us were in any great hurry to get out.

Eventually we slowly climbed the all too familiar stone steps. Would it turn out to be a bad move for us? We were in no hurry to go through the door to find out, but as we reached the top of the steps, the door began to open and squeezing out through the narrowest of gaps, our beloved Spot came dashing out to greet us.

What a welcome! We were overjoyed to see him and his mouth broke into a canine grin as he darted from one to the other, jumping up and licking our outstretched hands and faces. He was deliriously happy to see us and his antics really softened our return.

The regime at St. Ediths remained tough and 'caring' staff not as caring as they should have been, but things did seem to have improved, perhaps it was just that I was now more 'in-tune' with the discipline and the regime. Whatever it was, it seemed better than being in Weston-Super-Mare, we were back with Spot and later that same day we found out we were now not far from mum and Bryan.

Our mother had always promised that at some point she could get us all back together and her faith in that never wavered; but first she had to work hard to establish a sustainable business. Taking on a full-time carer, she quickly gained an excellent reputation for the care and food she provided. Adelaide House was full within days and there was a growing waiting list.

Although Rosemary and I never got the chance to actually live in Adelaide House, we were allowed to visit and even stay the night on many a weekend. We had not seen Bryan, now eleven years old, for some time, so when we were allowed out for our first visit, we hardly recognised our 'chubby-chops' brother. He was quite a bit taller; but all that good food from mum's cook friend at the nursing home had piled on the pounds. We didn't care, we were so happy to see him, but he had certainly grown; in all directions!

Mum warned us not to remark on his size.

"It's only puppy fat" she said "but he's very touchy about it".

So we said nothing, but I could not resist squeezing his side which got me a playful slap on the arm. But no matter, it was truly wonderful to see him and be back together, even if it was only for a day or two at a time.

It never occurred to us that there was anything wrong with Bryan being with mum and us at the Home. Mum had made it clear that was how it had to be for the time being. Bryan attended the local school and soon made friends with a couple of local boys, although he always seemed happiest when helping the gardener and doing odd jobs for him.

During our visits Rosemary and I would change into nice smocked dresses mum had bought us and spend time with the residents, who spoilt us. We also enjoyed, what for us, were huge helpings of good, well cooked food.

We often sat in the front room window of Adelaide House watching as violent storms funnelled up the Bristol Channel and gigantic waves crashed into the sea wall, cascading plumes of spray over the windows. I was totally in awe of this as we sat, safe and warm within mum's new Home. We cherished every moment of being there.

Bryan took us to play on the beach or in the parks. We often walked up the road together as a family and listened to the Clevedon Brass Band playing in the ornate bandstand, which overlooked the sea at the top of the hill. We went for walks along the grand Victorian pier and could listen to the music from the newly installed jukebox in the pleasure palace there.

Mum would go in to buy us glasses of lemonade, a milk stout for herself and we each had a bag of Smiths crisps with the little blue paper twist of salt inside. Sometimes, as a very special treat, we would have cockles or fish and chips. We were so very content on those days with mum devoted to her new Home for the Elderly and beginning to build a new life for us all.

The gardener at Adelaide House, Mr. Parks, was a widower. A big man in his late forties, he often brought mum fresh produce from his allotment. He encouraged Bryan to help in the garden and tried to get him interested in the growing of flowers and produce, but Bryan switched-off when he became too bossy and constantly tried to discipline him. He would much rather be tinkering with friends' bikes.

Mr Parks became very attentive to our mother and I often overheard him asking her out for a drink or to the pictures. She always refused by saying that she had far too much to do to take time off. When Bryan asked her if Mr Parks was her boyfriend, she gave him the reassuring answer he was hoping for.

"No. Never in a million years. I really don't have the time for boyfriends and besides, I'm still married to your father."

Bryan told us later that Mr Parks (Parky to us) had taken against him after mum refused to go out for drinks with him. The gardener went with the house and was paid for by Mrs Barnett, so mum could not get rid of him. Bryan thought that 'Parky' moon-lighted in other gardens as well as his own allotment, which was why he now only turned up at Adelaide House a couple of days a week.

One Saturday morning the doorbell rang and mum, who was in the kitchen, asked Bryan to see who it was. He quickly returned.

"It's a lady to see you, mum, her name is Mary".

As mum hurried into the hallway, she had a premonition that something was wrong because Mrs Barnett's housekeeper had never called in on her before. It came as a jolt to mum to see that she was dressed in black.

"Hello Ethel. Sorry to drop in uninvited, but I have grim news and I thought it best to deliver it in person. Is there anywhere we can speak in private?"

"If you don't mind the kitchen Mary, do come through," she whispered as she led the way.

She turned to Bryan. "It's a nice day, why not go for a ride on your bike, but make sure you're back for tea."

As Bryan left, mum led her visitor into the kitchen. "Would you like a cup of tea, Mary?"

"That would be nice, Ethel. It's been a long walk." She wearily slumped into one of the two easy chairs in front of a welcoming fire. Mum moved the kettle onto the hob as her visitor removed her small, black veiled hat and for the first time noticed that Mary was crying. Through her broken sobs Mary gave the reason for her visit.

"Ethel, I'm so very saddened to have to tell you that my dearest Florence died three days ago."

Mums heart hit the floor.

"Oh, I'm so sorry, Mary. What happened?"

"It was very sudden, her heart has not been strong for some time, but at least she passed in her sleep, the way she would have wanted."

A long silence descended as they became lost in their own thoughts.

Mary broke the silence. "She was so proud of you, Ethel and how you have managed to get this place off the ground and seem to be doing so well. But, and this is the reason I have come to see you, in total confidence you understand. I know a little of the conditions on which you took on this place and, as you know, Florence's solicitor was never very happy about it. Well, I overheard him talking to her eldest son earlier today and they are going to ask you to leave. They will not be renewing the lease Ethel and want the house sold as soon as probate is obtained.

"What? After all I had to do to get the place registered; and what about my residents, where will they go?"

"I know" said Mary as she took Ethel's hand, "I'm so sorry to be the one to have to tell you this. Have you got enough money to buy the house yourself?"

Ethel shook her head. I've only been here for less than a year Mary. I would have to borrow from a bank and without some security, I'm sure they would turn me down. What about you, what will you do now?"

"Oh, I am well provided for thanks Ethel; but I will be moving to my widowed sister's home in Bournemouth within the next few weeks".

When Mary had gone, mum sat alone in her kitchen and cried. She had had so many set-backs in her life and she desperately wanted to take this devastating news in her stride but she momentarily succumbed to the shock of it all.

The following day the postman had to knock on the door and ask mum to sign for a Registered Letter. Knowing who it must be from, she took it into the kitchen and made herself a reassuringly strong cup of tea before opening it.

The solicitor had sent the official 'Notice to Vacate' her beloved Adelaide House 'within three months'. Her immediate thoughts were for her residents. How on earth was she going to tell them? She thought about gathering everyone together in the lounge to give them the bad news, but had second thoughts. If she talked to them individually it would be easier to soften the blow of telling them they were going to have to find somewhere else to live out their twilight years.

She chose one of her elderly gentlemen to break the news to first. Mr Sheldon was a kindly soul, always willing to listen to others and had a brilliant mind which the ageing process had yet to dim. She went upstairs and tapped on his door

"Come in."

She opened the door and peeped-in. He was sitting at his own mahogany writing bureau, which he brought with him when he moved in. As so often happened, she found him writing a letter and looking out on the sunlit garden for inspiration.

"Sorry to interrupt, Mr Sheldon, but I was wondering if we could have a talk. I would value your advice on a rather worrying subject."

"Not your roses Mrs Williams?" He stood-up and smiled. He was tall, slim and ramrod straight. An ex-military man whose wit and demeanour belied a man well into his eighties. His only deference to age was the half-moon glasses he used for reading and writing. As he removed them he quickly noticed her distress and apologised.

"Sorry about that, my dear, I've always had a facetious nature. How can I help?"

Mum walked over to join him by the window.

"I'm not sure you can Mr Sheldon, but I have some dreadful news and thought if I told you first, you might be able to suggest the best a way to break it to the others." She handed him the letter. He put his glasses back on, frowned when he saw the letter heading and carefully read the contents. Then he went through certain paragraphs again, this time reading them out loud. He folded the letter back to its original creasing and tapped it against his chin as he thought about all the implications. Eventually, he put the letter down on the writing bureau and placed his reading glasses on top of it. He put an arm around mum's shoulders and turned her so that they both looked out over the garden.

"Well, Mrs Williams, you are quite right, that is dreadful news and it has been imparted without a single ounce of compassion. But that, I'm afraid, is how many solicitors operate. The paragraph offering you the opportunity to buy this house, is, quite frankly an insult. He is well aware of your financial situation, but gives no credit to the hard work and dedication you have put in to provide us with this wonderful home. I look out over this beautiful garden every day and appreciate what you have achieved for us. But, you can't eat the roses, my dear, someone needs to help you. I have enough money to buy this property without resorting to a mortgage, so if you would agree to continue to run the Home, very much as you do now, I will buy it and rent it to you for the same amount you pay now."

Mum looked at him with relieved amazement.

"Do you really mean that, Mr Sheldon?"

"Of course, Mrs Williams. I shall write a letter to this solicitor with my offer to buy Adelaide House today, also a letter to my own solicitor to act on my behalf in the matter. Of course, this means there will no need to acquaint the other residents with the problem and I would appreciate your keeping my ownership of Adelaide House, as our little secret."

A couple of hours later, Mr Sheldon came downstairs with the two letters and asked mum if Bryan could jump on his bike and drop them into the letter box at the main post office. That way they would be sure that his offer would be received, first post on Monday.

On the Wednesday, mum was overjoyed when Mr Sheldon told her that, subject to obtaining Probate, his offer had been accepted. Mum wrote a letter to Mary to tell her the good news and walked to Mrs Barnett's house with Bryan to post it through the letterbox, in the hope that it would be forwarded on. As they walked down the tree-lined avenue the estate agent's 'For Sale' sign was prominently displayed at the entrance to the drive. Other than that, the house looked much the same as it did when she walked up the drive over a year before saying a prayer and with hope in her heart.

Bryan was very impressed with the house.

"It would make a good nursing home, mum."

Mum laughed. "That's an idea above our station, my love." As she went to push the letter through the letterbox, Bryan stopped her.

"I think there's someone inside."

"I wouldn't think so." Despite her doubt, she pressed the door bell and as they waited.

Bryan put his ear to the letter box. "I can hear someone coming!"

They stepped back from the door and it was opened by a surprised Mary, who was even more surprised when Ethel told her that one of her residents was buying Adelaide House and renting it to her so that she could continue caring for everyone. Mary invited them in, apologising for the state of the place, but the family had asked her to sort through all of Florence's belongings, catalogue them and pack them into boxes.

"That's wonderful news, Ethel. Let's celebrate with a pot of tea." She turned to Bryan. "I hope you like shortcake biscuits young man."

Adelaide House 1953

Ground floor Flat in Princes Road, Clevedon.

14

TOGETHER ONCE MORE

Mr Sheldon was sound of mind when he moved into mum's care, but being an astute man he thought it wise to give his son Power of Attorney over his affairs. It was a decision which spectacularly backfired! He wanted nothing more than to spend his twilight years in Adelaide House, but with an exchange date only a few weeks away, his son was made aware of the impending purchase and put a stop to it.

Mr Sheldon was mortified and mum devastated. She had no option other than admit defeat and inform the other residents and public authorities. The original time frame for vacating Adelaide had to be adhered to. Mrs Barnett's solicitor would not or could not budge. Time was short! With Ethel's unstinting help, all her clients were suitably re-homed and a 'For Sale' sign was erected in the front garden.

Mr Parks heard the news and attempted to benefit from mum's dilemma. He asked her to divorce Tom and marry him, but with one proviso; he would not have Bryan living in his house. He was, of course, firmly refused and a frantic search for a new home began.

Eventually, a large ground floor flat to rent in Princes Road came to light. It had a massive front room, but, as before, it only had one bedroom. However, it was a very large one which enabled mum to take an existing resident with her and receive a basic, regular income.

Mum, Bryan and an elderly lady moved into the furnished flat in the summer of 1952. This meant we were separated by the length of Dial Hill, with St. Ediths at the top and mum and Bryan in Princes Road at the bottom. To reach the local church, the whole school had to walk, two by two, in a long line down the hill and through Princes Road for the Sunday Family Service and again in the afternoon if we had to attend Sunday school. Every time we passed we could only give a furtive wave as we had been warned not to make a fuss or any overt gestures. To see mum and Bryan waving from the window or the top of the front steps was heart-breaking for us all and continued for some weeks until mum decided it was finally time to get us 'home'. She went to see Sister Helen Irene at St Johns. St. Ediths would not put anything in her way as they had constant demands for accommodation, so together with Sister Helen Irene, arrangements were made for us to be freed from the care of St. Ediths.

We were overjoyed when we were told that we were to be 'released' back into mum's care. It was agreed that it would be best for Spot to remain at St. Ediths. He had been their dog over the two and a half years and the all the children loved him as much as we did. It would be cruel to take him away and we could always go back and see him at any time.

So it was that on December 20th 1952, a glorious pre-Christmas day, which was also Bryan's twelfth Birthday, mum and Bryan walked up Dial Hill to collect us. We were up early and instead of the usual uniform, put on the prized dresses mum had deposited with Sister the previous day. We were packed and watching for them long before they arrived. Then, suddenly, there they were, coming along the front pathway. Not being allowed to run, we skipped to the front door. Sister beamed at us as she opened it and we rushed out to greet them.

Bryan looked so grown-up in a smart new coat and cap; a birthday present. Mum, in her grey coat and perpetual silk headscarf, knelt down and cradled us both in her arms. We all cried and laughed at the same time. At long last, my prayers were answered and we were all together again.

Once the formalities were completed and discharge forms signed, we shook hands with Sister, saying that we would be back to see Spot now and then. We thanked them all for looking after us for so long and set off for the happiest ever walk down the hill towards Princes Road and our new home.

Poignantly for mum, it was exactly 28 years, to the day, that she had walked out from Princess Marys for the final time.

When we arrived in the hallway of the flat, mum said, "close your eyes girls, we've got a surprise for you."

We were guided into the front room and when we opened our eyes, delighted to see a fully decorated Christmas tree, festive decorations and an extravagantly laid-up party table. Jellies in frilly-paper trifle cases, pink and chocolate blancmange in the shape of sandcastles, sandwiches, cake and sweets. This was to be the combined celebration party of my brother's birthday, Christmas and our reunion.

The property had a vast, dark and dismal entrance hall, with an original Victorian diamond tiled floor in brown, yellow and red. A bird and flower patterned wallpaper, darkened with age covered the walls. The etched glass in the front door let in just enough light to reveal a dark mahogany table, which was the platform for domed glass cases of very scary, stuffed animals and birds. They all had staring glass eyes which glittered in the half light and seemed to follow us as we passed by. We lived on the ground floor so had no need to mount the foreboding bare boards of a dark oak staircase. The mahogany, panelled door to the kitchen, then another into a large bedroom were on the left and our sitting room door was further along, on the right.

As much as the atmosphere in the hall was depressive and dank, opening that door led to a different world. Light streamed in though tall bay windows.

That huge, sunny room became our world by day and when we collapsed the sofa bed, our sleeping quarters by night. But, best of all, it had that wonderful window looking out onto the real world and across the road to the local bowling green. Bryan and mum slept on fold-away camp beds, with us girls on the sofa bed.

Our dining table and chairs were in this room, together with a large sideboard and it had a huge ornate, but boarded off, fireplace with a marble mantle above it.

To make ends meet, mum accepted another ambulant convalescent in the generously sized rear bedroom, which had glazed, French doors leading onto steps down to the back garden. She cared for them both in there. She also worked, just one night a week, in a Maternity Home. The routine was that she would look after her elderly people during the day and, on the night she was away, because they were both mostly self-caring, Bryan and I would keep an eye on them. As Bryan was twelve and I was almost eight, this seemed to work well; for a time anyway.

Our lives settled down and it was bitter-sweet when we watched every Sunday as the line of children from St. Ediths passed by on their way to church. We never lost sight of just how lucky we were not to be in that line any more.

When mum took us to church or Sunday school, we walked by a house on the corner of Princes Road, where a tiny elderly lady would greet us as we filed by and ask us if we enjoyed the service. She seemed lonely so we often used to stop to exchange a few words with her. One day we were invited into her home for a cup of tea and she chatted with mum as we played in her fragrant garden. Rosemary and I soon became regular visitors and often joined her for tea. It was not like the tea we got at home, it was presented in a delicate china cup with a matching saucer and it smelt like flowers. It was also served with a slice of lemon, not the milk we were used to. Mrs Mundy told us it was 'China Tea'. Rosemary could not help but wrinkle her nose as she shook her head to refuse hers. This pale, delicious tea was always served with a thin slice of home-made Madeira cake. She often gave us a small gift, like a little note pad and tiny pencil, an ornate button, a piece of lace or ribbon or something else quite trivial, but these things became terribly precious to us and we kept them in the small, hand-painted biscuit tins she passed on to us. We treasured those lovely tins and the trinkets.

Mrs Mundy's was an enchanted house. The comforting, but exotic smell of mothballs, lavender and spices as we walked in was not of our ordinary world. Her home was brim-full of the most beautiful objets d'art: lace chair backs and arm covers, deepest maroon velvet curtains, embroidered rugs and cushions depicting exotic flowers and birds. She would show us her paintings and silver photo frames containing sepia images of her family and talk of her own childhood in India and Ceylon. I never wanted to leave after our tea with this lovely little bird of a lady. I felt privileged to be in the sanctuary of her charming home.

Mum also became very friendly with another neighbour, Mrs Toombs, who lived around the corner. She was the cook and housekeeper to a wealthy, somewhat autocratic and highly demanding old lady who owned an imposing detached house, set within its own grounds. Her husband was the gardener, come handyman, come chauffeur. We used to visit Mrs. Toombs and have tea and crumpets in the very large, warm kitchen. She had a son, also called Brian who was about the same age as our Bryan. The two boys were to become the best of friends and got up to the most awful mischief, such as taking a gun from the house and shooting small birds and rodents in the owner's back garden, playing truant from school to go swimming, pinching candles from the church and building camp fires in private woodland. They were always in some scrape or another and invariably got caught!

On Friday's, one of mum's friends from the maternity home would come to look after the residents and we could go to 'the pictures' and watch all the big films such as, Moulin Rouge with Jose Ferrer, Ivanhoe with Robert and Liz Taylor and, my favourite actor at that time, Alan Ladd in Shane. As soon as the 'sitter' arrived, we would leave her to it and walk down to the town centre and join the inevitable queue for tickets from the lady in the kiosk. After the woman with a torch showed us to our seats, the Pathé News would play, followed by the 'B' Film, normally a cowboy movie, then the main event, the 'A' Film. When the main film star came on screen, mum would give me a nudge and whisper, "here he is." or "here she is and at that point many in the audience would clap and cheer.

During the interval we were allowed to run down to the girl standing at the front of the theatre and buy ourselves a tub of Lyons Maid ice cream or an Orange Maid ice lolly or a pointy, paper bag of warm peanuts. After the film everyone clapped their appreciation. When we emerged, minds full of what we had seen, we stopped to buy fish, chips which we ate on the way home.

Thanks to mum, life was good again and we were very content.

There was huge excitement in the early summer of 1953 when, on the coldest June 2nd day for over 100 years, Princess Elizabeth was crowned Queen Elizabeth the second. Mum managed to rent a black and white TV which was set-up in our sitting room. Our two lady residents came into our front room and we all watched the Coronation in Westminster Abbey. We followed it from beginning to the end. Whenever the National Anthem was played mum always got to her feet. She said it was out of respect for our sovereign, so we stood up too. We drank tea and ate sandwiches mesmerised by the pomp and splendour of it all. The Queen and Duke of Edinburgh journeyed from Buckingham Palace to Westminster Abbey, as the commentator told us, in a golden coach pulled by eight grey horses, although of course we were seeing everything in black and white, but no matter, it was a magnificent spectacle. The service lasted three hours and the return procession took almost another hour, but the residents managed to stay the course, only returning to their own room after the first balcony appearance of our new Queen.

Our Christmas 1953 again saw a fully decorated tree, also paper-chains we made ourselves by licking the glue on the tips of strips of coloured paper and making them into chains, which we then hung from centre to each corner of the room, with brightly coloured, honeycomb paper bells in each corner.

We awoke to find a stuffed-full Christmas stocking by our beds, inside was an orange, apple, walnuts, a cracker and a Fry's Five Boys chocolate bar.

We were not expecting much in the way of other presents, but were in for a big surprise. When the main lights went on, we noticed a sheet draped over something beside the tree. Mum beamed as she slowly pulled the sheet away to reveal what she termed our "proper presents". We screamed with delight and couldn't believe our eyes. Rosemary and I both got a scooter, mine was blue and Rosemary's red. We also had Rosebud baby dolls: mine was dressed in blue and Rosemary's in pink. Mum had knitted them full outfits whilst on night duty. Bryan was overjoyed to receive a second-hand bike, an upgrade on his old one and a huge box of Meccano.

We rode our scooters and bike down the hill to church for the Christmas Family Service and shifted impatiently on the benches as we listened to the Vicar repeating all the stuff we had heard a hundred times before, but the Carols were worth the wait. As we came home we called in to present Mrs. Munday with a gift and she gave us a large tin of toffees with a Christmas scene on the lid.

Mum cooked the most wonderful Christmas dinner I can ever remember and Bryan was dispatched to deliver a Christmas lunch to Mrs. Mundy, then the residents were invited through into our room and we enjoyed our turkey Christmas dinner together. The Christmas pudding was on fire when it was brought to the table. It was rich, delicious and there was a silver sixpence in it somewhere, so we were all warned to chew every mouthful carefully before swallowing. I can't remember who the lucky finder was, but it was definitely not me. Not that it mattered, we all had a lovely time and at 3pm sharp we listened to the Queen's Speech on the radio before the residents went back to their room for a long and peaceful nap.

A very cold, snowy New Year followed which saw us penned indoors, unable to get out on our prized Christmas presents. But, Bryan's Meccano was used to build lots of different things and he even got the mechanical pulley system working. The two new dolls became the focus of attention for Rosemary and me. Clothes on! Clothes off! Clothes on! Clothes off!

During that time, mum taught us both to knit. Mrs Munday had loads of odd bits of unused wool she passed on to us so over that winter and our dolls, Rosie and Mary, became the best dressed dolls in the Kingdom, or certainly in Clevedon.

We attended the same school we went to when we were in St. Ediths and I hated it! We were outsiders because the other children knew we originally came from the orphanage. We were also singled out because we were allowed free dinners. A great idea, but a 'free-dinner' child was immediately stigmatised as teachers read out the names of those excused from paying every Monday morning as they collected the dinner money.

One day in early spring, Rosemary and I simply decided to stop going to school. So mum would not know, we left the flat at the usual time in the morning, but hid in some trees and bushes in a field, all day. This went on for nearly a week and if anyone walked by we simply stopped talking and hid in the bushes until they had gone. We had no food or drink at lunch time; we even tried spitting into an old rusty tin for drinking water but that just made us sick. We would gobble our tea when we did get home, at about four o'clock, because we were ravenous and dying of thirst by then.

We came unstuck on the Thursday when we arrived home too early. Mum was standing on the top step, arms folded, looking very angry.

"Where on earth have you two been?" She snapped out the question. Unprepared, I could not think of anything to say, but Rosemary blurted. "We've been in a field all day, it was Betty's idea."

She began to cry which softened mum, who mellowed her tone.

"You've just missed the School Inspector. He called in to see why you have been away from school, all week – ALL WEEK girls?"

She told us how worrying it had been to find out we had been missing and how embarrassing it was to admit that she didn't know where we were.

When we told her, through floods of tears, what we had been up to since Monday, she was furious with us and said she was going to tell the school and see what they made of it. We were told to put our dolls and scooters in the kitchen and would not be allowed to play with them for four days, the same amount of time we had played truant. We were allowed a supper and then made to get into our beds, be silent and think about the lie we had lived for four days and the trouble it had caused.

We went to school the following day and of course mum provided the note to tell them what we had done, how sorry we were and it would not happen again. This was accepted by the Head Teacher who gave us a verbal warning, but we had already decided not to do it again. We missed our free school lunch and it tasted especially good that day.

Our brother was for the most part very kind to us. He ensured, as much as he could, that the school teasing stopped by making frequent appearances at the school gate and threatening anyone we asked him to.

He also helped us with our homework and, best of all, when we were all in bed he would tell us the most wonderful made-up stories about 'Tommy and his Matchstick Gun'. He was of course always the hero, but I loved him for his daft stories and forgave him his rare off days. An older brother is a super hero and that's what my big brother was to me. However, glitches began to arise on some of the nights mum was working. Bryan could sometimes be very annoying; he would tease my sister and try to make her run around after him, he knew he had no chance of me doing any such thing.

One evening, when my sister and I were busy in the kitchen, we heard the 'snap', 'snap' of an air rifle from the sitting room. We ran in and to our horror, we saw that he had lined our new dolls up against the wall, on top of the bed and shot them right between the eyes with the air rifle he and Brian Toombs had 'borrowed' from the house where his mother worked.

"Look. Smack-bang between the eyes," he told us with a proud but stupid grin. Screaming loudly, Rosemary fell down and began thumping her hands and kicking her legs on the floor. Distraught and furious I launched myself at him, scratching his face. We then had a full-on screaming, hair-pulling fight. The appalling ruckus quickly brought the neighbours down from upstairs. They came rushing in, separated us and promptly called mum, at work. They insisted she come home immediately, which meant she had to find someone to cover for her at the Home, so she could get back pronto to sort matters out.

All was calm by the time she arrived, but the woman from upstairs was still with us. She had cleaned me up and sent Bryan upstairs with her husband. I could see mum was fuming and knew we were in deep trouble. She thanked our neighbour for her help, apologised for the distress we had caused and asked her to send Bryan down. Rosemary was clutching her injured doll and sniffing tears away as our brother came into the room. As soon as she saw him, my normally calm little sister charged across the room and began beating him with her clenched fists. Mum pulled her away.

"Stop it and be quiet, all of you! If upstairs hear anything more from you tonight, they'll call the police and you'll be taken away again. Do you really want to go back to St Ediths?

Her words struck home and Rosemary stopped yelling, ran to her bed and hid under the covers. Mum removed her coat, sat on the bed and stared at us. Bryan began to say how sorry he was, but she stopped him with the flat of her hand held in the air.

"Not a word from you, do you hear me? Not one word."

He stood silently against the wall as mum calmly uncovered Rosemary.

"Can I see Rosebud please? And your doll please, Betty."

After pretending to examine them, she opened our first aid box and removed things from it. We watched as she soothingly talked to them and expertly bandaged their broken foreheads and handed them back to us. Rosemary actually smiled at mum as she accepted hers.

Mum then turned her attention to Bryan and asked him to follow her into the kitchen. We knew better than to follow and listen outside, but got the gist of what was being said. On his return I could see he had been crying, so I assumed mum had given him a really severe telling off and this helped me feel gratuitously avenged for his thoughtless act.

Everything was calm again, but our beautiful dolls never did look quite the same. The following day Bryan was made to return the gun to Mrs Toombs with an apology he had to write himself. It wasn't long after that incident that her employer died and she left Mrs. Toombs the house, everything in it and all her money. We didn't see much of her after that and Brian Tombs went out of Bryan's every day orbit.

Our brother had many extra chores to do for a week following the dolls' incident, but the punishment which was the longest lasting and I took most delight in, was him having to knit two long, narrow scarves, a pale pink one for Rosebud and a pale blue one for Mary.

On another extremely fateful night, as it turned out, Bryan was telling us a story and I told him we had heard that one before and couldn't he think of something new. As a response, he picked up one of mum's cotton reels and lobed it towards me. It caught me smack in the middle of the forehead. The first I knew that I had actually been cut was when I put my hands up to my face to rub my forehead and felt the sticky wetness of warm blood seeping over my hands and into my eyes. I screamed. The sight of all the blood that gushed out of that small wound also terrified my brother and he immediately ran to get help.

Unfortunately it was not only him it frightened, my screams alarmed and alerted the upstairs couple, even before Bryan started banging on their door. They again came rushing to see what on earth was going on. The gash would not stop bleeding until they laid me down and placed a pressure dressing on the wound, which eventually sealed it. But, mum was called home again to sort out the rumpus. This time a kind neighbour took us to A & E and I was stitched up.

When we returned from the hospital, because I reassured her that he did not mean to hit me with the cotton reel, mum did not punish Bryan. She just sat on the bed, looking so woefully tired and told us that this incident could lead to us losing the flat and having to find somewhere else to live. I don't think Bryan fully believed her as, when he got into bed, he sheepishly grinned and whispered, "With that bandage around your head Betty, you look more like your doll!"

However, my mother's fears were not misplaced, a complaint went into the local Child Welfare Officer that three children were being left on their own at night, were out of control and possibly trying to kill each other. A stern Children's Welfare Officer duly arrived, demanding to see Mrs Williams and inspect the premises. As they walked through the flat, she was taking down notes and when they came back into the sitting room, we all listened to her warning.

"I'm sorry Mrs Williams, I realise that you and your family have had a hard time, but a complaint has been made and I must act upon it. An investigation will take place and you will be informed of the outcome within four weeks." She then added, looking at the three of us. "If there are any further disturbances, the children will be taken back into care. Not into St. Ediths, mind, but into a state-run orphanage. Do you understand Mrs Williams?"

Mum certainly understood and so did we. We all nodded as if our heads would fall off.

"Yes, I understand," mum said as she glared at us three. "I can promise that there will be no more quarrels. I have given up my job and will be here every night from now on,"

However, the Welfare Officer had not finished.

"Yes, that's all well and good, but I notice you are caring for two ladies in the rear bedroom?"

"Yes, that's correct" Mum responded, looking quizzical.

"Well, I'm afraid that you can't do that. You must register that room with the Social Services if you want to nurse patients in your own home. Surely you knew that?"

"No, I didn't" mum replied. "I'm a trained nurse, give professional care and they are both very comfortable here."

"That's as maybe, but either you properly register or they will have to go."

After she had gone, mum seemed to be in a daze as she sat and considered what the Welfare Officer had told her. She knew she would never be able to afford the compliant alterations demanded by social services to register even one room. She had no option other than to tell her ladies that they would have to find another Home.

One lady had a stroke a week later and died, never having the worry of knowing where she might move to. The other lady eventually found a place in a local care home.

With zero income, we would soon have to move on. Our mother vowed she would never allow us to be separated again and made another determined search through the classified advertisements in the local papers.

Woodside Farm, Doynton (2021)

15

MAKING HAY

"It's a long way to go for a job interview. Not quite what I was looking for, but I hope and pray something will come of it, we're fast running out of time."

Mum had been assiduously ploughing through the local papers but nothing suitable came up. Her good friends, Colin and Anne were aware of our plight and suggested that perhaps she should look further afield. Colin said he would put the word out to his taxi driving pals and it was not long before he brought in a pile of local papers including the Bristol Post, Somerset County Gazette, Wiltshire Herald and Bath Echo.

A small ad in the Bath Echo for a housekeeper caught mum's eye. It was for a young farmer and there was good accommodation on offer. Mum sent off a letter to apply for the job. Stating that she was a trained nurse, had a wide experience in caring which included housekeeping and was a highly accomplished cook.

"Sometimes you have to blow your own trumpet, no one else will blow it for you," she told us with a smile, She sealed the enveloped, licked the stamp, made sure it was square to the top right-hand corner (another sign of respect for the Queen) and gave it to Bryan to post.

A few days later, the stamped addressed envelope she had enclosed for a reply, dropped through the letterbox. We gathered around her, fingers crossed, as she opened the letter. She read it and smiled. She had been shortlisted for an interview and had been asked to take us with her.

"He wants see for himself that you're all angels," added mum. "So you will have to be on your best behaviour and use your 'Sunday voices'.

We laughed; mum was always telling us to use our 'Sunday voices'.

So, there we were, smartly dressed in our best clothes, on our way to a village called, Doynton, somewhere near Bath. We were up early to catch a bus to Bristol, then a bus to Bath and then after quite a long wait, our third bus, which meandered through villages to the north of Bath. It was early-summer and far from being bored we enjoyed travelling through the lovely countryside. Finally, the bus dropped us off in the small, attractive village of Doynton. Most of the village was owned by Squire and Lady Blathwayt of nearby

Dyrham Park. All the cottages were built with warm, cream, Cotswold Stone. Many had thatched roofs and they all had well maintained gardens. We walked past a small school, a village hall and a splendid ancient church, before we found Watery Lane, the narrow lane leading away from the village to the farm. We trooped along the rough lane with open fields on either side for about half a mile until we came to stream flowing across the lane, as mentioned in the directions mum had received.

"Crikey mum, that's a really appropriate name for this lane. Look out girls, wet shoes all round!" called Bryan as he cheerfully stomped through the water.

The rest of us carefully picked our way through the ford by balancing on large stones, obviously placed there for that purpose. It helped keep our newly polished shoes out of the deeper pools of water. A little further along, Watery Lane curved to the left and as we came out from the bend we could see the entrance to the farm.

For me, walking towards Woodlands Farm was like stepping into paradise. Apple trees in an orchard on the left were betwixt blossom and fruit formation with several enormous pigs snuffling and chomping on whatever they could find under them. On the other side of the drive there were open, buttercup meadows with cows and a few young calves. It looked heavenly and I felt so excited at the prospect of living within such a beautiful landscape.

As we entered the farm yard we were greeted by several excited black and white collie dogs. We wanted to stop and play with them, but mum, looking directly at my rascal of a brother, reminded us to behave and keep ourselves clean. Woodlands Farm house was a comfortable looking Cotswold stone property with weathered, white painted windows, in dire need of a lick of paint. It was semi-detached with a similar, slightly smaller property adjoining it. We grinned at each other, obviously liking the look of it. As we were ushered inside, I prayed Mum would get the job and we could make this lovely house our home.

We sat in the farmhouse sitting room, amongst several other hopefuls. Most were young ladies, several years younger than mum and without three children tagging along. We already knew the job came with ample living accommodation and the housekeeper was to look after and support the unmarried bailiff farmer.

Mum was eventually called in by the farmer's Personal Assistant who had arranged the interviews. She was gone for what seemed ages, much longer than those we had seen go in before. When she finally emerged she stood in the doorway, smiled and beckoned us in.

"Come in and say hello."

My heart leapt. I dared not assume that our talented and clever mother had landed the job. What if it was down to us?

The young farmer, Mr Prichard, seemed very relaxed and I was relieved to note that he appeared unconcerned that we three were included in the arrangement. Mr Prichard was in his late-twenties, recently out of agricultural college and this was his first position as a Farm Manager, for the owner, Mr. Pitman. He asked us how we felt about coming to live at Woodlands Farm and we left him in no doubt that it was just what we wanted. He nodded, smiled and turned to mum.

"Well, the job is yours if you want it Mrs Williams."

Rosemary and I could not contain our joy and we leapt about clapping our hands. Mum immediately accepted the post.

Mr Pritchard's PA was highly amused at the joy shown by two small girls. She laughed with us as she walked towards the door, but put on her serious face as she left the study to thank the other applicants for their interest. The post was filled.

Mum beamed at us and called to my brother who was staring out of the window. Bryan was deep in his own world as he watched a herd of black and white cows being herded across the yard and into the milking shed. He turned and the penny dropped.

"Wow, really?"

For once, he really did look genuinely 'wowed', especially when the PA came back to usher us all into the kitchen where a lady offered us all tea, bread and butter with jam and cake. Then Mr Prichard showed us our three furnished rooms and told us that we had full use of the house, except for his sitting room and study which were private and out of bounds. Mum would cook for him and his very rare guests. She would clean the house; deal with any laundry, plus any other duties she felt able to undertake, such as helping out with the smaller animals, hens and ducks. She would be given a free hand, £3 a week wages and a decent budget. He then took us on a short tour of the farmyard and introduced us to Clive, the cowman and his wife, Margaret (the lady who had served us tea), who lived next door. They were very pleasant and Clive chatted to mum as he drove us to the village to catch the bus back to Bath for our reverse journey to Clevedon.

We were beside ourselves with joy on that trip safe in the knowledge that not only did we have a wonderful home to go to, but Mr Prichard, according to Clive, was a very kind, fair minded young man.

Our spirits were high as we packed for our move, but there was a downside and that was having to say goodbye to dear Mrs Mundy. Tears were shed but we promised we would all be back to see her one day, which brought a measure of comfort to us all. She waved goodbye from her garden gate as we prepared to leave in two taxis organised by Colin. He and Anne were thrilled when they heard our good news. We managed to load most of our worldly goods into one taxi, including our scooters, but there was no room for Bryan's bike. He left it with Bryan Tombs to look after, with the veiled threat that he would be back for it one day. We crammed into Colin's taxi, with mum in the front passenger seat with her most valued possessions in the foot-well and the three of us in the back seat with Rosemary in the middle, surrounded by bags which could not be wedged into the boot. One last look at the lovely flat which had brought us back together again and we were off.

It was a dull, miserable day and the countryside did not look quite as beautiful as it had on our first visit to Doynton, but Colin did not follow the route we were forced to take on the three buses. He drove across the vast, open countryside between Bristol and Bath and the journey to our new home took little over an hour.

As we entered Doynton, mum directed him to

195

Watery Lane and warned about the ford, which was no more than a trickle across the lane on that day. Colin kept his taxi moving and said we were lucky. Any deeper and the cars would not have got through.

As we drew into the farmyard I was hit by an overpowering stench of something sour. I was to learn it was the smell of rotting grass which would become silage, a winter feed for the cows. The farm would be a smelly place at certain times of the year, but it nestled below soft green hills, with fields and woodland rising behind which gave it a most beautiful and protected setting.

It was apparently small in the general scale of farms and was built around a large cobble yard. Our new home faced an assortment of tall hay barns and animal shelters with huge double doors.

Mr. Prichard came out from the farm cottage to greet us He was not tall, but he was a very muscular, fit young man with fair curly hair. Mum introduced him to Colin and told him what a good friend he was and it was through him that she found the job advert in the Bath Echo. Mr Prichard thanked Colin, shook him warmly by the hand and insisted that he and his fellow taxi driver should have some refreshment before their return journey.

The taxis were unloaded, our worldly goods stacked in the hall and mum went into the kitchen to make a pot of tea, determined to begin her housekeeping duties as quickly as possible.

After a couple of cups of tea, Colin wished us luck and said he and Anne would keep in touch. Mum thanked him and gave him a hug and Mr Prichard walked out into the yard with him as mum organised us to move our belongings from the hall to our respective rooms.

Mum had her own pretty bed-sitting room. Bryan had a very tiny bedroom, but it was all his own. Rosemary and I shared our room, but we each had our own, normal sized bed, a luxury we had never known. Margaret, the cowman's wife, had put pretty cotton curtains at the windows and there were clean sheets, blankets and floral feather eiderdowns on both beds; just for us, how exciting was that?

The view from our window, beyond the farm buildings, was rolling fields and woods. Looking down into the yard I could see Mr Prichard standing by Colin's taxi having a chat. As they shook hands and Colin got into the taxi, Rosemary and I shouted and waved. A smiling Mr Prichard looked up at us and Colin waved his hand through the open window as he drove the taxi out from the farmyard.

We all met back in the hall, where Mr Prichard expressed amazement at how quickly we had cleared all our belongings away. He invited us into his study where he explained firmly, but kindly, the house and farm rules. We were told where we could go and where we definitely could not go, ever! A farm may look idyllic, but it could be a dangerous place. We were warned never to feed the farm animals, unless given permission to do so and to stay away from the barns where loose grain and feed was stored. However, as long as Clive the cowman agreed, we could play in the hay barn and go into the dairy to help with milking under his supervision. We could also go into the pigsty, but be very careful if there were piglets. A sow could be very protective of her young. We were never to feed the pigs, unless requested to, because they would eat anything and everything they could get their snouts around. He laughed when he told us that and we immediately knew we were going to love living on Woodside Farm We were the luckiest kids in the world and longed for bedtime to arrive so we could have a proper, warm bath in the upstairs bathroom which had a real bath, running hot and cold water and a flushing toilet. There was also an indoor toilet downstairs.

We soon settled in and adapted to the routine of farm life. The farm house needed a good clean, 'a woman's touch' as Mr Prichard put it. Mum worked hard and had the house cleaned from top to bottom in a week, but she did not stop there. During the second week, she turned her attention to the outside, scrubbing down and painting the outside windows and front door and climbing a ladder to deal with the bedroom windows.

Bryan took to life on Woodside Farm as if he was born to be a farmer. He was never bored, never misbehaved and was happy to take directions from Clive, the cowman.

The tallest and biggest of the barns was the hay barn. It was piled from floor to ceiling with hay and straw bales. This homely hideaway was to become the favourite place for Rosemary and me to play in. It was always warm and held the sweet fragrance of dried hay.

We were especially enamoured with the pigs and calves. The pregnant sow soon got used to having me around and as she was due to 'farrow' (give birth) she needed regular, high nutrient feeds of grain and green leaves. I was instructed on how to give this to her and to report to Clive if she became restless and started making a nest. Her litter arrived whist I was asleep one night and I missed it, but Bryan was there and later proudly told us how he helped rub her udders to relax her and get her to lie on her side, ready to give birth. She produced a litter of ten, healthy, squealing, pink piglets. The first ones to arrive got onto the best teats early, which gave them the richest milk, so the weaker ones needed bottle feeding. That became my job, using sugared milk.

We regularly attended the local church, mum sometimes taken there on the back of the farmer's motorbike. We also joined in with parish and village life as much as we could and were welcome. The local village school, which was about a mile and a half walk away, was friendly, with none of the stigma or bullying of our last one.

Mum and Mr Prichard got on very well; Rosemary and I, being so young, never noticed the age difference and I hoped they would fall in love and marry one day. In preparation for this, I made Rosemary practise with me for their wedding day. We picked field flowers to make posies, draped flower chains around our hair and walk in a stately fashion, as we were the brides maids, humming 'Here comes the Bride'. Bryan laughed, told us we were daft and said it would never happen, but I thought, "What does he know?"

The months passed by very happily. During the weekends and school holidays Bryan and I would get up early and help Clive bring the cows in from the fields. We helped in the dairy with the milking and got stuck in with sanitising and cleaning up, before returning the cows to the fields. The whole process was repeated in the evening, so we quickly learned how to herd the cows. They always knew when it was milking time and clustered by the field gates, so if the herd were in a nearby field we could manage without Clive's help.

He taught us how to milk by hand which was brilliant! But, best of all, he showed us how to supplement-feed the summer calves who had arrived late. He taught us how to first gain their trust by stroking their warm velvet-like fur, then gently put our fingers into their soft mouths and carefully lower their heads into a bucket of warm milk to help them learn to feed themselves. We tied fresh grass in clumps onto their pens so they could also eat juicy meadow grass Clive explained the important difference between green grass, hay and straw: Grass contains moisture and all its unprocessed nutrients so helps feed small calves: hay is dried grasses and used as a nutritious feed: whereas straw, the dried stalks of wheat or barley, was used mainly for animal bedding. Although both hay and straw were comforting in the hay barn when we were rolling around in it!

Living on the farm was just great and it taught us how to care for animals responsibly. Bryan swore he was going to be a farmer one day and I vowed I would marry one and we would have our own, adjoining farms.

One warm and sunny day, whilst Bryan and Rosemary were out in the fields and I was playing with the pigs in the sty, a taxi pulled into the yard. A man sitting in the back called me over. He smiled.

"Hello Betty, do you remember me?"

I was taken aback and said no, although some sort of recognition stirred in my mind. My brain was working on it when he climbed out from the car and put his arms around me.

"You're so grown-up, Betty and so pretty."

I pulled away. He let go and stepped back. "Is your mother here? Could you run and fetch her for me please. I would like to talk to her urgently?"

I was about to ask who he was when my brain came up with the answer. Brimming over with excitement, I ran into the house and found my mother in the kitchen talking to Mr Prichard. I blurted out my message.

"Mum! Dads here! He's come to see us and wants to see you outside. He says it's urgent."

"Who is out there" demanded Mr Prichard as he looked at my mother.

Mum looked stunned and just stared back at me. Thinking she would be as excited as I was that my father had finally come to see us, I was confused. Why was she not as delighted as me that he was here and wanted to see her?

Recovered and with a face like stone, mum told me to go and tell him that she would be out in a minute or two.

When she eventually emerged she was accompanied by an angry looking Mr Prichard who demanded to know what my father thought he was doing there. He asked mum if she wanted him to escort my father off the property. I was dumbfounded to see such a hostile reaction to his visit.

"Hello Tom. I didn't expect to see you today." Mum's face looked as if she had seen a ghost.

I held my breath as my father, who was leaning back against the taxi said "Hello Ethel".

Ignoring Mr Prichard's glare, he stepped forward, took my mother's arm and led her away. He was speaking earnestly to her as they crossed the yard and mum turned to say that she would not be long.

Mr Prichard disappeared indoors, but I stayed and watched as they walked high up into the top field behind the farm and talked for a very long time. When they eventually returned Mr Prichard had left to collect the cows with Clive. Mum invited Tom and the driver inside for a cup of tea, but when Mr Prichard returned from the fields, he was still very angry and I overheard him say, "The bloody cheek of the man, Clive, turning up out of the blue like that. Imagine how Ethel must feel."

Not waiting for Clive's reply, he strode into the house and ordered my father to leave.

Tom shrugged and told Mr Prichard that he had come to see his wife, not him. Then he called back through the open door.

"Thanks for the tea Ethel. Think over what I've told you. I'll be in touch again, very soon."

I stood, dumbstruck as I watched the taxi disappearing out of the farmyard. I then began to chase after the car, shouting as I ran. The car slowed, then stopped; my father stepped out and came back towards me. Putting his arms around me he said "Don't cry Betty, everything will be alright, you'll see."

Kissing me on the forehead, he walked back to the car and climbed inside. With tears running down my cheeks I watched the taxi drive away, not understanding why Mr Prichard had been so rude and ordered him to leave. It was so confusing. It had been a thrill to see my father and think we could go back to living together again. Why was mum not feeling the same?

Bryan and Rosemary, who were nowhere to be found during Tom's visit, joined me in the lane. After the initial disappointment of missing him, they jabbered excitedly about the possibility of him wanting us back as a proper family again. But Mum was visibly upset when we got back to the house and remained strangely quiet, locked in her own thoughts, as she prepared supper. Later, I heard her weeping in her bedroom when she thought we were all asleep.

The following morning, after eating breakfast in silence, mum called us all into her bedroom and asked us to sit on her bed; she wanted to discuss my father's visit. With Rosemary on her lap she said she thought we were now old enough to know the truth behind my father's departure from our lives and the reason for yesterday's visit.

She explained that we had to move out of our home in Oxford, because Tom told her it had to be sold to pay off his business debts. It transpired that he had in fact set-up home there with Hilary Kilby, his actress 'friend' and they had a daughter. During that time his debts grew and the house was forcibly sold to pay everyone he owed money to.

Hilary Kilby had not secured the lucrative acting career that beckoned, so he had to take a job as a chauffeur and they lived in the gatehouse of his employer's grand estate near Oxford. Kilby started an affair with the head gardener and became pregnant with her lover's child. When Tom was away on a trip with his employer, she left him and went to live with the gardener, taking their daughter with her. He had told mum he didn't know or care where they were living and would not try to trace them. He had moved back to Yorkshire a year ago and was living with his mother in Redcar. He now knew he made the biggest mistake of his life in leaving us and loved us all, very much. He sought to make amends for everything he had done and the pain he had caused. He desperately wanted us back together again and had promised mum that as soon as he was settled in Yorkshire, with a job and a house, he would write to her and ask her if she would return to him and begin again. He implored her to at least think about it and take the time she needed to consider all that he had said.

"So," she concluded, "now you know the full story, but the good Lord will forgive me for suspecting that he may not have told me the whole truth. I told him I would think about it, if and when his letter arrives."

"But don't you want us all to be together mum?" I blurted out. "He wants us to be a family again!"

Mum gave me a sad smile. "The trouble is Betty, your father may never send such a letter, so the real question for now is, are we happy here, living on Woodlands Farm?"

"I don't want you to go back to him". Bryan huffed. "He left us and just walked away mum, I love it here and I'm not going back to him, ever."

"Me too!" Rosemary piped-up. "I want to stay here as well."

Bryan, calmed down and surprised me when he argued his case.

"Mum, he split up our family, allowed the girls to go into orphanages, you to survive as best you could and now you're telling us that we have a sister! How can he expect you to go back to him just because he is now the one left on his own? You could never trust him again. Could you?"

Mum looked stunned by his summary of the facts. "Bryan, what you say is true, but life's not as simple as it may seem. Let's wait and see if any such letter arrives. For now we're all together again, we're happy here and as that promised letter might never turn-up, it's time to enjoy what we have and not dwell too much on the past."

Although I was only eight and Bryan twelve, we grasped what we had been told and appreciated why my mother found it so difficult to accept that our father had turned up, without any prior warning, simply because the person he had left us for, had left him. With that, she gently lifted Rosemary off her lap, slapped her knees and gave us one of her best smiles.

"So that's it then, now you know. You also know how much I love you and nothing will ever change that, nothing. We're all happy living here and I promise we will not be parted ever again. So let's enjoy our good fortune."

Later that day, us children met in the hay barn, where Bryan and I discussed what mum had told us. We couldn't get over the fact we had a sister we didn't know existed. But we both agreed that mum was very happy caring for Mr Prichard and anyway, why would she want to go back to a man who had run off with another woman? Bryan said he now understood why mum had been so troubled for so long and how much he hated his father for what he had allowed to befall us.

Although I never completely forgot my father's visit, we agreed that we wanted to remain on the farm and were soon lost in the pure fun and joy of harvest time. There was so much to do and it was all so new and exciting for us.

Everyone mucked-in during harvesting and other local farming families arrived to help. It was back breaking work for them all. The combine harvester was shared between the farms and everyone visited each farm in turn to bring in the harvest. They heaped the baled hay in high stacks and then transferred it into the barns. Bryan was truly in his element and relished the physical labour. He was up with the dawn and stayed in the fields until he was made to come in, as a result the weight was falling off him. Rosemary and I simply enjoyed larking about in the cut hay or straw. When it was all quiet and everyone had gone for a communal supper, we made warm, cosy nests within the sweetly perfumed haystacks. It seemed summertime would go on forever in those wonderful, balmy days.

Not long after all the crops had been gathered in, Mr. Prichard received an invitation to attend his brother's wedding in Bristol. He told mum that, although he had a lot of work to do and really couldn't spare the time, the wedding was an important family occasion and he would be taking a day off.

His brother and fiancée came to visit us all at the farm and my mother made them a traditional tea. We, together with Clive and his wife, were invited to join them for the tea party and we all drank their very good health with tea and squash. Rosemary and I were so happy to be a part of their celebration; we felt that at long last we were living a family life, albeit with a man who was not our father. But Mr Prichard was good humoured, very kind and we felt cared for and included.

So it was that Mr. Prichard took a very rare Saturday off. We had never known him do it before, unless it was to attend a working farmer's college day.

He organised that Clive would take over the farm for the day and asked Bryan to help with the milking in the early morning and late evening. Bryan, delighted to be given this huge responsibility, willingly agreed.

Early on the Saturday morning, we were in the farm kitchen demolishing our regular weekend breakfast, when Mr Prichard walked in. We all stopped eating and stared. It was the first time we had seen him formally suited and booted. He certainly looked different and extremely handsome with his fair curly hair shiny and slicked back. In his dark suit, starched white shirt and striped tie, he was a striking, good looking man.

It was obvious that mum was impressed. She beamed at him and commented on how smart he looked. He self-consciously grinned back and thanked her for starching his one and only white shirt and getting such a deep polished shine on his shoes.

He told us he would be very late back and asked mum to leave a cold supper out for him. Mum said she would leave it in the pantry and wished him a happy celebration day with his family. He began to leave, but took us by surprise as he turned, looked back at us from the doorway and in a surprisingly paternal way said, "Look after your mother and make sure you do as she says." He smiled at us and hurried away. We all gathered at the window to wave as he left to make the most of a very rare day off. The scent of bacon and toast hung in the air and the kitchen felt warm and cosy. I felt comfortable and safe, as if we were firmly where we belonged.

That evening my mother left his supper on a tray in the pantry; cold ham, cheese, her own home made pickle, crusty bread and butter. It had been raining for most of the day and we went to bed with rain lashing against the farm house windows. As I snuggled down, I wondered how the wedding party was going and hoped the rain had not spoilt their big day. I would have to wait until the morning to hear all about it.

However, as bad luck would have it, Mr Prichard could not get back to the farm that night. The brook which flowed down from the hills and ran across Watery Lane, usually no more than a trickle, had become a torrent and the lane was flooded to a depth of several feet. There was nothing unusual or untoward in that as it often happened after a period of heavy rain. Tractors could get through, but it was wise for cars and pedestrians to wait until the water had subsided. Mr Prichard assessed the situation, decided to wait until the morning and spent a restless, uncomfortable night in his car. At first light, he judged the water low enough and finally arrived back at the farm, in the early hours of Sunday. Tired and hungry, he welcomed the tray of food mum had left in the pantry and totally exhausted, fell into a deep sleep on the sofa. Knowing he wanted to get a day's work in, when mum found him there, she dutifully roused him at 8 am and he went off to change out of his wedding suit, freshen-up and put on his working clothes.

When he joined us during breakfast he explained what had happened and that although he was feeling unusually tired, he had an unfinished task to attend to. The silage heap in Lower Field, down the lane, had to be compacted to squeeze air out. Driving a tractor slowly up and down the steep heap of silage was a slow boring job, but it had to be done if the cattle were to be fed throughout the coming winter. Without compaction the silage would spoil.

He left after breakfast, saying he would be back in time for a late lunch at about 3pm.

There were two tractors on the farm, a single-seat, grey Massey Ferguson, known as 'Little Grey Fergie' and a much larger, bright red, David Brown Cropmaster which had two seats. We heard him drive the Cropmaster out of the yard and down the lane as we helped mum clean away the breakfast plates and dishes and prepare for the traditional Sunday roast. She decided to make a fruit pie, which would require fresh soft fruit and rosemary and mint would be needed to go with the lamb.

Mum was going to the Family Service in the village church. Bryan was excused because he was helping Clive and Rosemary and I were excused because we had been forced to attend so many religious outings in our orphanage years. Mum fetched her bike from the barn and cycled off saying she would also collect some produce from the garden of an unoccupied cottage in the village. It was owned by Mr Pitman, who owned the farm and we were welcome to take whatever was there until he found a new tenant.

After mum cycled off, Rosemary and I roamed around the farm to make a fuss of the animals and play with our recently acquired guinea pigs, but after an hour or so we got bored and decided to go and meet mum on her way back from the village.

When we were not attending a church service, we often walked down the lane to meet mum, usually finding her about halfway, wobbling along with garden produce heaped high in the large basket on the front of her bike. As we wandered down the lane we could see Mr. Prichard in the field to our left. He was slowly manoeuvring the huge red tractor up and down the steaming heap of silage. We called and waved as we walked past. I doubted he would hear us over the noisy tractor engine but he good humouredly returned our wave and we carried on walking to the village.

We found mum, busy in the garden of the unoccupied cottage. Whoever lived there before was obviously a keen gardener, for although weeds were taking over, rows of planted crops were still evident. Mum was having a lovely time and we helped her select the best of the abundant herbs and fruit and loaded it into the wicker basket on the front of her bike. It was warm and sunny in that blissfully scented garden and I thought how lucky we were, how good our life was, compared to a few months before. It was easy to see mum felt that way too.

With the basket heaped-up, mum sat Rosemary on the bike and pushed her along. I shut the cottage gate and ran to catch-up. I could hear the tractor engine as we wandered along Watery Lane, then it suddenly stopped.

"Sounds as if Mr Prichard has finished earlier than expected," said mum. "We'll have to put our skates on. Good job I put the lamb in a low oven, we can soon turn the heat up and…...."

We stopped in our tracks. The tractor was upside down in the ditch running alongside the silage clamp. The huge rubber wheels were still turning, but there was no sign of Mr Prichard. Mum lifted Rosemary off the bike and dropped it to the ground, scattering the garden produce across the lane. In an unusually strangled voice she told Rosemary to stay where she was and we both ran through the open gateway into the field where we were horrified to find Mr. Prichard trapped, beneath the huge tractor! Mum quickly pushed me away.

"Go Betty! Go! Run to the farm! Find Clive. Get help!"

I sprinted out from the field and dragged a shocked and screaming Rosemary up the lane with me. As we ran, I looked back to see mum picking her way down into the ditch.

I was yelling my head off long before we reached the yard. Clive and Margaret came rushing from their house, quickly followed by Bryan. After I gabbled incoherently what had happened, Clive told Margaret to phone for an ambulance and he sprinted, followed by me and Bryan, out of the yard, towards the scene of the accident. Margaret took Rosemary with her into the house to summon help from everyone and anyone she could think of.

"OH, JESUS CHRIST – WHAT THE HELL…………!" yelled Clive, as he ran through the gateway and took in the full horror of the scene before him.

We all saw the upside-down tractor lying on top of a half-submerged Mr Prichard with my mother kneeling beside him, sobbing as if she would never be able to stop.

Dyrham Park

16

SERVITUDE

There was nothing we could do other than wait for the arrival of the emergency services, Mr Prichard was dead.

Mum stayed beside him until the local doctor arrived. He was quickly followed by the police, an ambulance and a fire engine. The firemen arranged for a crane to lift the tractor off Mr Prichard's body and the ambulance drove away after the medic explained that they were not allowed to carry a deceased body.

Mum asked Clive to fetch an old door that was lying in one of the barns and a team of men from the village used this to stretcher Mr Prichard's body back to the farm, where it was placed on straw bales in the hay barn. After everyone had left, mum washed and changed Mr Prichard and carried out his 'laying out' there in the barn. Later, I heard her confide to the vicar that there was not a mark from the accident to be seen on his body, but he was totally crushed inside.

Bryan and I were escorted back to the farm where Margaret gave us all very sweet tea, to help us recover from the shock of what we had witnessed. We then sat numbed by the sudden demise of such a kind and considerate young man.

At the post-mortem it turned out that Mr Pritchard had been reversing the tractor down the silage heap and the outer tractor wheels had slipped over the edge. It was thought he had tried to jump clear, but being a two-seater became trapped and the tractor fell on top of him. It was further considered that had he used the single seat Massey Ferguson, he may have been able to jump clear. They said he had died instantly, but only mum knew if that was true and she never revealed what happened after Rosemary and I left her alone with Mr Prichard in that ditch.

After the funeral we were told by Mr. Pitman that we would most likely be able to remain on the farm, if Mum so wished, to care for the new bailiff. We remained there for some weeks whilst several young farmers were interviewed by Mr Pitman and Clive, but none of the younger men, fresh out of agricultural college, measured up to Mr Prichard. When a replacement was eventually found he had a wife and two small children.

Mr Pitman took it upon himself to tell mum that her services would no longer be required. We would have to leave, but he was grateful for everything she had done and would give her time to find another position.

A few days later, I answered a sharp rap on the front door to find a smartly dressed, past middle age couple, standing in front of a Rolls Royce with a uniformed chauffeur in attendance. The man spoke loudly and with upper class authority.

"I'm Squire Blathwayt of Dyrham Park and this is my wife, Lady Blathwayt. We wish to speak with Mrs Williams. She is in, presumably?"

"Yes" I stuttered. Not knowing whether to bow my head or curtsey. Lady Blathwayt, seeing I was flustered, stepped forward, smiled and spoke softly.

"Thank you for opening the door so promptly, young lady. We would like to have a quiet word with your mother, if that is possible?"

I returned her smile, wondered if I should call her 'my lady' or curtsey, but blurted, "I'll get her for you." and ran to the kitchen.

"Mum! Mum! The people from the big house are here and asking to see you."

"What big house?" Asked mum as she took off her pinny. I shrugged. "Something Park."

"Dyrham Park?" I nodded.

"Hmm. What can they possibly want?" Mum confidently walked to the open door, introduced herself and invited them into the sitting room. I followed, but she pulled a face and shut me out. I listened at the door and Bryan silently joined me. We heard Lady Blathwayt say how sorry she was to learn of the tragic death of 'the young farmer' and that we could not remain at the farm. However, perhaps my mother would give consideration to a proposal they had for her. Bryan and I looked at each other with eyes as wide as saucers as Lady Blathwayt continued.

"To come to the point, Mrs Williams, we've heard many favourable comments about your cooking ability and would like to offer you the position of head cook at Dyrham Park."

"That's very kind of you, Lady Blathwayt, but I'm a trained nurse, not a cook and I have three children to house."

Squire Blathwayt loudly intervened. "The children do not present a problem, Mrs Williams. We have ample accommodation available at Dyrham Park."

Lady Blathwayt spoke in a more persuasive tone. "I'm sure you have many things to consider, Mrs Williams, but if you could perhaps give the matter some thought, I will be in touch later."

"Thank you Lady Blathwayt, I will of course think about your offer, but in all honesty, I think you should be seeking a trained, experienced cook, not a nurse."

Bryan and I heard mum moving towards the door and scampered away. Through the window we saw the chauffeur deferentially touch his cap as he opened the rear door of the Rolls Royce for Lady Blathwayt and repeat the performance as he opened the front passenger door for the Squire.

Mum smiled at us she came back into the kitchen. "I'm sure you heard everything. I don't think

I'll hear from them again, do you?" and calmly went back to her kitchen chores.

Bryan and I just stared at each other, then Bryan said, "Crikey, mum, for the people from the big house to come here to ask you to be their cook? Well wow! You must be good!"

Mum, delighted with his praise, grinned broadly as she said, "Shouldn't you be helping Clive with the cows young man?"

Lord and Lady Blathwayt obviously thought she was good, because they wasted no time and their Rolls Royce whispered its presence in the farm yard later that afternoon. The chauffeur got out and tapped on the door and when mum opened it he touched his cap.

"Her Ladyship would like a word, Mrs Williams. Please follow me."

We watched from the doorway as mum followed the chauffeur to the other side of the car and opened the back door for mum to get into the Rolls Royce, next to Lady Blathwayt.

After a short time, the chauffeur opened the door to let mum out again. As she approached us she pulled one of her funny faces, before turning to watch the Rolls Royce drive off and Lady Blathwayt give us a rather 'royal wave'.

"I'm to be the new head cook at Dyrham Park," said mum, waving at the departing car. "The Blathwayts must be either mad or desperate."

"Wow! You can do it, mum," said Bryan.

Rosemary and I jumped up and down with excitement and I said, "Yes mum, you can do anything."

217

"I'll give it my best shot," said mum, putting her arms around us. "The pays not much though, only £2.10 shillings a week, but they say there's a delightful, rent free cottage which goes with the job. I can take up my duties and move in as soon as we like."

The wage was a pittance, but the rent free cottage made the offer irresistible for mum. She was clearly relieved to have been given a way out of our predicament. Another open door, as she called it. She told us she would have much preferred a position which made use of her nursing abilities, but, for now, thanked the Lord for opening that door for us.

The following day the Rolls Royce drove into the farmyard again. Mum had been told by Lady Blathwayt that a car would take us to Dyrham Park, but we never expected it to be the Rolls Royce. The chauffeur seemed more relaxed without his employer in the car and smiled as he opened the rear doors for us to climb in. Mum grinned and thanked the chauffeur as she joined us. It only took a few minutes to reach the grand stone entrance that led into the long wide driveway which swept through swaths of unkempt grassland. We were stunned into silence as the car rounded a bend and the magnificent mansion came into view. It sat in a wonderfully sheltered position, beneath the folds of the Cotswold Hills, with spectacular views towards Wales. I had never seen anything like it. It was absolutely breath-taking but we were about to find out that it was a view which was not meant for the working class.

We were stopped in the driveway by a man in a gardener's leather apron.

"What do you think you're doing coming in this way, Fred?"

"Her Ladyship instructed me to collect the new cook and her kids for a look around."

The gardener glared at us, then back at the chauffeur.

"You know bloody-well you shouldn't be coming in this way. Now, go back and enter by the servants' gate!"

The chauffeur swore under his breath as he turned the car around and drove back up the hill through the grand entrance and out onto the main road. We all sat in stunned silence.

Because the staff entrance to Dyrham Park is at the rear and totally separate from the main drive, we had to drive back through Dyrham village and negotiate narrow lanes, before we came to the rear entrance which was discretely hidden from view. The chauffeur drove up a shabby lane to the rear of the big house.

"Welcome to the world of those of us in service, Mrs Williams," he laughed, "for a moment back there I forgot my place."

"I hope we haven't got you into any trouble, Fred. May I call you Fred?"

"Of course, Mrs Williams."

"In that case you can call me, Ethel."

"Thank you, Ethel, I will, but don't be surprised if I call you Cook or Mrs Williams in front of Squire and Lady Blathwayt or any of their well-to-do guests, that's just the way of it. I have orders to wait until you've looked around the kitchens and Mrs Farrer, the cook, has told you what's what and then I'm to take you home again."

219

We clambered out from the Rolls Royce,, transfixed by the huge house and the unkempt, 'U' shaped quadrangle which faced us. Eventually mum broke the silence.

"Come-on then, in we go and don't forget. Best behaviour."

As kids we were intimidated by the grandeur of the place, but stepped out bravely towards one of the rear entrances. Before we reached the door it opened and Lady Blathwayt stepped out to greet us.

"Hello Mrs Williams, welcome to Dyrham Park."

She shook hands with all of us, asking our names as she did so. We were then led through a stone-walled back passageway into a small, scruffy sitting room, off the kitchen.

She turned to my mother, "I hope you will enjoy your time here Mrs Williams and that you and the children will soon settle in."

She had that superior, cutting-edge to her voice which made me think of the way the Queen spoke. My mother assured her that she felt everything would be fine. Lady Blathwayt bid us goodbye, saying she looked forward to seeing mum again when we moved in and that she would leave us in the capable hands of her head cook.

She swept out and left us sitting by a log fire in that faded little room. I looked at mum; we were all clearly overawed by that formidable place and our situation. Mum laughed and jokingly referred to the chauffeur's suggestion that henceforth her name would be, 'Cook' and perhaps they should leave before 'Cook' arrived. Bryan did not laugh; he grimly reminded us that we had nowhere else to go. We fell silent, each deep within our own thoughts awaiting Mrs Farrer's arrival.

After a few minutes, Mrs Farrer bustled in. She was a short, round woman with a chubby red face and a pleasant radiant smile. She exuded energy and it was only her greyish hair which gave any clue she was heading for retirement. If she thought mum was not up to taking her place, she did not show it as she rattled on about the history of Dyrham Park.

"There was a manor house on the site in 1311. In 1571 it was owned by Sir Walter Denys, a courtier and soldier for Henry VIII. In 1601 it was listed as a 'Richly furnished house of 22 rooms and sold to William and George Wynter for one thousand eight hundred pounds. Subsequently it was inherited by John Wynter, an active Royalist who was impoverished by the Civil War. Fortunately his daughter married William Blathwayt in1686 who deemed it necessary and had the funds to build a new grand house, most of which you see today. But, from 1765, Dyrham Park went into decline with Blathwayt after Blathwayt selling off art treasures to pay the running costs. Then, in 1844, Colonel George Blathwayt inherited and carried out extensive works to repair the roof, install central heating, a new kitchen and remodel the servants quarters. Not that you would think the kitchen very new now, Mrs Williams."

She paused to look at us with a twinkle in her eye, as we fidgeted in our seats. "But the tour can wait. I have a pot of tea brewing and some cakes which children always enjoy, not to mention the grown-ups."

She briefly left the room and came back wheeling a trolley, with a pot of tea under a woollen cosy, cups and saucers laid out and a three tier cake stand packed with a variety of delicious looking individual cakes. After ascertaining we all took milk, she poured the tea and told us to help ourselves. As we enjoyed the cakes and sipped the tea, Mrs Farrer continued with her potted the history of Dyrham Park.

"In 1938, the house was leased to Lady Anne Islington, the wife of a local MP and former Governor General of New Zealand. When World War Two broke out she transferred her children's nursery here from war-torn London. She cared for over eighty babies and small children, most from the Bethnal Green area of East London, which was badly bombed. She then brought in several aristocratic lady friends and gave them free reign to redecorate parts of the house and they slapped pastel paint all over the place, on the ornate, walnut panelling and the magnificent, baroque staircase. Squire, Justin Blathwayt inherited it in 1948. He and his family immediately took residence and are doing their utmost to return Dyrham Park to its former glory. But between you and me, Williams, it's an impossible task. I've been in service to the landed gentry for over thirty years and I can tell you that at one time, there would have been hordes of servants working here. Now, there are only a dozen of us permanently employed. People from the village have to be drafted in for special occasions when they have a houseful of toffs. They have so much leisure time on their hands that food is an over important part of their lives. That's why good cooks are so highly valued."

I saw mum smirk at that. Two Pounds Ten Shillings a week did not seem such a high value!

Once tea was over and we had scoffed all the cakes, we were escorted over the lower, rear quarters of the mansion. The cold, stone dilapidated area had an enormous kitchen with a vast black iron cooking range of hobs and ovens. Ceiling-high, wall to wall wooden cupboards all jammed with cups, plates, china dishes, copper pans, jugs and a varied selection of jelly moulds.

From there a door led into a dismal, long narrow corridor with numerous side rooms for storage with cold rooms, north facing, for dairy produce, raw meats, cooked meats. There were a multitude of other rooms, even one with a huge marble fountain in it, but they all had the same thing in common, they all had cold grey decaying walls, ceilings, woodwork and reeked of damp. Mum, who was taking great interest in the vast amount of space with rooms for just about everything she could imagine, stopped Mrs Farrer's flow with a question.

"How many people do you have working for you?"

"Ah, that's a very good question. If it's just the family and a few friends, it's just me and my kitchen maid, but as I say, help can always be drafted in from the village."

I could see mum's expression tighten as she tried to get her head around what the job entailed, but as Mrs Farrer continued to add to the list of tasks, her attentive expression turned to dismay.

"Only the best quality produce will be tolerated and you will have to ensure it is properly prepared, which means gutting, jointing, de-boning meats. You will have to use your experience to select only the finest cuts from the butcher. You are expected to make your own bread, pies, biscuits, chutneys, bottled fruits and jams. Tell the game keeper what deer or wild animals need to be caught and hung. Inform the head gardener what vegetables and herbs to gather for the day and the dairyman will need to know the required quantities of milk, cream, butter, cheese and eggs. All on a daily basis taking into account what is required to cook breakfast, lunch, tea and dinner for family, friends, important visitors and parties. On top of that you have to prepare food for the staff and keep the stoves and ovens clean, saucepans and dishes spotless and glassware sparkling."

Mrs Farrer's flow of information continued apace as she led us through the back yard to the huge stable block and beyond to the kitchen gardens. By that time Bryan had done a runner and Rosemary was telling mum that her socks had gone to sleep, her shoes hurt and she was cold. Fortunately a maid appeared to tell the verbose cook that she was required by Lady Blathwayt.

"See you soon Mrs Williams." As Mrs Farrer bustled off giving us a cheery wave we ran for the warmth of the waiting Rolls Royce.

As soon as we were back at the farm, Mum told us that being the cook and head bottle washer at Dyrham Park sounded like hard work, but she was used to that. However, she thought it was doable once she learnt the ropes. But, most importantly, we'd have our very own cottage, decent working hours and a regular wage. We then realised we had not been shown the cottage.

Bryan, who had spent the time he was missing, talking to one of the stable lads, thought it was marvellous. He couldn't wait to move there and help care for the horses and the wild deer.

It was soon agreed with Lady Blathwayt that mum could take-up her post with immediate effect, but, as Mrs Farrer was not due to retire for a few weeks, she could have two weeks unpaid leave to settle into the 'delightful cottage.'

Mr Pitman suggested that if we were prepared to vacate the farmhouse straight-away, he would pay mum one month's wages in lieu. This was gratefully accepted and the move was arranged for that weekend.

A van was sent from 'The House' to collect and transport us to our new home. It was driven by one of the gardeners, not the one who stopped the Rolls Royce and sent it back, apparently, he was the head gardener. Our gardener, was very helpful. He, Clive and Bryan loaded the van which took some time as Mr Pitman had kindly donated some pieces of furniture, including beds, chairs and curtains which would not be required when the new farm bailiff and his family moved in.

Mum thanked Clive and Margaret for all their help and friendship and they waved us goodbye as the van trundled out from the farm yard, with all of us crammed in the cab next to the driver for the short journey.

The van slowed and stopped before we got to the nondescript rear entrance to Dyrham Park. We looked for the 'delightful cottage' extolled by Lady Blathwayt but all could see was a dilapidated dump of a tiny hovel, set under a gloomy canopy of thick low trees. It was a property which would always sit, damp and dark in the shadows.

We were dismayed at what we saw and mum asked the gardener if he had brought us to the right place? He shrugged and looked embarrassed. "I'm afraid so, Mrs Williams. It's been unoccupied for some time."

"Good heavens!" said mum, through clenched teeth. It was obvious to her that we really had no option other than to make the most of it. "Can you just wait before we unload, please?"

We all went to investigate. There were two bedrooms, a sitting room with an open fireplace, a small scullery-cum-kitchen with a wood stove for cooking and one tap with running cold water. There was no indoor toilet and no bathroom. The place looked like it had recently been used by vagrants; it was filthy and reeked of urine and decay. The garden was a wilderness of nettles, brambles and weeds and the outside loo was inaccessible. I heard mum whisper, "Oh lord, what has thee led us to – and why?" For the first time I too wondered why her Lord kept putting such awful obstacles in our way.

The gardener produced a broom from the van and mum used it to sweep the floor of the sitting room. As we moved our things in and piled them up in there, I began to feel distraught. What lay ahead for us? How could we possibly live in such a place? How could mum cope with this and take over as cook at the big house? With all those negative thoughts whirling around in my head, I resigned myself to never living in a proper home again.

However, mum's spirit prevailed. She got us organised and we all went to work. We scrubbed and cleaned the house, the windows and the paintwork and yes, small as she was, Rosemary made a worthwhile contribution. The gardener returned with a scythe, cut a path from the scullery door to the outside loo and placed an old galvanised bucket under the wooden seat. He also arranged for a chimney sweep so we could safely light the fire.

Mum told us to make a wish when we saw the sweeps brush emerge through the chimney pot. My wish was that everything would turn out well in the end.

We had the place acceptably clean within a week or so. Kind members of the Dyrham Park staff, motivated by our friendly gardener, loaned mum some other bits and pieces We all worked hard on our new home and it looked more homely by the time we were done.

The garden was another matter, it took ages to clear and in fact we never really got on top of it. The gardener, his wife and their son helped to develop a tiny vegetable patch and clear spaces around existing fruit bushes and ancient apple, pear and plum trees.

We obtained a tin bath through Bryan's new best friend, the stable lad, who also loaned Bryan an old, but serviceable Raleigh bike. Mum was delighted: her very own errand boy was back in business!

There were obvious disadvantages to living in the shade of a gloomy wood, but the upside was the dead wood readily available and we had great fun running through the trees to see who could find the best pieces. We easily found enough for the sitting room fire, the oven and to heat water for the tin bath.

We began to embrace our new home, but it was a false dawn. Mum became withdrawn, very tired and began to ask strange questions, such as. "Why is the baby crying?" and "Where's Spot?"

Bryan and I buckled down and did more, thinking that given some rest, mum would soon recover. However, she was so tired she could not get-up to work on the appointed day.

Mrs Farrer came to see what was happening, took one look at mum and called for a doctor. The doctor diagnosed an emotional breakdown, most likely caused by the delayed shock of finding Mr. Prichard crushed by the tractor. The doctor arranged for her to go to hospital for a few days and told Mrs Farrer that when she came out, she would need complete rest, good nutritious food and no worries for at least a month.

After making sure we would be able to cope, Mrs Farrer went to see Squire and Lady Blathwayt to appraise them of the situation and offered to delay her retirement for another month.

Lady Blathwayt visited mum in hospital to tell her she could take a month's unpaid rest before starting her duties, but, true to the family motto 'His Ute re Me cum' ('Share These With Me') sent us a food hamper.

Food was also provided from the kitchen over the following weeks and we looked after mum as best we could. With rest and decent food, she began to recover and started part-time with Mrs Farrer within a few weeks of coming out of hospital. Mrs Farrer and her husband left a couple of weeks later and my mother took over. Her work initially involved obtaining supplies and cooking meals for just the family.

However, she was soon overseeing extra staff, for although austerity ruled and the Blathwayt's were said to be running out of funds, they still found money to entertain friends and people of influence.

Mum was expected to work five days a week, clean and lead-polish the black iron stoves, supervise other staff and cook for ten to twelve hours a day. Her five day week quickly increased to six and her one day off had to be a day when someone else was available who could take over the cooking. So we were never sure which day she would be free to be with us.

For the most part, we got ourselves off to school in the mornings and always returned to an empty house afterwards. In the evenings we would often wait for Mum beside the sagging railings at the rear of the house, sometimes until ten at night. We waited so we could escort her safely home through the back courtyard and along the stony lane to our cottage. It always seemed spooky, dark and menacing due to the thick canopy of low hanging trees.

Bryan would make up ghost stories as we waited in the dark. They always involved the big house, a phantom horse rider dressed all in black, save for a dark red mask. This spectre roamed the grounds in the moonlight, looking for his lost love who had fallen from her bedroom window on the morning of their wedding and died. Her ghost also wandered in the grounds, her lace wedding dress and veil in tatters, clinging to her skeleton. She could be seen, gliding amongst the lilies in the lake. They were often seen to be close, but never actually found each other. Should they meet, it would spell the end of the Blathwayt dynasty.

Rosemary would hide her face in my coat as he told his ghostly tales and although I did not entirely believe them, I was always relieved when mum finally arrived. We would walk her back along the dark lane, being careful not to fall foul of the broken paving slabs, pot holes and wheel ruts.

When we got indoors it was my job to make the cocoa before we went to bed. Even though she must have been dead-beat, once we were settled in our warm, comfy beds, mum always found the energy to listen to what we had been doing all day and then we'd talk about what had gone on during her day.

The Squire and his Lady never seemed to give a thought to mum's on-going health or that of her family. Mum had never really regained her full strength and was struggling after one long day after another. Living in a tied cottage you were expected to be at the beck and call of 'The Family'. We discovered there was a 'them and us' code which had to be strictly adhered to. Our first taste of that was when Fred, the chauffeur, drove us in through the main entrance and it was soon confirmed when mum became a permanent staff member. Servants were not to be seen or heard if at all possible and access was only allowed to the family's main living quarters if you had a specific role to fulfil.

Paradoxically, servants were desperately needed because most of 'The Family' could not live without their skill and knowledge, so they were valued and their off-spring, as in our case, were tolerated in order to enlist and retain decent staff.

Despite the class divide, Dyrham Park was a wonderful, magical place to live for us kids and with the vivid imagination of childhood we made the most of it. We were given a stern lecture by a senior member of staff, the butler, just after we arrived. He seemed very prim and proper in pinstripe trousers, a waistcoat and tie, but mum, who had to work closely with him, said he was very kind and helpful with a wry sense of humour, but we did not detect that when he first spoke to us.

"You must never, ever, enter the main house. If you should meet a member of the Blathwayt family, or their guests, you should stand still and not speak until they have passed by. You must never be seen within the grounds of 'The House'. Break any of those rules and you will be in serious trouble."

Being kids we naturally pushed the boundaries. The House was sacrosanct but not the wilderness of a garden. We would sneak into the not so well cared for areas, which only served to make them enticing and irresistible. We'd watch the birds and woodland creatures, especially the deer. I often hid in the shrubs and flowers or beneath the trees, sheltering from the pouring rain. We would pretend the garden was all ours, as it was most of the time. It became our own secret garden.

Rosemary adopted any and all animals she came across. She laid out food, built nests for fallen birds and watched over them until they either recovered or died. If she found a damaged mouse, in it came. This meant that small boxes and cotton wool were commandeered to make beds. Unfortunately, most died within a couple of days and then it was the inevitable funeral parade and prayers, but at least we now had plenty of burial space!

We climbed to the top of the tallest trees, made camps in the orchards and watched, for hours on end, as darting kingfishers flashed over the unkempt lily-clad lake. We hid patiently under the enormous Gunneras, waiting for a heron to arrive and pluck out a fish, then with a slow beat of massive wings, flyaway with its ill-gotten prize. Of course, the herons were not supposed to be there and neither were we, but like the herons we developed an uncanny knack of knowing when to stay away; although I did get caught, twice.

The first time, the dreaded head gardener spotted me as I lay day-dreaming about being rich and having a garden like the one I was in. He grabbed my ankle, pulled me out from under some bushes and glowered down at me.

"What the hell do you think you're doing here?" I was quite shaken, but replied, "I'm doing no harm, just watching kingfishers."

He gripped my arm so hard it hurt and growled, "You're so bloody cocksure of yourself, ain't you gal? You shouldn't be here, leave now and in future don't forget your place."

I pulled away from him and ran home. He was supposed to be working class the same as mum, but it seemed even the working class had their pecking order. I was never sure if it was meant to be that way, or in his case, self-assumed.

The second time he caught me I was swimming in the lake. I spotted him striding across the lawn, swam to the opposite bank and sprinted into dense bushes, where I hid until he gave up looking for me. But when I came out I discovered he had found my clothes and taken them away with him. I had to walk home in a wet vest and knickers. The stable boy brought my clothes back to me that evening. He thought it highly amusing but warned me to watch out for the head gardener because he thought he was in charge of everyone, not just his under gardeners.

At the time, I was not aware Dyrham Park had been built on the proceeds of colonialism, but I certainly knew that the upper class held the inherent belief that they were better than their middle and working class contemporaries. The advantaged family and friends, from London, Bath or Bristol, would arrive, decked out in their elegantly tailored clothes, with their posh accents. I watched them from my secret places as they wandered through the grounds and enjoyed the most sumptuous picnics. Trestle tables covered in flapping white linen sagging under the weight of silver trays laden with delicate sandwiches, chicken legs, game pies, pork pies, iced cakes and scones with fresh strawberries, clotted cream and jam.

The temporary servants who waited on them and kept the tables replenished were recruited from the families of regular staff or locals from the village. The waitresses were all very polite and subservient whilst in the presence of the guests, but once they got out of earshot, they complained of how badly they were treated, mainly by guests being rude, demanding and dismissive. The words please and thank you were never used. Members of the Blathwayt family were not so directly obnoxious to the unappreciated domestic staff, they needed to retain their services, but guests had no such reservations. They would demand, at all times of the day or night, food, drink, the running of a bath, clearing up after their children, laundering, or any other service whether required or on a whim.

One, long- retired army Colonel, found his way into the kitchens one evening and spoke directly to mum.

"I fancy a spot of hanky-panky m'dear. Shall we say my bedroom at 11 o'clock?"

Needless to say, he was given short-shift by mum, but she did laugh as she acted out the tale to us later.

For me, Dyrham Park was an insight into an unattainable world. I could only watch, with some envy, from my secret hiding places, but it taught me how the other half lived and what a protected and over-privileged life they led. And yes, it created a desire within me to experience some of the luxuries they took for granted.

As the days grew shorter, Bryan and I spent more time combing through the trees to stockpile wood for the winter. The ritual of waiting by the bent railings for mum to come out from the kitchen after work changed. Mum had her own pocket torch and insisted that we should not wait in the cold, not knowing when she would come out; she was quite capable of walking home by herself. So we always made sure there was a welcoming fire for her in the dining room hearth and a kettle on the hob ready for me to make the cocoa.

When she returned to the cottage late one evening, mum showed us a letter that the butler had given her. He had delivered it on a silver tray in the kitchen with a wry smile and mum thought it was a joke. But the small, white envelope on the tray had been written by hand and addressed 'Personal and Private, To Mrs E M Williams, Care of Woodlands Farm, Doynton, Gloucester.' It had been forwarded onto Dyrham Park.

We never received any post, so all eyes were focussed on the white envelope propped up on the table as we drank our cocoa. Eventually Bryan asked the question we all wanted to ask.

"Aren't you going to open it, mum?"

"Not now, my love, I'm very tired. Finish your cocoa and go to bed, we'll read it in the morning."

The following morning I knew something was afoot when mum came into our bedroom, but instead of the usual kiss goodbye she sat on our bed.

"I'm not going to work today and you can all have a day off school." She held up the white envelope.

"The letter is from your father and we have to discuss what he has to say."

After breakfast, she told us he recalled his visit to the farm many months before and how it made him long to have his real family back. He begged for mum's forgiveness and understanding. He wanted us to join him in Redcar where he had a home and a secure job as the manager of a furniture shop. He promised that he would make up for all the hurt and pain he had caused and give us a happy, decent life. He ended the letter by swearing he would never let us down again and enclosed a £5 postal order for our train fares.

Mum folded the letter and put it back in the envelope.

"We have to carefully think about what your father has said and whether or not we want to leave here and join him in Yorkshire."

Rosemary, who could not remember her father chirped up. "I would like to meet him; do you think he will like me Betty?"

I reassured her, "He'll love you just as much as we all do, Rosebud."

Bryan, being older was blunt.

"I don't want to go, I like it here and besides, he left us once, what's to stop him doing it again?"

"Well, I think its great news," I said enthusiastically. "It's got to be. We'll be back with our father and a long-prayed-for family again. I can't wait."

"It's up to mum," said Bryan. "If that's what she wants, then I'll have to go along with it."

We felt very grown-up by the way mum had sought all of our views before coming to an extremely tough decision.

Rosemary asked to see photographs of him and inquired what he was like and what life was like with him. I wanted to know all about him too. I remembered him at the farm, that he was handsome and had a lovely smile.

Bryan was still reticent. He clearly remembered what we had all been through and did not want to leave the place we had made our home on the chance his father had really changed.

Mum was between a rock and a hard place. She told us that, had we still been with Mr Prichard, she would not even consider going back. Even at Dyrham, she was wary of giving up her secure job and the home that went with it. On the other hand, she could see that the hours she worked took her away from us too much and was unsustainable. She had also heard on the grapevine that 'The Family' were running out of money and might have to sell Dyrham Park before too long. The opportunity on offer might not knock a second time. It was a chance to become a united family again, yet she had been the long-suffering wife of a weak, deceitful man and would she ever be able to love or trust him again? She knew he was a master carpenter and could command good money. The letter spoke of a home and a respectable, permanent job in Redcar which would offer the family a decent standard of living. She deliberated and we all discussed the pros and cons for the rest of that day.

Eventually she called us all together for our thoughts. Rosemary and I wanted go, Bryan wanted stay. Mum patted his shoulder.

"Bryan, I understand your reservations my love, I have to admit I have some myself. But after weighing everything up and considering all aspects, I've decided that we should take the chance and go to Yorkshire."

Bryan frowned and gave us his raised eyes acceptance, but said nothing.

Mum replied positively to the letter and a week later, she was surprised to be summoned into the Squire's estate office and handed the telephone. It was our father. He told her how delighted he was that she was giving him another chance and again promised that he would not betray her trust and could not wait to see us all, very soon.

When she came back to the cottage bearing this news, it looked as if a heavy weight had been lifted from her shoulders, she appeared younger, happy and relaxed as she told us she would hand in her notice to Squire and Lady Blathwayt the following day.

Rosemary and I were overjoyed and started jigging about with glee. Bryan conceded that maybe it wasn't such a bad idea after all. He put his arms around mum, told her he loved her and how it seemed that things might be alright after all.

Mum smiled at us, put her hands together in mock prayer and said, "Lord, I do hope so."

The Main Kitchen at Dyrham Park

Lake at Dyrham Park with Gunneras

238

JOHN B SMITH TIMBER YARD STOCKTON-ON-TEES

17

A BROODING SHADOW

Following a seven hour train journey, with several changes, the train for the final leg of our journey slowly came to a stop at Redcar Railway Station. I recognised my father who was already waiting on the platform, looking very smart in a suit, white shirt and tie. As we opened the carriage door, he smiled and walked towards us. Mum told us that sometimes he had to use two walking sticks, but on that day he was using just the one. He greeted my mother and surprised me by putting his arms around her and kissing her full on the mouth. I found that very strange

239

as I could not remember seeing anyone kiss her like that, but she smiled nervously as they stepped apart and he returned her smile, but he too seemed nervous.

"I'm so happy to see you, Ethel you must be very tired after such a long journey?"

Mum nodded. "It's been tiring in more ways than one, Tom, but here we are."

Turning to us she said, "Say hello to your father. They're all a bit dishevelled and travel weary I'm afraid, but looking forward to seeing you."

My father turned to Bryan first. "You've grown into a fine young lad, Bryan."

He held out his hand and Bryan shook it but remained silent. I noticed with a feeling of unease that he did not smile.

My father seemed unfazed as he bent down to embrace Rosemary and tell her how pretty she was. She returned his smile before shyly backing away behind mum's coat.

Finally, it was my turn. "So Betty, we meet again, I told you it wouldn't be too long."

I allowed him to hug me but felt unsure if I should hug him back.

We returned to the railway carriage to collect our belongings, behind our mother and father who were walking side by side. I took Rosemary's hand in mine and tweaked it to make her look up at me. I cocked my head towards our parents and she and I shared a secret smile.

I turned to smile at Bryan. His mouth remained determinedly pressed shut, but for me it was the crowning moment of a long battle to leave Dyrham Park.

****

When mum handed in her notice it was rejected and she was summoned into Lady Blathwayt's presence and I was fearful mum would be persuaded to stay. To start with Lady Blathwayt adopted a high-handed approach.

"You have only just arrived; you cannot possibly leave. We expect you to remain within post for at least three years."

Mum stuck to her guns. "Apologies Lady Blathwayt, but I'm on one month's notice and that's how it must remain."

"No, that's not how it works, Mrs Williams, we have to have loyalty. You remember how loyal Mrs Farrer was to our cause when you had your unfortunate illness? That was admirable and expected from one who is in service."

"I'm terribly sorry, but I have this opportunity to be reconciled with the father of my children."

"And where was he when you had your breakdown? You are a wonderful cook, Mrs Williams."

Lady Blathwayt segued into a softer approach.

"You need to consider your position. Our guests, people of rank, speak well of your culinary skills and should you seek to leave after three years with us, you will be highly sought after. In the meantime, I'm sure we can find a three bedroom cottage on the estate for you and your wonderful children; the one I have in mind has a delightful garden. So, it would be wrong of me to accept your resignation, Mrs Williams. I would never be able to live with myself if in doing so I denied you the opportunity to fulfil your potential."

241

She handed the resignation letter back.

"I suggest you give the matter some more thought."

When mum told us what had happened, I was aghast.

"You mean we're not leaving?"

"Of course we are, Betty. As I told Lady Blathwayt, we've made our decision and that's it, we have to go."

I was relieved, but Lady Blathwayt did not give up. She offered mum a substantial salary increase, shorter hours and more help. Every time mum told us of yet another offer, I dreaded that she would be talked into staying, but she declined all blandishments and worked out her notice.

It was raining when we left, wedged into a taxi with blanket bales and bags. I looked through the back window as we drove away. I would miss the bungalow we had turned into a cosy home, but not the long days we endured without our mother who was working all hours. On the other hand, the secret places in the wilderness of Dyrham Park's beautiful gardens, the animals and birds would stay with me forever.

The taxi took us to Bristol Temple Meads Railway Station. Mum had arranged a price, but when we were unloading, the taxi driver wanted to charge an extra five shillings. The porter who was loading all our mismatch of bags and bedding onto a trolley told him to buzz-off. As he took us to the correct platform, he commented that he had not moved luggage such as ours since refugees arrived at the end of WW2. He made the observation in a kind way and refused mum's offered tip.

242

****

My father recoiled when he saw our blanket wrapped bedding, soiled with soot and grime from seven hours of steam train travel. He summoned a porter who heaped everything onto a trolley and we followed him to the exit, where Uncle Ted was waiting with his car. He seemed to know mum because they hugged each other and he seemed genuinely pleased to meet us when mum did the introductions. Uncle Ted crammed most of our belongings into the boot of his big black car. My father sat in the front with Rosemary on his lap; mum, Bryan and I were in the back sitting on some leftover bedding, with me in the middle. I felt we were very special to be treated to such luxury and thought that my uncle must be rich to own his own car. The 1940's Austin smelled of polished leather and petrol fumes and unfortunately it was not long before I was travel sick.

Uncle Ted had to stop twice to allow me to vomit on the side of the road, much to the annoyance of my father who remained in the car as mum ushered me out and helped me.

As we climbed back into the car on the second occasion, he muttered something over his shoulder. Mum pulled a face at him, but smiled at me.

"It's been a long day, Tom. She can't help it."

"Not long now Betty," said Uncle Ted, over his shoulder, then glanced left towards my father. "You should show more tolerance, Tom, old chap, you'll have to adjust to having three children around again."

The remark was made in a light-hearted way, but when my father failed to respond, I felt uneasy. He looked uncomfortable for the rest of the journey and did not speak until we arrived at a small, terraced house.

"This is your grandmother's house. We'll be staying with her tonight." He put an arm around me as we were about to enter the house.

"Betty, I'm sorry for the way I reacted to your travel sickness, you must be worn out after being on trains all day, please forgive me."

I never reacted well to anyone touching me unexpectedly, so somewhat startled, I pulled away, said nothing and followed my mother into the house.

Uncle Ted took all our belongings into the narrow hallway which led into a kitchen, where he set about making tea for us and uncovered a plate of ready-made sandwiches. As we tucked into them as he set off to collect his wife, Auntie Ada, I could not help but wonder why Uncle Ted seemed to do all the work.

After washing our grubby hands and faces in the kitchen sink we were taken into the front parlour where our grandmother reclined in a huge armchair. Stern of face and not at all the kindly, birdlike old lady I imagined, she was huge, with a mass of bright white curly hair clinging to fat jowls. Under her grim, unsmiling mouth multiple chins hung down to rest on her chest. She wore thick stockings, held up by elastic garters tied above plump knees. An over long white slip showed beneath a front buttoned floral cotton frock and a beige hand knitted shawl was draped around massive sagging shoulders. A pair of grubby tartan slippers, with red pom-poms attached, completed her attire. She stared at us grimly. Finally, without the flicker of a smile, she spoke.

"Well, you're all here, at last. I hope you'll be happy, now you're back where you should be, with your father."

She stared at mum and her obvious hostility towards her made it impossible to relax.

Apart from grandmother's armchair there was only a small sofa in that pokey room. Our father instructed us to sit on the floor as he and mum sat on the sofa. Mum sat stiffly on the front edge, looking far from comfortable.

Grandma Williams exchanged small talk with Tom, her only son and the youngest of her five children, as if we were not there. It was a relief when Uncle Ted arrived with Auntie Ada, the youngest of Tom's four sisters. Ada and mum knew each other from their Oxford days and they entered into an animated conversation which was cut short by Grandma Williams who wanted to go to bed. Ada took her upstairs and when she returned, helped organise our sleeping arrangements, such as they were, with mum. Beds were made on the floor in the front parlour with the bedding we had lugged along with us. We were allowed to wash our face and hands in the kitchen sink again and given a china potty to use during the night.

We were used to roughing it, and accepted the situation without question. After such a long day we were almost sleepwalking by that time anyway. As I lay in my makeshift bed, I was thinking of the new life which would begin in our new house the following day. Mum, dad and Ada were in the kitchen and I drifted off to sleep to the sound of their hushed, but passionate, conversation.

The following morning we found our way into the kitchen. My father and mother were already in there; apparently they had been there for most of the night. Mum looked at us as we entered, then closed her eyes, shook her head from side to side, put her hands to her face and began to sob. She was in total despair, her shoulders heaving up and down and wailing like a wounded animal. We froze, terrified in the doorway. We had never seen our mother so distressed, yet our father just stared at us and made no attempt to comfort her. Without a word, he turned and looked out through the window.

Bryan, looking as frightened as I felt, eventually went over to mum and put an arm around her heaving shoulders.

"What's wrong, mum? What's happened?"

Mum spluttered between sobs. "Your father has no home for us. No job."

Bryan swung round to meet Tom's angry gaze. "What?"

Tom blustered and stammered something about being best qualified for the job, but arriving too late for the interview.

"So you lied in the letter to mum?"

"I expected to get a job before you arrived, but it didn't happen," he glared angrily at Bryan "Don't you get cheeky with me boy!"

Bryan would not back down. "You lied to mum and you lied to us. Mum would never have agreed to come to live like this. We had a cosy, comfortable home."

"Well this is what you've got, so you'll just have to put up with it!" Walking stick raised he lurched angrily towards Bryan, and I thought for a moment he was going to hit him with it, but at the last moment he lowered it and hobbled out from the kitchen. We heard the front door slam, followed a few seconds later by what sounded like a motor cycle engine starting up and driving away. We were to learn later that it was his 'Invacar' a motorised carriage for disabled drivers.

After a silent breakfast mum recovered her calm demeanour and took us for a walk so we could talk in private. Although she must have been forlorn and fraught with guilt, she managed to sound convincing when she said we would have to try and make the best of things; we were where we were and we would all be fine once Tom found a job and the new home he had promised us.

It was at that point mum began to refer to him as Tom, not 'your father'. Somehow, we returned to grandma's house with a renewed spirit and resigned to hope for the best.

The house was a typical red brick, smoky northern terrace home; two up, two down and back to back. There was a narrow alley running between the rows of houses and the toilet was in the back-yard. The bathroom was a zinc bath in front of the fire, which we were used to. We were told to continue using the china chamber pot at night as the toilet door creaked and would wake-up grandma. We were to ensure that we emptied and washed it out each morning and of course, being the oldest girl, I landed that job!

Life in this tiny house in the narrow Redcar streets soon became impossible. Tom's mother was an all-powerful, domineering woman who was jealous of any attention her son showed us. She would call him into her room to interrupt any interaction. We could only use the front parlour at bedtime, so spent most of our time in the kitchen or back yard.

The four daughters did everything 'personal' for grandma, whilst she just sat in that large grubby chair for most of the day. At night she retired upstairs to a huge feather bed with many pillows to support her vast bulk. But the daughters gradually withdrew their services and mum became the housekeeper for Tom and his mother. He seemed more than happy to do nothing and remain at home, unless he went for a jaunt in his Invacar. So if mum was out it fell to me to deliver snacks and hot drinks to my grandmother.

I feel sure it was very difficult for her to have us all turn up at her small house and she probably believed her son would find a job and a house for us, although he did not seem to be making much of an effort. However, she was needlessly and openly hostile to my mother from the start and delighted in causing trouble between my mother, Tom and my aunts at every opportunity.

One day, when Tom was out, Uncle Ted paid a surprise visit to tell us he had advised Tom not to entice us up to Yorkshire on a false premise. He felt that Tom realised his mistake and was not coping well with the consequences. It had occurred to me that my father was as unhappy as we were. Being an atheist, he was intolerant of mum's honest belief in God and would delight in ridiculing her if she ever gave God any credit for anything good which happened; not that it did in his mother's house. He soon began to find fault in our behaviour, especially Bryan's. He had no patience with my mother and would chastise her for the most minor of things. Something had to give and it did!

Mum began to question the demands Grandmother Williams was making upon her and why his sisters had stopped attending her needs? She spoke her mind one day when we were all in the kitchen.

"I didn't come up here to care for your mother, Tom and I'm not going to do it, I need to find a job and bring some money into this house."

Tom erupted in a blinding rage.

"You selfish bitch!"

He hit mum so hard across the face the force knocked her backwards, onto the kitchen table. He immediately went to her, picked her up and said he was sorry. Mum sobbed and tried to twist free. He held onto her and said through gritted teeth, "I'm sorry, I said, I'm sorry. I didn't mean to hit you, but it's your own fault, you shouldn't have made me so angry."

We rallied around mum as he stomped out. This was the beginning of a dark, violent chapter in our lives. He began to turn on mum, Bryan and Rosemary; but for some reason, he never bullied me. I know I possessed an arrogant, independent streak and I can only think he recognised that in me and knew I wasn't going to be intimidated by him or grandma. I quickly learnt to read his mood as soon as he entered the house and would react appropriately. Rosemary was too young to be able to do that and Bryan seemed impervious to Tom's moods. He hated him from the moment he knew he had lied to us. He was not yet old enough to protect mum, but was beginning to gain confidence in his growing body strength.

Everything came to a head on Bryan's fourteenth birthday. He was given a small amount of money to spend as he liked, so as soon as the corner shop opened, he shot out and bought himself one of his favourite things – a small tin of sardines in olive oil. He loved to eat them straight from the tin. We all thought Tom had left the house to visit one of his sisters, but he had crept back into the hallway to listen to what was going on. Bryan was opening his tin of sardines when, without warning, Tom charged into the kitchen with a face like thunder.

"You little thief!" he shouted, "I'll teach you to steal from your grandma!"

Mum leapt up to protect Bryan, but it was too late. Tom brought his walking stick down on Bryan's arm with all his angry might. We heard the unmistakable sound of breaking human bone a split second before Bryan's agonised scream.

An unholy commotion ensued with mum wrenching the stick from Tom's hand and threatening to hit him with it, before throwing it across room. Tom quickly retrieved it and stomped out through the door before any recriminations could be brought to bear.

"What the bloody hell's going on, Ethel?"

Grandma Williams had somehow managed to get out of her chair and make her way into the kitchen.

Mum glared at her. "It's your son, Ada. He's a cowardly bully and needs locking up."

Mum eventually calmed us all down, strapped Bryan's arm and took him by bus to the hospital. On the bus she told him not to say his father had attacked him as that could have consequences she might not be able to control. So Bryan told the emergency doctor that he fell out of a tree. Considering the lack of trees in the back streets of Redcar it was hardly plausible, yet it was accepted without question. He came back home a hero, with his arm in a plaster cast up to his shoulder, to celebrate what was left of his birthday.

Tom remained at his sister's house for several days, only returning because his mother insisted.

"It's his home Ethel and he should be allowed to come back. Things must be forgiven and forgotten."

It was clear that mum was not going to get much sympathy or support from grandma Williams, but when he arrived she ushered him into his mother's presence and closed the door. I heard her say her piece in a very firm voice.

"If you ever hit any of us like that again, Tom, I will call in the police and have you arrested and don't for one moment think I won't. And, Ada. If you condone this thuggery by your son, I will never forgive you."

I could hear my grandmother admonish her son and my father apologise and promise that it would never happen again. But he never apologised to Bryan and remained a menacing, brooding presence in our lives.

On one occasion I overheard mum ask one of Tom's sisters why she thought he was so angry all the time and was disillusioned when I heard her response.

"Tom is not a happy man, Ethel. There must have been faults on both sides in your marriage or he would never have gone off with Hilary in the first place. By coming back to him you've made your bed and you'll just have to lie in it."

We discovered we had many relatives when we moved to Redcar, but with the notable exception of Uncle Ted and Aunt Edna, we were not welcome and being Yorkshire people, they made no bones about it.

They remembered Tom as a charmer, which still held true, if he wanted something and I thought he really did want life to work out for us as a family again, because he became quite courteous towards me.

His Invacar was a motorised three wheeled invalid carriage, supplied free by the Ministry of Pensions. There was room enough inside for him and one child. Bryan was too big, but if he was in a good mood he would take me to the coast near Redcar beach to watch the Northern Lights as they floated and weaved across the sky. He would tell me stories of his youth as a gymnast and musician, of how he met and married mum and some of his family history. During these outings he was kind and smiled a lot. So I forgave myself for thinking that, given time, everything might be alright. I thought he really did care about us and just needed to get used to having us around him again.

But, eventually, living in grandma's tiny house, with her attitude, took its toll on all of us. In desperation, mum found a caravan to rent, on a farm near Redcar. Unusually for him, Tom insisted on taking Rosemary to see the caravan before we moved in. They were gone for some time and Rosemary was very straight faced and withdrawn when they returned. She told me she never wanted to go there or anywhere with him again. I led her into the garden and asked if dad hit her. She started to cry and whispered that it was dark and smelt of pooh and she hated it. She hated daddy and did not want to go there to live in that horrible place. When I later asked Tom why she was so upset he said, she hated the mouldy brown marks on the walls and the horrible smell of damp and decay and did not want to live there.

When we moved in I could understand why. The ancient, 21ft caravan, which was really only a summer holiday let, was damp and grubby.

****

It was many years later, when we were at my daughter Lucy's home in Devon, watching a local news item concerning the husband of her friend who had killed one of their children, that the horrific details triggered something in Rosemary. Memory of her dreadful ordeal in that caravan came flooding back and she shocked me by blurting out that Tom had sexually abused her. She would not go into details but at six years of age it terrified and sickened her.

She assured me he never attempted anything like it again and was sure mum never knew.

****

There was no bathroom in the caravan and the only toilet was in a shed across the yard, so we had to travel by bus, once a week, to grandma's for a bath, but it was better than living under her roof. However, it soon became obvious that we had to find other accommodation as soon as possible. It was a particularly wet winter and due to the invasive damp and associated mould spores, we all went down with bronchitis.

Mum found a small, first floor flat. It had two bedrooms, sitting room and kitchen, with a bucket style toilet in the back yard, shared between three flats. It was near grandma's which meant we could walk for our weekly bath. Tom was allegedly looking for work, although nothing came of it, so once again it was down to mum. She managed to get a nursing job in the Redcar General Hospital as a night nurse. This meant she could grab some sleep during the day and work two or three nights a week. Life settled down for a short while with mum working and Tom, when he was not at grandma's, spending time at home with us.

Mum slept in the day so Tom took us to the beach or to relatives so she got some peace and quiet. She got up and made us supper before leaving for work at 7pm. At weekends we went out together, either to the beach, cinema or local parks. They both appeared to be happier and Tom a lot calmer. Perhaps they were beginning to feel they had not made such a blunder after all.

Twice a week, we made special 'let's find fuel' trips to the beach. Armed with buckets and spades, we descended on the wet Redcar sands to scoop up black coal dust which lay in drifts on the sands as the tide went out. We then carried it back to the flat and wrapped wet coal dust as tightly as we could in newspaper; this made 'briquettes' which we used, most efficiently, to keep the fire going when coal could not be afforded. Tom also showed us how to fold old newspapers to make first-rate firelighters.

Then there was cockling on the sands. This entailed sifting out cockles from the wet sand and taking them home to soak in buckets of sea water with porridge oats at the bottom, boil them in sea water, then pickle in vinegar. Cockle and crisp sandwiches were a delicacy!

We sometimes went crabbing with just a piece of line and a hook and caught crabs, or maybe even a fish from the pier, which gave us a nice supper.

Mum was eventually offered a full-time job at Eston General Hospital, but it was on permanent night duty so the treadmill intensified, working five nights a week, trying to catch- up on sleep during the day and taking care of us.

Tom, who could not find a job, became irritable and started spending more time at his mother's. His bullying gradually became a problem and we lived under a cloud of violence again. He found fault with the meals he was getting, the flat not being as clean as it could be, the noise and mess we children made. Just about everything really. He did not seem to be able to cope when things became challenging.

The menacing atmosphere was becoming more intolerable by the day and, combined with her long working hours and lack of sleep, it soon began to tell on mum's health. Rosemary was still not fully recovered from her bronchitis and had developed painful mouth ulcers. Bryan had found new friends and spent as much time as he could away from the flat, so we never knew where he was or who he was with.

He would say to mum. "Don't worry ma. I'm just going to see my mates and will be back for supper, let me know if dad gives you any grief and I'll sort him out."

They both laughed as he grabbed his jacket, gave mum a peck on the cheek and sauntered out, whistling. He was never back in time for supper and mum would leave it on top of a simmering pan of water. If Tom spotted it, he would turn the gas off, but Bryan did not seem to care.

"Hot or cold, Betty, it all goes down the same way."

Angry, because he was being ignored, Tom attempted to start an argument one evening as Bryan was about to go out.

"I don't like the sort of friends you've got in with. They're a bad lot."

Bryan stopped by the door. "You don't know them, dad. Do you know their names?"

"I don't need to know their names to know you shouldn't be mixing with them."

"Come and meet them. Then you can tell them what you think of them." He smiled, which infuriated Tom.

"Bugger off!" he snarled. "Don't come knocking at my door when you're in trouble."

Bryan smirked as he left; he knew he was winning the battle against his abusive father.

It was impossible to know if Tom was seriously looking for work, but mum forced the issue when she answered a job advert in the local paper. It was for a married couple to care-take at a local timber yard in Stockton-On-Tees. It came with a three-bedroom house. The husband was to be the caretaker, timekeeper and stockman of the wood yard and the wife was to clean the manager's office, the workmen's tea huts and ensure supplies of hot drinks from Monday to Friday. She said nothing to Tom until she received a letter inviting them for an interview. We knew about it and watched in some trepidation as mum handed him the letter. - would it be another frightening moment of fury? No. He actually gave mum a beaming smile.

"That sounds wonderful, Ethel. Where did you hear about it?"

"It was in the local paper, Tom. I thought it was worth a try. Of course we haven't got it yet, but at least we have an interview."

"That could be just what the doctor ordered" he said as he gave her peck on the cheek."

They were both very excited by the security that job could bring and our flat took on an air of lightness and hope. We even heard them laughing together, a sound we were not used to.

On the day of the interview they came into the sitting room and we stopped what we were doing to gawp. Mum looked beautiful in her lovely floral frock, topped with a black jacket she had borrowed from auntie Ada. She was wearing a new pair of high-heeled shoes and a pearl necklace. Tom had slicked his hair and was in his smart suit with white shirt and plain tie. We were amazed, he still looked like a film star. They both did!

We wished them luck, even Bryan, after hugging Mum, he tapped his father on the back and said he would keep his fingers crossed for them.

Mum and dad left the flat, arm in arm in search of a new beginning.

They landed their dream job! The double placement paid over £8 a week, Monday to Friday, with no weekend working. It came with a substantial, fully furnished, three bedroom house, with two sitting-rooms, an upstairs bathroom and a second, downstairs toilet. Mum could give up her night work altogether and Tom finally had a respectable and remunerative job.

On their triumphant return, they both celebrated with whisky and ginger ale. We only had the ginger ale but were nonetheless delighted.

The job would take us to Stockton-On-Tees, County Durham, a large, manufacturing and chemicals town on the north bank of the River Tees. The J B Smith Timber Yard and Sawmill fronted the river, a few hundred yards downstream from Victoria Bridge. As it sat opposite the Boathouse Lane Bus Depot and beside a branch railway line to Stockton Quay, it was certainly not Stockton's most salubrious area, but it seemed wonderful to us.

For Tom it meant a move away from his mother, grandma, but as he had his own vehicle, he could visit and maybe stay there as much as he liked.

We moved into the roomy, clean, fully furnished house a couple of weeks later. It was the fresh start I had been dreaming of and hoped it would prove to be a happy home.

Tom was delighted to find a separate, second front-room, with its own, lockable door from the hallway and its own outside door. It was an ideal space for a workroom where he could set up his own business on the side, making and upholstering furniture.

We arrived at the onset of winter and deep, dank smog covered the area. It seemed to be hanging over us for most of our time there. The timber yard covered several acres with ton after ton of clean, sweet smelling timber stacked over twelve feet high in row upon row.

The team of men employed there spent their days receiving, storing, treating and cutting timber.

From inside the house we could hear the high pitched scream of hefty and extremely dangerous saws. It hardly ever stopped from 8am to 5pm every weekday.

One of Stockton's claims to fame is that has the widest High Street of any town in England and every week there was a street market running its full length. Everything you could think of was sold here: fish, meat, abundant fresh seafood, fruit and veg, clothes, shoes, household wares and garden plants. We spent many hours just browsing the stalls or listening to the street vendors in that noisy, bustling place. But, street market or not, the sickly-sweet smell of hops and barley always emanated from the town centre brewery. It was a smell which reminded me of the potato peelings mum cooked to a mash to feed to the chicken on the farm at Doynton.

Due to our ages, we attended three different schools in Stockton. Bryan hated his and played truant on a regular basis. His continued absence was reported to mum, but to keep the peace she stopped it from reaching Tom's ears. With the pressure off, my father seemed far more relaxed there. When he was not working in the yard, he was busy setting up his upholstery business and working towards becoming his own boss again.

He also spent some of his time trying to teach us different things, such as how to make him a decent cup of tea. He liked his strong, "so you can stand your spoon up in it lass" and with three huge spoonfuls of sugar. I recall some evenings of great contentment with him during these early days in Stockton. We would sit together and listen to the radio. He showed us how to peel a pomegranate and pick-out the sweet fleshy seeds with a pin. He told us of operas and plays he had seen and how comedians were the best entertainers because they made people laugh and to do that was a great gift. He demonstrated how strong he was by lifting our small armchair above his head with one hand gripping a back leg. He could do one hundred press-ups using one arm, and then do another hundred with the other. He was strong in his upper body, no doubt about that and he could be entertaining. He played the spoons, where he held two, wide-handled spoons back-to-back and between the thumb and two fingers and could somehow click them together on his other hand, knees, elbows or arms to produce a tune. He tried to teach Bryan, but he never seemed to latch on to how it was done and Tom mocked him. That was when he revealed his bad side. He was on Bryan's case, mostly because he stayed out too long; but he would tease him about being tubby and make sarcastic remarks at mealtimes. This naturally led to Bryan refusing food, not that there was that much and certainly no treats other than the lemonade and pomegranates.

So Bryan began to lose weight. He slimmed down and shot-up. Without a target for his sarcasm, Tom turned on the rest of us and would fly into a rage without giving a thought to the threatening atmosphere he was creating. Mum told us he was a complicated man. Because of his disability, he had been bullied throughout his younger life and she felt perhaps it was that which bred the inner demon within him, which he could no longer control. I thought mum was being supportive and making excuses for him, although I had never really been the object of his fury. But my time was to come!

One day, as I ran through the market, I fell and suffered a deep cut to my forehead. The bleeding would not stop and Tom was called to collect me in his invalid car. When he arrived there were several shoppers trying in vain to stem the flow of blood. He looked horrified, but remaining calm, gently lifted my blood soaked hair out of the way and pressed his handkerchief firmly on the gash until the bleeding stopped. With the wound sealed he proceeded to wipe blood from my face, but stopped when he realised I had lipstick on. I had been playing at a friend's house and we tried some of her mum's lipstick. Tom went berserk and the anger in his eyes frightened me more than the blood on my clothes. He rubbed and rubbed at my mouth with the blood stained hankie until it was sore, all the while warning me never to put make-up on again, he said "only easy-girls wear lipstick." I didn't even know what an 'easy-girl' was.

His anger episodes became more intense as time passed. Although only nine years old, I could prepare a reasonable meal for Tom and often did so. One evening, mum was out shopping so I got his supper ready, loaded it up onto a tray and placed it on one of his carpenter's footstools, in front of him. The stool was about 2ft high and 4ft wide and had a lift-up upholstered lid, covering a deep storage box. He made it himself and it held much of his upholsterer's sewing paraphernalia such as cutters, tacks, buttons, needles, threads, measures and many other items. Bryan and Rosemary were messing about and Bryan accidentally knocked Tom's supper tray onto the floor. All three of us froze wondering what on earth was going to happen. I knew it was unlikely be good and so it transpired.

261

Within seconds Tom leapt up and screamed at us, "You bloody savages, I wish to Christ you would all go back to Oxford." He kicked the tray across the room and lifted the big stool above his head, held it there for a moment before hurling it at Bryan, who leapt to one side as it crashed into the wall, narrowly missing his head before smashing down to the floor, scattering the contents everywhere. Tom followed the footstool across the room, grabbed Bryan by the neck and shook him violently.

"Pick-up every piece. Do you hear me boy? Every last button! And do it before your bloody mother comes home."

He was in a terrible fury. Spittle was flying from his rage contorted mouth and he was tightening his grip around Bryan's throat. Rosemary and I screamed at him to stop, but he seemed to be in a trance. In desperation we started to beat him with our puny fists and he was so surprised he stopped and turned on me. I thought he was going to put those powerful hands around my neck as they reached out towards me, then, as if someone had thrown a switch, he looked at his grasping hands in horror and fled into his workroom. Bryan fell to his knees with such a wallop, we thought he was dead. But, although badly shaken he quickly began to recover. Gasping for air he croaked, "Jesus, I thought the bastard was going to kill me."

We were relieved when we heard Tom slam out of the house. As we set about picking up all the scattered contents from the stool, we knew he would be gone for days this time. I later looked at my big brother with a new respect and thought, "bastard" that's a new word I haven't heard before.

Tom didn't come home for two weeks and when he did, he was on a charm offensive. We had seen this many times before, but overtime, or due to one incident, he would suddenly lose his temper and we would enter another period of fear. But on my birthday in January1955 all was well and I was excited to be called into the, usually out of bounds, inner sanctum of Tom's workroom. As I entered, both he and mum were smiling with each of them holding out a wrapped present. As I skipped forward to take them, there was a loud thumping on the door. "Blast!" said mum and left us to see who was there.

She opened the door to find a stern looking, pinch faced woman on the step. She spoke in an official, demanding tone.

"I wish to speak with Mr Thomas Williams, is he in?"

Tom immediately reached past mum and closed the door in the woman's face.

"Take Betty into the sitting room to open her presents, Ethel, I'll deal with this."

He rushed to the front door. Mum and I trailed behind, but instead of going into the sitting room we waited for him in the hallway. I was holding the present Tom had given me and mum was still holding hers.

When we heard the woman say she was there in her official capacity as a debt collector, mum put a finger to her lips to warn me to keep quiet. We listened and heard Tom tell the woman that Ethel Williams, his wife, had run up massive debts in his name. She drank a lot, was an alcoholic and the misuse of his money caused him to get into debt. The collector commiserated with him on his bad luck and left, saying that although a husband was normally responsible for his wife's debts, but she would reissue the debt paperwork in his wife's name.

When Tom came back through the front door, he was mortified to see us standing there and could tell from mum's face that we had heard every word.

Mum asked him why he had lied and sullied her good name; he pushed her into his workroom and slammed the door. I heard him slap her face and screamed at her.

"I left you once Ethel and I'll bloody well do it again. You mark my words, the kids will all leave you too one day. You'll be forever alone, just wait and see."

As he stormed out through his workshop door, as an aside, he called out. "Oh yes. Happy Birthday Betty!"

When I went in to comfort mum, she tearfully put her arms around me and said how sorry she was to have exposed us to Tom's violence. It could not and would not be allowed to continue. Nothing could be as bad as trying to live with our father.

The final straw came a few days after his return. During a tense evening meal, Rosemary, who was again suffering from painful, mouth ulcers, asked for a glass of cold milk during supper. Milk soothed the acidic soreness of her ulcers. Tom told her that half way through a meal was not the time to ask for a drink. She made the mistake of asking a second time, so he quickly stood up to fetch her a glass of milk from the kitchen.

"Drink it, all of it." His voice was as cold as ice.

Rosemary, not noticing this grave change in him, gave him a grateful smile and drank it. Then without a word, Tom went back into the kitchen, refilled the glass and told her to drink that too. She stammered that she couldn't and started to cry. He grabbed her head, tipped it back and poured the milk into her mouth. It came out through her nose and she began to choke, but Tom continued to pour. Mum leapt up and for the first time, so did Bryan. Mum pushed Tom away and he turned and slapped her across the face, sending her reeling. In a fit of rage he grabbed Rosemary, carried her out of the room into the hallway and threw her halfway up the stairs. My brother went after him, grabbed hold of his jumper, twisted him round and yelled in his face.

"Leave her alone, you bullying bastard, you cowardly cunt! Never! Never! Never again, will you touch her or mum. If you do, I'll fucking kill you, you mingy piece of shit!"

Tom was probably right about the boys Bryan associated with in Redcar, but the tirade of expletives he dredged-up from their foul lexicon, stopped him in his tracks. He did not know how to react to such verbal abuse. He froze, glaring at Bryan. Was he going to fight him? To my relief, he obviously thought better of it, tore himself away from his grip, took his keys and bolted out from the house through the front door.

Mum and I watched in awed silence as Bryan carefully picked up Rosemary and carried her to our bedroom. She had been sick and soiled herself. Mum bathed her, I made her a hot water bottle and then we put her into bed and climbed in next to her. Bryan gently assured her that was the very last time my father would touch her, enough was enough. She eventually fell asleep in Mum's arms, but sobs came from deep within her as he slept.

Bryan went out very early the following morning and came home with a small cardboard box. He was grinning.

"Where's Rosebud?"

"Still in bed," I told him. He called up the stairs.

"Hey Rosebud, I've brought someone home who wants to meet you."

Rosemary came slowly down the stairs, puffy-eyed and sullen. "Who wants to see me?" she suspected she had been lured out of bed for nothing.

"Here" said Bryan, handing her the box.

Rosemary took it with a puzzled look on her face which quickly changed when something moved in the box. There was a mewing sound. She slowly lifted the lid, peered inside and squealed with delight when she saw two tiny kittens. We all looked. One was black and the other tabby, but they both had the biggest, bluest cat's eyes we had ever seen.

Rosemary was beside herself with joy as she scooped them out and tucked them under her chin. Mum looked like she wanted to say something sensible, like, "two more mouths to feed," but held back and joined in the combined, "Ums" and "Ahhs" and finally commented,

"Looks as if we have two friends to find a new home for, as well as us."

Although we knew our home would be 'Tom free' for a short while, Mum was determined to find a new position with accommodation, to get us away from him, she blamed herself for exposing us to Tom's cruelty. He was a man she no longer recognised.

However, as Stockton was such a grubby, hard-working, northern town with shipyards, railway yards and breweries, no one was looking for, or could afford to hire, a housekeeper or private nurse. Mum realised she would have to broaden her search but events soon made the need to find somewhere, desperate and imperative.

Because Tom was so often at his mother's, mum carried out most of his duties as well as her own, but he was supposed to carry out late-night security rounds, to deter drifters seeking a warm refuge in one of the woodsheds. They never caused any trouble, but the management did not want them close to dangerous wood-cutting machinery. As Tom continued to stay away for days on end and the site security was not a role my mother could take on, those checks were not being made.

The first we knew about a fire was when we were rudely awoken by fire engines, streaming past our house. We wondered where they were going; never dreaming it was in the wood yard. By the time we were out of the house the cutting sheds and wood stores were on fire and a fierce blaze was spreading across the yard. More fire engines noisily arrived but it took hours to bring the fire under control. In the morning the yard was still smouldering, but luckily no one was injured and the offices and our home were unscathed.

During the subsequent investigation, it was discovered that Tom, who should have been on duty, had not been there. The undamaged clocking-in machine clearly showed that he had not clocked in that night, or many other nights for that matter.

The source of the fire was thought to be sawdust under a cutting machine set alight by the discarded cigarette butt of a sleeping tramp.

Within days Tom and mum were summoned to see the yard manager. Tom's negligence had allowed a growing number of tramps to use the shed as an undisturbed night shelter. Both were given immediate dismissal: with no notice: no references and no pay 'in lieu of notice'. They were also told to vacate the house within a week.

Tom stormed out, but mum remained and asked to see the owner. She had spoken to him on several occasions whilst cleaning the offices. She explained our dire situation and pleaded with him to be allowed to stay until she could find another situation for us. The owner, who admired mum's work ethic, was sympathetic and did not want to throw us out on the street. The house would be needed for a new caretaker, but mum could stay-on to clean the offices, and receive £4 a week, whilst the sheds were being re-built. That would give her two months grace, but on no account was Tom allowed to return. Mum thanked him for his generous offer and we all rejoiced in Tom's ban. He only returned to pack his things and empty his workshop.

Uncle Ted and Auntie Ada, who had once known good times with the carefree, young couple during their 'salad-days' in Oxford, came to see us. They again said how sorry they were about us being enticed up to Yorkshire by Tom and promising to keep in touch, gave mum £25 and wished us well in our new home, wherever that might be. They were the only ones within the Williams family who actually seemed to care what happened to us. We never heard from Grandma Williams or any of the others.

Stockton Market 1950's

Low Gill Cottage

18

THE SILVERY MOON

Back to the local papers! Mum combed through them searching for a job with accommodation, knowing we only had weeks to find somewhere. She came across an advertisement offering a vacant cottage in a place called Dale Head, Rosedale. It was out on the vast North York Moors, just eight miles from the market town of Pickering. No matter it was unfurnished as that meant the rent was an affordable, five shillings (twenty five pence) a week. It seemed that salvation had arrived as she would able to obtain separate work as a District Nurse. She made enquiries and was assured that one was badly needed in that area and to apply as soon as she had the new home address and signed the lease. The owner of the cottage said she could have it as soon as she signed, paid the deposit and the first month's rent.

Now, all we had to do was tell Tom when he sneaked into the wood yard to collect the larger carpentry tools he had left behind, mum joined him in his workroom and left the door ajar for us to hear what she had to say.

"Tom, I've have found a cottage at a very low rent and have decided to move there with the children."

Tom snorted. "We all know we have to move somewhere. Where is it?"

"On the North York Moors."

"WHAT! You expect me to move up there?"

"No, I don't Tom." Mum spoke softly, a counter to Tom's shouting. "We're reconciled to going there without you."

He became petulant. "Suppose I do want to come? What then?"

"I think you need the time and space to think about what you really do want, Tom," said mum, soothingly. "It's been obvious that you bitterly regret asking us to come to Yorkshire and you may decide not to join us. We're at a crossroad and you must be very sure about what you want. So, for now, we're making the move on our own and we leave in a weeks time."

Tom said nothing. Mum had skilfully manipulated our first move towards freedom.

It was sometime before Tom emerged from what had been his workroom; obviously, having thought things over, he looked remarkably happy and could not disguise his delight.

"Ethel, I think you are right. We both need time to come to terms with the position we find ourselves in. It's good that you have found somewhere for you and the children. I'll take the time to consider what you've said and perhaps join you later."

Standing to one side where Tom couldn't see her, mum reassuringly shook her head, so we knew that this was never going to happen. We were relieved, but taken by surprise when Tom said he would go and take a look at the cottage for us.

He travelled all the way to Rosedale in his invalid carriage and returned very upbeat. He couldn't keep the smile from his face as he told us how beautiful it was on the Moors and how much we would love living there; "It's nothing like here in Stockton," he said, "it's clean, freshest air I've ever breathed and you can see for miles and miles."

"What's the cottage like, Tom?"

"Well, I couldn't actually get inside, Ethel, it was locked. It's quite small, but as far as I could see it had two bedrooms and two sitting rooms. Plenty of space for the family and as I say, it's in a wonderful position."

To our utter surprise, he then told us he would find the money for the deposit, the first three months' rent and on top of that, settle any removal costs, about £5 in total. He also vowed he would send a Postal Order for £2.10 shillings a week. This was great news to us as it meant we would have some money left for daily living costs until mum got the district nurse job.

As soon as everything was paid and signed, mum asked if we could move in the following week. The owner commented that it was short notice, but it would be fine so long as we were prepared to clean the place up. At that time we were not sure what he meant, but we had the experience of clearing-up the hovel at Dyrham Park and nothing could be as bad as that!

On the day of the move, early spring 1955, mum was 46, Bryan was 14, I was 10 and Rosemary 8. The two very helpful and friendly removal men collected our things from the house. We had managed to scrounge some items, armchair, small dining table, two wooden dining chairs and a large upholstered trunk Tom had made, from his sisters. We also had three beds and a wardrobe from the house in Stockton, so we left Stockton-On-Tees better equipped than when we moved in. By the time we got our stuff packed and onto the van it was mid-afternoon. I was unnerved to notice my father smiled broadly as he waved us off, but shouted that he would 'see us all again, very soon'. I caught my mother's twinkling eyes as we waved back, but we all kept our thoughts to ourselves.

It was not an easy journey, it was getting dusk as we began to climb onto the moors and heavy fog swirled in the van's headlights, shrouding everything. We took the wrong road, completely bypassed Pickering and ended up in Scarborough!

The quickest way back to Rosedale was to take a high, bleak road, directly across the North York Moors. Dense fog made the journey slow and nerve-wracking and by the time the driver found the steep hill which took us down to Rosedale Abbey Rosemary and I were asleep, We woke-up during the slow descent to find less fog in the valley as the van slowly trundled along narrow lanes until the driver found the rutted track leading up to our new home.

It was well past mid-night by the time we finally came to a stop outside the cottage. The two men, tired and fed-up, looked at each other, then at mum. "Sorry Mrs Williams," said the driver, "but we seem to have come to the wrong place."

Mum jumped down from the van to take a look. She shouted to the driver. "Nope, I can see from this old photo that this is it, we're here."

We grabbed our bags, jumped down from the van, stood next to mum and stared in silence. Bryan was first to voice what Rosemary and I were thinking,

"Bloody hell Mum, it's a shack! This can't be where we're actually going to live, can it?"

Mum looked frustrated, but pushed open the unlocked front door. "This is it Bryan, so let's just get in, shall we?"

We followed her inside and fumbled for the matches and candles we had in our bags. The removal men opened the back of the van and followed us in. As they entered it was clear they were concerned.

"We can't just leave you here Mrs Williams. We could find you a bed and breakfast for the night and see how you feel about this place in the morning."

Mum shook her head. "No, we've been in worse places, please help us bring everything in."

She grinned at us in the flickering candle light as she added. "It really is very good of you to be concerned, but please don't worry, we're well used to managing.

She lit more candles and we mooched about to see what we were going to have to deal with. We were dismayed to find there was no water, no electric, no gas and no toilet. It was a shack of a cottage which might have once been a very pretty farm worker's home, but that must have been a long time ago. Judging by the droppings, feathers and broken eggs covering the floor it had been used, fairly recently, to house chickens. A cracked window had a huge spider's web draped across it and the place reeked. The owner's warning that it needed a clean was an understatement of massive proportions but at least the chicken mess seemed to be restricted to the ground floor as the stairs had been boarded off. The removals men removed the boards and went up to take a look and reported that although the boards kept the chickens away, it was very dirty and in dire need of serious repairs to floors and walls, although one room was just about habitable. So it was agreed that everything 'bedroom' should go in there. Bryan had already lugged in the boxes containing food, so mum began to prepare some supper and we mucked-in to get the van unloaded, either upstairs or into a lean-to shed at the side of the main cottage. As soon as everything was safely gathered in, we enjoyed an ad hoc supper with the removal men, who had been marvellous.

When it was time for them to leave, they hesitated and hovered awkwardly in the door way.

"Are you sure you're alright, Mrs Williams?" asked the driver. "We're not happy leaving you here like this."

"Off you go!" ordered mum "There's no need to be concerned, we're used to dealing with adverse situations. Thank you so much for all your help. Have a safe journey home."

The fog had completely lifted and it was a bright moonlit night as we waved them off.

"They should find it much easier to find their way home," observed mum, as their lights disappeared around a bend in the track.

We were finally on our own and in the dark – except it wasn't dark. A mesmerising bright silvery moon seemed to be smiling down on us. We gazed up into the clear night sky at the biggest, brightest display of stars we had ever seen and when, at last, we looked around us, the brilliant moon was bathing the moor in a ghostlike, silvery glow.

We went back inside the cottage. Rosemary was holding her kittens, safely tucked under her chin. Bryan was finishing off the last of the bread and I was watching a huge spider crawl across its web, probably came out to see what all the noise was about. It was enormous– ugh!

I jumped as mum started laughing. She laughed so hard I thought she had gone mad, but then I realised she was laughing with tears of released emotion. Seeing this we all began to laugh. We laughed at the ridiculous place we found ourselves in. We laughed at the absurdity of our last few years: the bad luck: the violence: the mental torture of it all: and, just when we thought things could not get worse, we found ourselves in the middle of nowhere, in a condemned cottage surrounded by chicken shit and feathers.

What was left of that first night at Dale Head was a strange mixture of wonderment at the moonlit beauty we had just seen, fear of what was to come and relief to be away from my father.

We awoke to the reassuring, familiar rumpus of a farmer shouting, 'cush-cum-on' and 'aye-up', as he drove his milked cows back into the field next to our bedroom window. The window looked out across the track the removals van had driven up and provided a splendid view onto the rising fields leading up to the moors, placing the cows on the same level as our upstairs window. Beyond them were fields with hundreds of sheep and lambs frolicking around them.

We agreed that we were lucky to have found a place in such a magnificent location. It was a world away from anything we had ever known but we were under no illusion: the cottage was in a dreadful condition. However, based upon our previous experience, we believed we could eventually make it habitable. But, there were major repairs it would be impossible for us to make, all we could do was clean and bodge-up.

The ancient, Yorkshire stone cottage was under an unevenly tiled, weathered roof, which we suspected would let rain into our bedroom. Attached to the right of the cottage was a large open-fronted lean-to building full of obsolete farming equipment and broken gardening implements. We discovered a dilapidated toilet building on land just below the house. It must have collapsed many years ago. The heap of stones just lying there, waiting for a strong young man, such as Bryan, to put them back together again.

The cottage front door opened directly into the left-hand sitting room. To the right was another small room, but the holes in that ceiling and floor, meant that it was out of bounds for anything but storage, certainly for the time being. The room we could use, however, had a window which enabled us to see a bend in the lane, about half a mile from our home, which would serve to give us a five minute warning of approaching visitors.

The 12' x 12' sitting room had an open, cast-iron fire place, with a small, black oven built into the wall beside it with a single, round hotplate on the top. The use of the oven and the hotplate was totally reliant on the fire being lit.

The interior walls were of dirty, roughly plastered stone. The floor was simple wood planking. The ceiling was the bedroom floorboards over woodworm ridden beams.

A tiny scullery led off the sitting room, it had a brownstone sink, a wooden table and a couple of rough wood shelves, but that was it, apart from the creepy inhabitants of more huge cobwebs. There were, of course, no taps over the sink.

We only had the one useable bedroom and even that had a long crack running down the northern wall. All the beds had to go in there as we could see there was real danger of falling into the unusable sitting room below if we even stepped into the other bedroom.

Rosemary and I slept top to toe in one single bed, but mum and Bryan had the luxury of one bed each. We did manage to squeeze in a large chest of drawers, but that was it for the bedroom. Thank goodness we had also brought plenty of bedding, as come the winter, we were definitely going to need it. The bedroom window wasn't weather proof as some of the panes were loose or cracked, but it did provide those splendid views.

After a short rest, we all had to set-to and clean-up the downstairs space. It was a mammoth task and Bryan was summoned many, many times to remove gigantic spiders which seemed to have taken over the place as their own. There was red spider mite, rotten eggs, wet feed, chicken droppings, straw and filth everywhere. It took us days, but we did it and it looked as good as it possibly could when we finished. However, it might have been clean, but it was still dilapidated!

Bryan did the best he could, he rebuilt the collapsed toilet by utilising some of the large stones already there and two rusty corrugated metal sheets we found lying around the place. There was a rusty old bucket in the lean-to shed and this took pride of place under the existing wooden seat. The toilet still resembled a pile of old stones, but it worked for us.

From day one, we had to deal with the problem of no mains water. Not even a well! We had to collect water, in every available container, from a stream at the bottom of a steep hill behind the house. Bryan and I shared this chore as Rosemary was too small to lug water back up the hill.

Taking a day off from our labours, we walked to the Rosedale Abbey, closest village about three miles away. This picturesque village sits at the bottom of a steep, lush-green valley on the River Severn. It is sheltered within an area of rolling hillsides and wonderful scenery. We soon discovered that the village had a post office, an inn, a small primary school, a butchers and bakers shop and a church with an acre or two of seriously ancient graves. On the perimeter were the remains of an old priory tower.

The postmistress was very chatty and Bryan was excited to learn that despite its quiet beauty, the village was associated with the old iron ore industry. At its peak, the mining boom of 1880 saw over 2,000 people employed and many of them living in the village. Stones from the Abbey ruins were used to build many of the old miners' cottages in the village in the 1880's.

She was surprised to hear we had moved into Low Gill, the cottage had been condemned years ago. It was originally built for mine managers and their families. There was another called 'High Gill', about half a mile above ours, but that was now just a couple of outer walls and no roof. It was used to pen sheep during the winter. Other relics of mining activity, Rosedale Branch Railway and Iron Ore Mines were still there on 'Bank Top' and 'Chimney Bank' which just happened to be immediately above Low Gill. Bryan was jubilant when he realised there was so much to be discovered and especially so when the postmistress invited him to accompany her and her son on a walk up to Bank Top. He eagerly accepted and we agreed to see her again, very soon.

Whilst in the village, mum called in on the local doctor to introduce herself and register us. He was out on a call, but mum asked his wife if she knew anything about the district nurse post. She didn't, but said she would inform the doctor of her visit and that he would call on us one day soon.

Basic food supplies for a couple of weeks, more candles, a mantle lamp and a gallon of paraffin, had to be carried on the long trek back to Low Gill. Rosemary hitched a ride, high on Bryan's shoulders.

We soon learnt that we had to be very careful with the mantle wick in the lamps. Once lit, they became gossamer-like and fragile. They could disintegrate into a fine dust at the slightest touch, even breathing on them too hard could destroy them. They were kept alight with paraffin, which had to be gently pumped up from a brass container at the base of the lamp up onto the mantle, which could then be turned up to a full white light or turned low for a comforting, more economical, yellow glow. Keeping it alight for too long was not an option due to the cost of fuel and mantel, so most of the time we used candles.

Our next outing was much more exciting, we went by bus from Rosedale Abbey to Pickering, a small, typically northern, agricultural market town. There was every shop we could wish for there, from fresh fish, meat and vegetables to clothing, shoes and household goods. We were able to buy all we needed, the only restriction being we had to be able to carry it, and my sister, on that three mile hike from the bus stop in Rosedale Abbey, to home.

By that time, we had used up quite a bit of the money mum had managed to scrape together before we left Stockton. We prayed Tom would do as promised and send a £2.10 shillings Postal Order every week, but after a couple of weeks nothing had arrived and given his history, the signs were ominous.

We had to begin some serious patch and repair work. The landlord provided some thin hardboard sheets. Mum and Bryan put them, side by side, against the inside walls of the bedroom and sitting room. Without any experience of how to fix them, Bryan hammered nails through into the wall and prayed!

The plan was to stick wallpaper over them, literally papering over the cracks. A pale rose and trellis pattern wallpaper was only six pence a roll at the hardware store in Pickering and when mum told the owner what we wanted it for, he kindly let her have the lot for two shillings and threw in loads of paste and a paste brush.

We took it back to the cottage and all mucked in. I was responsible for cutting off the borders that always ran the full length of the rolls and applying a generous helping of paste to mum's cut lengths. Bryan and mum would then line it up and hang it onto the hard-board walls. We filled the cracks in the north facing scullery and bedroom walls, as best we could, by jamming in screwed-up wet paper and using white distemper brightened-up all the other interior stone walls. We never could stop the draughts coming in through the cracks in that north facing wall and the hardboard would flap when the wind blew strongly, but, one bonus was that food and milk stayed cool and fresh in the scullery.

Mum managed to persuade a shop owner in Pickering to let us have a small, battery operated, transistor radio, on the understanding we would pay as soon as money came from Tom. At first we were very sparing in the use of it, mostly in the evenings when we would lie in bed and listen to plays or music. It was a great comfort to be in touch with the outside world when we were warmly wrapped up in our beds. I enjoyed this time, as it was too late for us to enrol at the local school and then it was the summer holiday period.

The local doctor eventually came to see us and made an arrangement for mum to be interviewed for the District Nurse's job. She duly attended for interview and all went well until they realised we lived in a remote cottage and mum did not own or drive a car. They could not offer her the job or any job, unless she had a car, which was a huge blow. There we were, stuck in a condemned cottage on the North York Moors with no money.

Mum would ride her borrowed bike to the local post office in Upper Rosedale to collect the post, not that we often had any. As we watched her cycle back over the top lane we hoped Tom had sent a postal order and mum was bringing the money home; but she never did.

There were only four other properties at Dale Head. Our nearest neighbour, just above us and to our right, was Mr and Mrs. Barraclough and their family, at Dale Head Farm. With its back to the steeply rising Moors, Dale Head Farm was the highest and most remote farm on the Moors and marked the end of the road through the Dale. Opposite us, about two miles across the other side of the Moor, sat Frank and Ella Hebron's family farm. Mr and Mrs Reece owned the farm just below us, to our left. Mr and Mrs Metcalf owned the farm with land either side of the public lane leading up to those three farms and Low Gill. Mr Metcalf was a most objectionable man and uncharacteristically unfriendly for a Yorkshire farmer. We were always wary when we saw him standing outside his farm. It was our habit to climb over the five bar gate which was kept shut to stop farm animals leaving the Moor, but he would shout and tell us to open the gate the same as everyone else. But everyone else was either driving a car, tractor or bike, or riding a horse! The gate was hard for me to open as it was latched on a very strong spring. Bryan could manage it easily enough, but it was impossible for my little sister who was beginning to thrive in our new environment.

Rosemary had her two cats and animals and an abundance of insects in her boxes and jars. One day I was outside playing with the cats, now both pregnant, when Rosemary staggered up our track with a new born lamb which she claimed to have found abandoned.

She was quickly followed by an angry woman running and shouting:

"Put that lamb down girl. Do you hear me? Put that bloody lamb down!"

Without slackening her pace, the woman barged into Rosemary and snatched the lamb from her arms. She seemed furious, but immediately softened when she saw the look of fright on my sister's face. She held the lamb, expertly cradled in an arm, and began to gently stroke Rosemary's blonde hair with the other.

"I'm sorry, love. I didn't mean to be so sharp, but mother sheep often stray from their lambs for a while and get very upset when they can't find them again."

Mum came out to see what all the fuss was about and the woman introduced herself as Ella Hebron from Hebron's farm. She said she was sorry if she upset Rosemary, but ewes sometimes won't accept their lambs back if they've been taken away from them. Mum apologised on behalf of Rosemary and invited the farmer's wife in for a cup of tea. Ella declined the invitation as she had to get the lamb back to its mother, but we were welcome to go back to her farm to see the new born lambs in their barn and meet her husband Frank. We did visit them and were to become friends with the Hebrons for the rest of their lives.

Mum explained to them that when we moved there she was hoping to fill the vacant position of

District Nurse, but without a car, that had been ruled out and it was difficult to get any paid work. Frank reassured her that as the summer progressed there would be loads of work on the local farms for her and Bryan, but payment would need to be in produce, not cash and that's how it turned out. We helped with the haymaking, fruit and potato picking and it never ceased to amaze me that mum could create so much from dairy products, bread, eggs, a decent potato and some swede.

Bryan was ever-so happy. His mood had lifted now he didn't have to worry about Tom and he became very protective of us girls and my mother. If she was out after dark he always went to meet her and walk her home. He was growing-up and the man of the house. He had lost some weight in Stockton, but now he had slimmed right down. His voice was deeper, he shaved and he was getting taller by the day. The farmers knew they were onto a good thing when they saw Bryan and even more so when they saw how hard he was prepared to work.

About two months after we moved into Low Gill, Bryan came rushing into the house yelling "Look out, Dad's here! I just saw him coming round the top bend towards the cottage. It has to be him, because he's the only person I know who drives an Invacar."

We all froze and stared at each other.

"Just stay calm and act as if his visit is the most natural thing in the world". Mum said trying to allay our fears. "He won't be staying, that's for sure."

After the carriage wobbled its way up the rutted track, we all dutifully trooped out and watched as he folded back the Invaca's weather protection canopy and climbed out. He was dressed in black slacks, a white shirt, no tie and a fawn cardigan. I thought how nice it would have been had we all been happy to see him instead of wondering if he was going to cause problems. It had been so peaceful without him and mum was so much more relaxed. I was glad Bryan was there, but as he caught my eye I could see he was not happy with Tom's unannounced arrival.

After bidding him a guarded, "hello" I ducked back inside, purportedly to make him tea; but more to get away from the feeling of unease that accompanied his arrival. From the scullery I heard Tom telling mum how fortunate we were to have found such a place. Mum agreed that it was lovely, but we had to work very hard to make the place habitable, but even then we could only use one bedroom and one downstairs room.

He paid scant attention to what she was saying and as I came out with his cup of tea, said he might like to come back to live with us one day. We all shrank from the thought and uttered not a word of encouragement. After asking us individually how we were and receiving subdued responses, he handed me his empty cup, dug into his inner pocket and pulled out a large harmonica. This took us by surprise as we kids had heard him play the spoons, but never a mouth organ. He ambled over to the wall and smiled before he began to play, 'Genevieve' from the hit 1953 film of the same name. Then he played Clair de Lune and Night and Day, his playing was spellbinding. I could see M=mum becoming overwhelmed and unable to bear it, her face crumpled into tears and she walked away. He continued to play and cows wandered over and stood the other side of the wall, listening to him. He continued for fifteen minutes or so and when he stopped, grinned, obviously relishing our stunned admiration.

I was not sure how to react, I was dumbfounded. Mum re-joined us to tell Tom his playing reminded her of their time in Oxford and she had forgotten just how well he played.

We all gave him a round of applause and even Bryan was impressed.

"Crikey dad, you'll have to teach me how to play like that."

"Maybe one day lad, who knows, maybe one day."

The spell was broken as he slipped the instrument back into his pocket and asked Bryan to show him what he had done to make the cottage habitable. After a tour of the interior Bryan went through a list of other work which would need to be done before winter set-in. There was not much that could be done with the lean-to attached to the cottage but Bryan proudly pointed to the toilet he had rebuilt, stone by stone.

"Well done, lad. You have been busy, you must be a great help to your mother. I'll just use the toilet, it was a long bumpy drive up here."

We waited as we heard him clanging about in the toilet. The sounds made us nervous and when he emerged he banged the door so hard it fell off its hinges. His mood had darkened and he had morphed back into the intimidating menace we had seen much to often. He glared angrily at Bryan.

"I've torn my trouser leg on a blasted nail sticking out of the wood in there. You've been here long enough, why the hell haven't you finished the job?"

Bryan visibly stiffened and pulling himself up to full height replied angrily. "Christ dad, give us a break will you? You've stayed away and left Mum to cope all on her own, so don't come here and expect everything to be all hunky-dory!"

Rosemary and I were paralysed with fear. Mum stepped forward as Tom made a hostile move towards Bryan. My brother stood his ground and before Tom could launch any attack, he roughly pushed him away and brought his fists up in a boxing stance.

"Come on then dad, it's about time".

The two of them stood defiantly facing each other as mum stepped in between them and glowered at Tom.

"Your days of intimidating and bullying us are over Tom. Never again will you raise your hands to me or the children, do you understand?"

Bryan was fuming, but out of respect for mum, strode away, shouting over his shoulder. "Leave now or I'll knock your fucking head off."

Mum steadied my father, who looked pale and shaken.

"WHY Tom, WHY?"

"Why what Ethel?"

"Why did you entice us back to you, it's obvious you don't want us".

I had never heard her directly ask that question before and held my breath as I waited for his answer.

"Oh, Christ, I don't know Ethel. When I wrote, I thought that I would get that job. But things just seemed to escalate out of control and I couldn't find a way out.

Please don't give up on me. Things will get better, maybe not just yet, but I won't let you down again".

Mum had obviously heard enough.

"Stop the lies Tom, we both know you will never come back and live with us. What has happened, to turn you into such a vile bully and liar? What happened to the money you promised to send to us every week?"

Tom who had been standing meekly, head bowed, suddenly reverted to type.

"You don't think I would ever have come back to you and live here in this God-forsaken place, do you Ethel?" he snarled, "I won't be sending you any money. HERE! That's my last £3, you money grabbing bitch! You'll have to drag me through the courts to get another penny."

He threw three, one pound notes onto the ground.

"This is the last time you'll see me. Even the kids will desert you one day Ethel and you'll be an old maid, all on your own."

He scowled as if he hated the very sight of us as he climbed into his carriage and prepared to leave. As the engine fired Bryan wandered up to the side of the carriage, tapped on it, bent his head down and looked in.

"Hey dad, if you ever need to earn a few quid, why don't you play the spoons and harmonica together, you could become a one-man band!"

Tom looked as if he wanted to kill him, but must have decided it was best not to get out of his cart. Instead he thrashed the tiny engine and wobbled off down the track. As we watched him go, we were all too stunned to take any pleasure in this transformation and mum and Bryan's triumph.

We all understood it meant the end of our mum and dad being together again. Bryan, having calmed down, reminded us that never again would he allow his father to touch any of us. Having seen the look on his face when he challenged Tom, we totally believed him. I recognised a change in my brother that day. He was no longer a boy.

As we watched Bryan hang the toilet door back on its hinges, I realised we had learned to accept, even become fond of, our ramshackle cottage. By the time Tom arrived, it no longer mattered that we had to carry the water from the stream and because we knew there could be a dead sheep carcass upstream, boil it. Emptying the night-time potty every day became part of our normal routine. We did not have much food and certainly no regular money, but there was peace in the house and that was the main thing.

We all looked forward to having the radio on. It was the first time, apart from the jukebox on Clevedon pier, that modern music came into our world. We had it on most of the time now and heard all the news and the music of the day. The music in the early 50's was, by today's standards, innocent and inoffensive and we listened to all types of music from the aforementioned Larry Adler's 'Genevieve': 'Doggy in the window' by Patti Page: 'Secret Love' by Doris Day: 'Three Coins in a Fountain' by Frank Sinatra: to the early Elvis Presley and Bill Hailey stuff. Rosemary and I would dance outside to all this music and could sing our hearts out because no one but the cows could hear us. But our musical interludes were about come to an end for a while.

Returning from a walk up on Bank Top, I spotted someone walking away from the cottage. I didn't think much of it as we thought mum was there. When we got indoors, we found she was out and the shop owner, who loaned us the transistor radio, had been in. We found a note on the table to say that the wireless had been taken back and we could have it back when we paid for it.

We were bereft. Our wonderful radio had gone. How would we entertain ourselves in the evenings and how would we keep abreast of what was happening in the world? We would just have to find the money to get it back – and quickly.

Without the radio and no Weather Forecast, we had to decide for ourselves what the day had in-store for us, but if a thunder storm was due, birds and animals became ominously quiet and still. On one particular occasion, as dark clouds gathered, mum called out to us.

"The calm before the storm girls, in you come."

We lingered for a moment as the threatening dark grey cloud base rolled towards us. Then we watched as flashes lit up the hills way over the other-side of the Moors. Already smelling the dampness from the falling rain over there, we were well indoors, with Rosemary safely under the table covered by its thick cloth, by the time we heard the first distant rumbles of thunder. Then in it came, accelerating towards us as we watched white veils of rain sweeping across the Moors. It started with big, sopping drops of rain landing here and there on the corrugated tin roof of our toilet. Then, within seconds it was pouring down in torrents, followed by a vicious hail storm, whipped into a lashing frenzy by violent winds, which sounded like an express train tearing through the land. Next came the blinding flashes of lightning. On each flash we began to count – one thousand, two thousand, three thousand and then the most God-almighty bang. This was followed with another hot white flash and one thousand, two thousand – bang; this time it hit ground behind the house. Then – flash/bang with no count-time, a simultaneous flash and a bang that sounded like an explosion right above us. The house shook and we thought it was about to cave in and dived under the table with Rosemary. Petrified we huddled together in the improbable hope that, if the cottage did fall, the table would protect us. A few more immediate flash-bangs, then, as the storm ambled off towards the south; we came out from our safe-place and went outside to see what had happened. We fully expected to see a hole in the cottage roof, but it was our prized toilet which had taken the full might of a lightning strike and reverted to a pile of stones and scorched corrugated panels. But to our combined amusement, the seat and new shiny bucket we had recently bought, remained in place. The storm had gone but it became an unforgettable memory. It was one of the scariest, most exciting moments of our young lives, but easily the best storm ever. There were quite a few of them whilst we lived on the moors, but never again one quite like that.

During warm summer evenings, Bryan and I would head up onto the Moors to explore. Sometimes we stayed out until well after dark. Although there were many dangerous places up there, especially at night, mum had faith in Bryan's abilities and common sense so turned a blind eye. Sometimes we walked as far as the mysteriously haunting, deserted iron ore mines and quarries at Dale Head, Sturdy Bank and Bank Top. On the way back, with the huge harvest moon shining above us, we felt as if we were on the top of the world and would sing the Doris Day hit 'By the Light of the Silvery Moon' at the top of our voices and hoped this way of living could go on forever and ever.

Rosedale's High Moor's abandoned Iron Ore Mines above Low Gill

Dale Head Farm from Top Bank

TEACHERS & PUPILS OF ROSEDALE SCHOOL 1955

19

UPDALE LIFE

On 6th September 1955 we were enrolled in the small school in Upper Rosedale. After our long summer of total freedom it came as something of a shock, but we could not have been in better hands. The headmaster, Mr Curtis was a kind, patient man and his wife, also a teacher, pleasant and caring. I found it very difficult to concentrate during lessons and would look out through the window to the huge expanse of Moor and daydream. By the time I snapped back to reality, I had lost the thread, especially in Maths and English, so in exams I took to copying answers from a friend. Mr

Curtis soon noticed what I was up to and must have decided I needed another kind of lesson!

"Well done Betty. That multiplication answer is correct, perhaps you would like to go the blackboard and show the class how you worked it out?"

I walked over to the blackboard and he handed me a piece of chalk, but of course I had no idea. He let me stand there for quite some time, before he smiled and took the chalk away.

"Sit down, Betty."

The class giggled.

"Anyone want to come up and complete the sum for Betty?"

The giggling stopped.

"I thought not, carry on with the exam."

Mr Curtis came over to my desk, drew-up a chair and sat next to me.

"Now Betty, it really is not as difficult as you might think, but through no fault of your own, you've missed opportunities to learn. So let's look at the question and find the answer, step by step. If there's anything you don't understand, you must say. I don't mind explaining things time after time, that's what I'm here for."

As he worked with me a flea dropped from my hair onto the page. He said nothing, merely flicked it away and continued with his one to one tutorial. However, as I left school that day Mrs Curtis handed me a small paper bag to give to mum. When mum opened the bag she found a dreaded nit comb, some lotion, a bottle of shampoo and a note asking her not to send any of us back to school until we were flea free. Mum was not affronted, head lice were a problem in those days. She combed and lotioned our scalps and when we went back to school mum came with us to thank Mrs Curtis. They became friends and as a result mum was introduced to her neighbours and word of her nursing qualifications spread. As a result, she was called upon to deliver babies in emergencies, nursing duties and 'laying out' the deceased. In other words, she became an unpaid District Nurse! But, it helped us integrate into village life.

Sometimes there would be an evening game of cards or dominoes which involved tables and chairs laid out in the village hall for locals to get together. As the evening progressed, everyone changed tables so we got to meet a lot of new people that way. The ultimate winner took the collective winnings, made up mostly of produce from farms and maybe a small amount of cash. Tea and home-made cakes were always on offer and very often we were given a cake or pie to take home as it would have only gone to waste

Once the harvest was in, apart from potato picking which came much later, the farmers held barn dances to thank the locals. Everyone was invited and barns which normally held bales of hay were transformed into dance halls. They were festooned with field flowers and pine tree branches. The bales were stacked to the sides as seating, and the centre cleaned and swept for dancing. Home-made sandwiches, pies, trifles and cakes were laid-out on long side tables and hot tea, cold milk, squash or home-made cider for the adults was freely available. Village musicians played live music for dancing and we all let our hair down.

Neighbouring farmers got mum up to dance; she looked so relaxed and happy and it was lovely to see just how young and gay she could be. Rosemary and I danced together or with friends we had made at school, while Bryan made the most of it in a different way. He chose the best looking local girl and disappeared with her for most of the evening. When I asked him where he had gone and what they were doing, he smiled and shrugged.

"That's for me to know and you to find out; nosey!"

There was frenzied whispering at the school the following week. One of the girls in the school photo became his particular favourite which upset some of the others, but he did not seem to care.

When we later discovered the school photo in the village archives, all the children were named, but Bryan, the tallest boy in the back row was the only child with a nickname. He was identified as 'Bryan (Buffalo) Williams', a nickname Mr Curtis obviously knew about and condoned, but we never found out why. I'm front centre in the photograph and Rosemary, kneeling on one knee, is three to my left.

By that time, Bryan was doing odd jobs for different farmers. He liked mending anything mechanical, which they found useful. Also, being young and full of energy he was good at helping drive flocks of sheep from the moors into pens for dipping or shearing. Dogs, which had been purposefully bred over many years, did most of the work and we were welcome to visit the farms and play with the gorgeous collie puppies when they arrived, sometimes as many as ten in a litter. Rosemary desperately wanted one as her own, but they were bred to be instinctive sheep herders and far too feisty and valuable as working dogs, to go to domestic homes.

Rosemary took off on her own one day and we couldn't find her. Bryan immediately sprinted up to the Moor where there was a pool, which he and I swam in in the hot summer months; it was always cold, but just bearable at that time. On the last occasion, mum and Rosemary came with us and we had a picnic. Rosemary could not swim at the time and contented herself with paddling in what was no more than a puddle. Mum watched as she moved further away to another puddle, stepped into it and completely disappeared! We heard mum's scream and Bryan immediately scrambled from our pool and ran over to where mum was crouched with her hands desperately reaching into the deep, black water which Rosemary had mistaken for a shallow puddle. Without hesitation he jumped in and like Rosemary, completely disappeared. After what seemed a long time, but was probably only a few seconds, he re-surfaced with Rosemary who coughed and spluttered as he handed her to mum. The only reason she had escaped serious injury was because she always held her breath if she got into trouble.

Mum forbade any of us to return to those pools on our own, but Brian wanted to check. From the pool he would make his way across the valley to the Hebron's. I set-off to the Barraclough's and mum went down the lane to 'Mr Misery' - farmer Metcalf.

We all returned with no news of any sightings and were desperately trying to think of where Rosemary may have gone, when we heard sounds on the other side of the cow field wall. Bryan heaved himself up to look over and there she was, tucked-in behind the wall, playing with two four-week old puppies from the Barraclough's latest litter. She had walked up to their farm and carried them back without being seen.

We were so relieved to find her and her grin was so wide, it was impossible to tell her off. We brought the puppies into the house for a while and then she and I returned them to their mother. Mrs Barraclough saw us and came over to the barn. She too could not be angry with Rosemary and gently explained that the puppies had to stay with their mother for at least another two months. She could go and play with them as often as she liked, but must not take them away from the barn. After that, whenever Rosemary went missing, we knew exactly where to find her.

Picking summer fruit was as enjoyable as it was gratifying, because it was usually warm and sunny and we could stuff our faces with the ripe, soft fruit. When apple and plum picking followed in the autumn, that too was fun, and the dark red plums were delicious; but wasps had the same idea, so great care was needed.

The Harvest Festival Service in Rosedale Abbey Church took place on the first Sunday in October. Flowers, fruit and vegetables were arrayed in impressive displays and the church smelled sweet and wholesome. There were baskets filled with potatoes on display, but those were the ones dug-up from cottage gardens. Farmers would not dig their potato crops until the autumn and the foliage on the plant had died off, which was a sign that the potato skins had set and they would last a long time in storage.

Potato picking took place at the end of October and it was awful! We walked behind a tractor with a rotating device which turned over the soil to expose the potatoes. With freezing rain working its way down the inside of our coats and necks, we had to bend down and pick them into a metal bucket. When that was full we had to tip the contents into a sopping wet sack. Everything was cold, wet and muddy. It was bone-chilling, back breaking work, but we got paid in potatoes or one shilling per one hundred-weight sack, which made our discomfort tolerable.

We earned enough to add to mum's meagre savings and get our sorely missed transistor radio back!

In November, the temperature on the Moors dropped below freezing overnight. The fire in the sitting room was our only means of heating, but when lit, some of the warmth crept through the cracks up in the bedroom floor so when we went to bed the room was not freezing. Even so, we were always loath to leave the warmth of the fire and go upstairs. We had to dress in jumpers and long socks over our night clothes and sometimes even gloves and woolly hats to keep out the cold. Rosemary and I would cuddle up together and even with coats piled on the top of us, we were still cold and any water in bedside glasses could be frozen over by the morning.

First one up would light the fire, which was usually mum. Logs were in short supply and had to be paid for, so we could not fill the fire with logs to keep it in overnight. Outdoor farm work had dried-up and without any money coming in, mum had to raid our emergency tinned supplies of corned beef, meat in gravy and pilchards in tomato sauce. We would have those with free mashed potato and swede we pinched from the fields. This food would all have to be cooked over the open fire or in the fireside oven.

Mum, wrapped in a sheepskin lined coat, a gift from Ella Hebron, a shoulder blanket, thick socks and a pair of brown, second-hand fur boots, trudged to neighbouring farms. She would bring home milk, eggs or bread from her labours, but there was never enough cash for a load of logs.

One bitterly cold day mum and I walked the Moors searching for odd pieces of wood. To our surprise, we found a large, flat piece of slatted wood, in the middle of nowhere. We dropped the few sticks we had collected and went for the bigger prize. Dragging it back to the house was not going to be easy, but we were slowly getting there when we were yelled at by a farmer from one of the farms across the other side of the moor.

"What the bloody hell do you think you're doing? That's the door to my sheep enclosure. Damn well put it back. Now!"

With great difficulty, we dragged it back to where we found it.

"No! Not there! There!" The irate farmer pointed to a tumble down miner's cottage on Bank Top.

"This is where we found it," protested mum.

"Aye, that's as maybe," grunted the farmer, "but if you don't put it back where it belongs, I'll report you to the police for theft."

The door must have blown down the moor in a recent gale, but we were in no position to argue. The farmer watched us struggle up the hill with the door and made no attempt to help us until we reached the ruins of the old cottage which served as one of his moorland sheep pens. With a triumphant glint in his eye, he took the door from us, wedged it back in place and strode way.

Exhausted, mum and I staggered woodless, back down the hill to our cold cottage. On hearing our story, Bryan left to speak to a farmer he had often worked for and managed to get a load of logs delivered in return for promised labour. So he kept the home fire burning.

As the winter really set-in, we had to float two old footballs in the stream we collected our water from. The movement of the footballs kept a small area clear of ice.

Christmas approached and mum and Bryan suddenly found work at one farm or another. A farmer would often come and collect them in his tractor or truck. They helped prepare Christmas turkeys, geese and ducks for market. Plucking out so many feathers took a toll on their fingers which became painful and cracked. They had to rub a special cream (a mixture of honey and goose-grease: made by the farmers' wives) into their hands each night to ease the pain and stop their fingertips from becoming infected.

Mum also helped to make jars of mincemeat and chutney for the local Christmas Food Fairs. As a result we managed to get a good stock of food, paraffin and logs together. Some paid cash which was a godsend as it meant we would be able to go into Pickering and do some last minute Christmas shopping.

Prior to the unexpected pre-Christmas glut of work, mum was worried about what sort of Christmas she was going to be able to provide for us. Our doctor suggested contacting the National Society for the Protection of Cruelty to Children, the NSPCC, to inform them of our plight. It was not unusual for them to help people in distress. They would visit to witness things for themselves and in our case see that no abuse was taking place. Our problem was a lack of money, not affection.

Of course, only mum knew about this when the NSPCC officer called. He was wearing a black overcoat and peaked cap so Rosemary and I thought he was a policeman. He introduced himself as John and said "hello girls" to us. He looked kind, but we had a long experience of officialdom which had blighted our young lives and we still thought he looked 'official'. When mum told us to go upstairs and warned us not to listen to what was being said, we both feared she was about to be taken to prison.

We heard quiet conversation for about an hour and then John called up the stairs."Goodbye, girls, I'll be back to see you soon."

After he left, mum told us he was a very kind man who might be able to talk to Father Christmas for us. Rosemary was thrilled, but I had long stopped believing in Father Christmas and remained convinced that nothing good would come from his visit.

The following day saw a slight fall of snow; just enough to remind us that winter was upon us, but not enough to present any problems. However, there was enough for Bryan to build an ice-box in the snow to store our milk, bread and cheese.

As promised, John returned the week before Christmas. We were sent upstairs again, but because we knew the obvious connection with Christmas, we listened excitedly to everything that was going on downstairs. We could hear talking, laughing, the rustle of paper and opening of packages. John had delivered something! How exciting was that? But by the time we were called downstairs mum had hidden whatever he had brought. We stood and watched as he handed her five pounds to spend as she wished. He also gave her a soft, square parcel for her to open on Christmas Day and a bottle of Stones Green Ginger Wine.

"Happy Christmas, I hope you have a wonderful time."

John smiled at us as he left and we all wished him a Happy Christmas and really meant it. I briefly thought he could be Father Christmas in disguise, dismissed the notion, but told Rosemary anyway. We watched from the bedroom window as he drove away in his car through a flurry of snow.

"If he's Father Christmas, why isn't he driving a reindeer drawn sleigh?"

"Perhaps he is, Rosebud. Perhaps it's disguised as a car."

My answer satisfied Rosemary who continued to believe in Father Christmas. Of course, I remained an unbeliever but I must admit, John left a warm Christmassy glow in our cottage which was reinforced by our Christmas Eve visit to Pickering.

We trudged through light snow to get to Rosedale Abbey and excitedly boarded the bus to Pickering. On the bus mum gave us five shillings each to spend as we liked. When the bus arrived in Pickering we found ourselves in a surreal, magical place. It was like a Dickensian film set. A group of some twenty carol singers, dressed in heavy coats, scarves, woolly hats and long boots, holding lanterns with flickering candles, were singing carols in front of a huge

Christmas tree. Crowds of jovial shoppers gathered around them.

The street carnival atmosphere was a first for us and really brought home the Christmas spirit. Hot spiced wine, hot chestnuts, sausage rolls and mince pies, provided free by the shopkeepers were passed around. Shops were festively decorated and had inviting displays of toys, poultry, puddings, Christmas cakes and fresh fruit and vegetables. Everything you could imagine for a wonderful, Christmas Eve shopping experience. Everyone was smiley and cheerful, they all kept wishing us a, "Very Merry Christmas" and as kids we were offered soft drinks and food at every turn. It was truly magical.

When mum went off to shop by herself, the three of us gathered in a gift shop and took ages searching for something special for Mum. We eventually found what we were looking for, it was a gold coloured brooch with 'MOTHER' written on it. The shop owner put it in a box with some cotton wool and made no charge for cheerful, Christmas gift wrapping. We still had enough money left over for an equally well wrapped box of chocolates.

When we eventually met-up with mum for the bus back to Rosedale Abbey, she was laden down with carrier bags. It was obvious we would be burdened on our long walk home and we supposed Rosemary would just have to walk this time; however, mum still needed fresh bread. A bone chilling wind was blowing off the moors as we waited outside the village baker, huddled together, stamping our feet to keep warm. Then, as mum came out with the bread, in yet another bag, Frank and Ella Hebron stopped next to us in their truck and offered us a lift home. We could not believe our luck! Mum squeezed into the cab next to Ella and we piled into the back with our bags and huddled down.

Snow swirled around us. It was bitterly cold, but we shouted our grateful thanks to Frank Hebron when he drove us right up to our front door. The snow was much deeper than when we left and we wondered if we could have managed to get home at all without their help.

On Christmas morning we woke-up to find Christmas stockings at the end of our beds stuffed with nuts, fruit and sweets. After a hurried cup of tea we excitedly opened our gifts from Father Christmas (John). I had been given a brightly dressed, five stringed puppet which resembled Pinocchio, but without the long nose. When I opened another package and found a small red purse with a silver shilling in it. I thought I had been given the best presents any child ever received.

There was a baby doll for Rosemary, with a spare set of hand knitted clothes.

Bryan had a second-hand, but complete, Meccano set with a battery run engine, a wallet with £2 in it, a comb and a huge jar of Brylcreem.

Mum's gift was the bottle of Stones Ginger Wine and in the soft packet, a long woollen scarf and knitted gloves. Mum had managed to buy us girls a knitted scarf, gloves, an amazing cardboard kaleidoscope and some sweets. There was also a diary for me and colouring book for Rosemary.

Bryan received a woollen hat, gloves, a mouth organ and some chocolate. Mum opened her presents and said she loved her brooch and would treasure it forever. "It's a truly wonderful, real White Christmas," she said with a smile, as we looked out of the window at the snow covered moors and passed her box of chocolates around of for us to select one each.

We were absorbed in our presents and mum was busy preparing our Christmas dinner of tinned steak, jacket potatoes and swede, when there was a loud bang on the door. We opened it to find Frank Hebron, standing in the snow with a huge grin on his ruddy face, carrying a large wicker basket.

"Just a little thank you Ethel, for all the help you have given to Ella and me."

Mum invited him in and offered him a glass of ginger wine. He stepped through the doorway like Father Christmas, but without the red coat and whiskers. Putting the basket down, he accepted the glass of ginger wine and raised it in a toast.

"Here's to a Merry Christmas," he chuckled.

"Here's to you and Ella for being such wonderful neighbours," replied mum, raising the small glass she had poured for herself.

Frank Hebron drank his in one go, blew out his ruddy cheeks and smiled.

"By heck, that'll keep out the cold!"

"Best have another then Frank," said mum.

"Just a half then Ethel – thank you very much."

He raised the glass again.

"That's grand. I'll be back tomorrow with a load of logs. Looks as if we could get snowed-in very soon, it 'appens a lot up here. Happy Christmas to you all!"

As if to endorse his weather forecast, snow blew in through the open door as he left.

As soon as she had closed the door, mum opened the basket and we explored the contents. It was full of the most wonderful things: a cooked stuffed goose, which was still warm: roast potatoes: a Christmas pudding: mince pies and an iced fruit cake: a large jar of fresh cream and jars of jam and preserved fruit to go with it. Talk about Christmas in a basket! There was enough food in there to take us through to New Year 1956. Mum welled up, but we kids just danced with sheer joy. The Hebron's probably never knew just how much it meant to us; but then again, perhaps they did?

We had the most wonderful Christmas Day and Frank, as good as his word, arrived with a load of logs early on Boxing Day. He also brought us 50 candles, four gallons of paraffin and two mantles for the lamp. As he left he warned us that heavy snow was definitely on the way.

Early in the New Year we just might have been able to get to school by hopping onto the milk waggons, but, walking back through deep snow would have proved impossible and by mid-January it became too deep anyway. Up to that time, Frank Hebron was able to get through to collect mum in his tractor to work in their house, which meant we received some food to help us get by. We believed Ella engineered this because she enjoyed mum's company, but there came a time when Frank could not reach us, even with a snow-plough on the front of his tractor. So we became totally isolated.

In between Christmas and the New Year we had fun in the snow. We built a snowman and used the biggest tin trays from the scullery to sit on and slide down to the brook where we collected our water. Rosemary and I were cautious, we started to slow down even as we took off, not wanting slide into the beck, but Bryan was deliberately reckless and on one occasion shot off the bank and through the ice. Mum came running out to see what Rosemary was screaming about and saw Bryan clambering back over the bank, laughing, soaking wet and carrying his tray up the hill for another go.

One morning we awoke to an eerie silence outside and a lighter than usual radiance coming in through the bedroom curtains. Bryan was up first and tugged back the curtains.

"Wow! Wow!" he yelled, "come and see, just come and see!"

We all shot over to join him and couldn't believe our eyes. Everything, Moors, fields, the track to our cottage, the stone walls, everywhere was glistening white and completely covered in the deepest snow we had ever seen. It came right up to the bedroom window!

The predicted winter snows had blown in with a vengeance. The Christmas snow was only a light dusting by comparison. As the weather worsened we could only leave the cottage, to go to the toilet or collect logs from the lean to. Bryan excavated a pathway to both locations and worked hard to keep them clear. We were not as experienced as the farmers so had not stored enough tinned and packaged food for a marooned winter. Our supplies began to dwindle and due to a lack of nutritious food we all went down with bronchitis.

It hit Rosemary the hardest and she became very poorly. Mum made a bed for her in the Ottoman Tom had made in Stockton and she slept in front of the sitting room fire. The doctor couldn't possibly have got to us so we used home remedies. Mum mixed crushed aspirin with honey and made hot drinks with it. She filled bowls with hot steaming water, adding a teaspoon of salt and a tiny drop of Vick inhalant. Rosemary had to put a towel over her head, bend over the bowl and gently breath in through her nose and out of her mouth; she hated it, but it helped. Vick was also be rubbed into her chest. She couldn't eat much so we made her sip warm sweet tea and vegetable soup laced with Bovril.

There came a time when mum was sitting-up with her all night, worried that she might not survive. Mum was desperate, if her bronchitis developed into pneumonia there would be nothing she could do. Bryan decided to attempt to get up to Dale Head Farm, to see if Mr and Mrs Barraclough could help. He wrapped himself up in just about every garment he had, with double, even treble layers, lined his boots with newspaper, put on his warmest hat and gloves and a scarf around his neck, and another around his face.

From the bedroom window we watched as he began the mammoth task of digging his way down our track and then up to Dale Head Farm. We soon lost sight of him.

Many hours later, the Barraclough's were amazed to see an exhausted, snow covered figure at their door. They dragged him in, thawed him out and once acquainted with our situation accompanied him back, through his tunnelled track, with fresh milk, eggs, cheese, bread, butter and jam and to mums utter relief, some prescription medicine. They promised to keep us supplied as long as we needed their help and Mr

311

Barraclough would go for the doctor as soon as he could get a tractor through the snow drifts, some of which were over fifteen feet deep!

We still had flour, sugar and honey in the house and some root vegetables stored in the lean-to. So, with the fresh supplies from the farm, we slowly began to recover.

Mr Barraclough eventually managed to get through to the doctor's house and brought some prescribed medication for Rosemary. Once on the medicine she slowly began to recover, but remained frail and needed to stay in the Ottoman in front of the warming fire.

Towards the end of February the cold spell began to ease. It had isolated us for weeks, but it seemed more like months to me. The roads became passable and we were linked to the real world once again. The batteries for our radio had run out.

Bryan began going to the shops by hitching rides on any farm vehicle going that way. The doctor eventually paid a house visit and thought mum had done a great job in caring for Rosemary. He only wished she had a car and could take up the vacant district nurse post. Mum told him that even if she could drive, there was no way she could afford a car, so it could never become an option.

Within days of the track becoming passable, there was a loud thumping on the cottage door. I opened it expecting to see yet another benefactor, but there were two menacing looking men on the doorstep. They were debt collectors and they had come all the way from Stockton to collect the money for our removal from there. Tom never paid them, as promised, and when they chased him for it, he told them it was his wife's debt and gave them our address.

Mum tried to explain that it was Tom who arranged the removal and my father had offered to pay it, but her pleadings fell on deaf ears - they were bailiffs.

"Sorry Mrs Williams, we're sympathetic to your situation, but we have instructions to collect the money owed or goods to the value of."

"But I have no money, nothing of value and cannot possibly pay you; you will have to go and see Mr Williams in Redcar."

"Sorry, that's your problem. We've come a long way and we can't go back with nothing."

They barged into the living room. Bryan stood in front of them but the bigger of the two merely pushed him aside and told him to sit down, being Bryan he did not do as he was told and went outside.

"Not much of value here," said the smaller man.

"You're right there mate, but that Ottoman could be worth a bob or two."

My mother protested, "You can't have that, can't you see my sick child is using it as a bed."

"Nothing personal, Mrs Williams, but it seems the only thing in here worth having. Come on little-un, hop out."

Mum quickly lifted Rosemary and her bedding from the Ottoman and watched in dismay as he motioned to his colleague and between them they carried it out to their van. They returned for the brass companion set by the fire place and mum's cherished tea caddy.

"I'll take those to the van, you see to the rug."

The small man crouched down to roll up the large rug which served to cover cracks in the floor and stop draughts.

It was ready to go when the large man returned.

"What about that?" asked the smaller man, pointing to mum's brass crucifix on a shelf.

"Nah, religious icon. Can't take them."

As the big man lifted up his end of the rug he dropped a receipt on the table.

"As I said, nothing personal love, just doing our job."

Mum and I followed them out and watched as without saying another word, they pushed the rug into the van and drove off. Bryan joined us to watch them as they rounded the top bend. He began to grin and neither of us could understand what he had to be happy about until he bent down, riffled through some long grass and triumphantly pulled out our beloved brass tea caddy. He pinched it from the back of the van when both men were preoccupied with the rug.

The following morning, over breakfast, mum told us that we would not be able to survive another winter on the North York Moors, we had been in our ramshackle cottage for almost a year and taken the rough with the smooth, but we had now reached rock-bottom. Then she surprised us.

"I want to discuss something serious with you. I think we have all suffered enough. I can now see that coming to Yorkshire and returning to your father was a big mistake, we gave it a try, but it has been a very sorry experience for us all. It could have worked here on these lovely Moors had I been able to get the district nurse job, but we now know that is not possible without a car."

She began to nervously rub her hands together and her voice became croaky, always a sign she was under stress.

"How would you all feel if I said I was thinking of taking us all back to Oxford? I would like an answer from each of you."

We were taken aback, it seemed a good solution, but how would she ever be able to get us all back there?

Bryan was first to agree. He thought it was a great idea. Rosemary seemed very happy to confirm her agreement, as long as she could take her cats. I was delighted and so relieved that mum had come up with a way out of the dire-straights we found ourselves in.

Mum went on to explain that nursing jobs would be much easier to come by in Oxford, she had family there and some very dear friends who would be more than willing to help us.

She wrote that very day to her mother, Ellen, explaining what we had been through and asking if she would help by sending copies of the Oxford Times and Mail to help her seek employment in the Oxford area.

OXFORD

20

OUR CITY OF DREAMS

My maternal grandmother wrote back within the week. She sent a large brown parcel which contained a month's worth of local newspapers and a very kind letter with five one pound notes tucked into the envelope. She wrote that she would be very pleased to see Ethel come home, but only had a small property and would not have room to house us all for more than a transient night. Having experienced cramming into Grandma Williams's house, I thought she must be a very wise lady.

Mum became upset when she read some very sad news: William, mum's step father, had died in the

Cowley Road Hospital two years earlier from a haemorrhage due to throat cancer and her sister, Ruby, was in Brookwood Mental Hospital due to alcoholism brought on by the fire which gutted the very successful Public House she ran with her husband. The shock of losing everything led to the end of their marriage and a downward spiral for Ruby. Mum was badly shaken by the news and replied to her mother to say how sorry she was to hear about William and Ruby. She thanked her for the newspapers and said it was our fervent wish to return to the Oxford area as soon as she found suitable employment, with accommodation for us all.

It was at that time mum told us more about her early life and the part played in it by Ellen and Ruby. We thought it was a dreadful thing her mother had done, but mum was not resentful. She said it all happened a long time ago when things were very different and certain actions were considered acceptable for survival.

We scoured the papers and circled any jobs we thought might suit mum, but there were very few offering accommodation. Eventually mum wrote off to several of the advertisers requesting interviews for jobs. It was a long way to travel on the off-chance, so she had to be very explicit in explaining her need for accommodation for all of us and asking what they could offer. She received several replies and some of the positions seemed perfect for her nursing ability and came with decent pay and accommodation, but not for a family of four. One would have taken us girls, but not Bryan, so mum crossed them off the list.

However, amongst the replies was a position for a cook/housekeeper to a lay preacher and his teenage son in Littlemore. Mum wrote to them and received a very encouraging response. After some debate between us, a telephone conversation with the son took place from the phone box in Rosedale. The son asked some basic questions about mum's nursing background and offered her the job. Mum was assured there would be enough accommodation for us all and on top of that, mum would get £3 a week. It was not a lot, but it afforded the opportunity to move back to her much loved Oxford. She decided there and then to accept the offer.

Bryan and Rosemary were delighted to be 'going home', but strangely, I felt sad to be leaving our remote, North Yorkshire Moors cottage, with its beautiful views which changed dramatically with the seasons. It was an exciting place to live, but mum made going back to Oxford sound like the best thing in the world, so I joined in her excitement and thought of the life which beckoned us back to the city in which we were all born.

We said good bye to all our neighbours and the friends we had made in Upper Rosedale and Rosedale Abbey. We packed what we could carry into just a couple of bags each. Rosemary was sad to have to re-home her precious cats with the Barracloughs, but knowing the daughter, Mary, loved them as much as she did made it easier.

We bid farewell to our ramshackle cottage, wondering if anyone would ever live in it again.

On a morning in the early spring of 1956, we clambered into Frank Hebron's truck. Frank was kindly taking us to Pickering Railway Station. As he drove around the bend in the track which overlooked Low

Gill and we were looking back to watch the place which had been our home for a year disappear from sight, we heard him shout.

"Hey up! Who's this in't middle of road?"

We looked past the cab to see a small vehicle straddling the centre of the narrow track, hurtling towards us.

"Christ, it's your father!" shouted mum, "duck!"

We cowered down behind the cab as Frank veered off the edge of the lane and missed Tom's carriage by inches. Tom was too intent on avoiding Frank's truck to see us. We watched his Invacar, bounce and skid as he brought it back under control and disappeared around the corner.

We wondered if he had somehow heard we were leaving or was his visit purely coincidental? He said he would never come back, so why had he? Had he come to gloat because the bailiffs had taken most of our home? Or had he come to apologise and make some miserable excuse for letting us down – yet again? What would his thoughts be when he realised we had moved out? We would never know the answer to any of those questions. We watched the road, expecting him to drive up behind us at any moment, ready to cause a scene on the railway platform at Pickering, but, as it turned out, that was the last glimpse of our father any of us ever had, or wanted.

****

When we arrived in Oxford we were met by Vincent, the son of the lay preacher. He had naturally blonde hair, fair eyebrows and eyelashes; I thought he looked very strange. He was about the same age, but shorter, than Bryan. He waved as he saw us and energetically thrust out his hand to mum and Bryan. He ignored Rosemary but gave me an unpleasantly rude 'once over', which somehow made me feel grubby.

Picking up one of mum's bags he spoke sharply.

"Let's get a move on, there's a taxi with a meter running outside."

He was self-assured and bossy, too much so for my liking. He led us to the taxi, where he jumped straight into the front passenger seat leaving us and the driver to load up the boot. We journeyed in silence to the house in Littlemore. It was on a large housing estate and semi-detached, not at all what I had expected. The bottom half was red brick and the top was brown tiled from the roof top to just above the sitting room windows. It was in a cul-de-sac. All the houses were the same and did not look very inviting. My heart sank as we pulled up outside, the house seemed to be frowning at us and did not appear big enough to comfortably house us, the 'preacher' and his son.

As we entered the house, we were hit by the heavy reek of what I was to soon discover was stale urine, whisky and cigarettes. Rosemary immediately screwed up her nose and was about to voice her disgust but mum gently put her hand over her mouth and motioned her to stay silent. We assembled in the hallway as the taxi driver plonked our few possessions at our feet and left us to it.

"Welcome to my world," breathed Vincent as he took our coats and quickly ushered us into his father's bed-sitting room. The 'lay preacher' was spread-eagled on his dishevelled bed and after witnessing the shenanigans of the Rosedale farmers after a few pints of cider, even I could see he was drunk. The room was obviously his day room, bedroom and lavatory, by the look of the half full, lid off, commode chair beside his bed. Newspapers were strewn all over the floor and full to overflowing ash trays covered the top of the bedside cabinet. His letter told us he was in his early fifties, but he looked much older. He was strangely heavy-eyed, his striped pyjamas were filthy and his hair had clearly not been washed nor had he or shaved for weeks.

Thankfully, he did not get up to greet us, merely propped himself up on one arm, waved with the other and slurred, "Ah, Mrs Williams, welcome to our home. Do make yourself comfortable dear, I'll see you later." As we were about to leave he added, "I don't really need your help you know dear, it was my son who placed that idiotic advert in the paper and then wrote to you, not me."

Bryan looked at mum and shook his head. Mum nodded in silent agreement and turned to Vincent.

"Can you show Bryan and the girls the rest of the house please, Vincent, while I have a quiet word with you father."

Vincent accepted mum's request without dissent, which surprised me and meekly led us into a kitchen with a dining area, where he began to make us some tea. Mum joined us within a few minutes.

"Your father tells me he has no intention of mending his ways for me or anyone else, Vincent, and it was your idea to employ help. There was little point in discussing the matter with him as he is clearly drunk, so I'll talk to him again in the morning, but tell me, what is the true situation?"

As we drank our tea, Vincent apologised.

"I'm sorry Mrs Williams. It's true. I placed the advert and wrote to you because I desperately need someone to take complete charge of my father's needs: the cooking, shopping, household cleaning and laundry. You can have weekends to yourself, other than providing us with a roast dinner on Sundays. I'm sure he'll agree to our agreement tomorrow and pay you £3 a week and cover your food and heating costs. Please excuse my slight deception. Please, please, say you'll stay."

Bryan gave a scornful laugh. "So my mother can have the weekends off, but you expect her to cook your Sunday dinner and pick up any slack from your father on a Monday morning?"

"Well, I wouldn't put it quite like that," said Vincent.

"So how would you put it then?" asked Bryan sharply.

Mum could see Bryan was getting heated and interrupted. "I suggest we discuss this in the morning, with the preacher, after a night's sleep."

Bryan reluctantly agreed and after we finished drinking our tea, Vincent showed us upstairs. The house was roomier than it looked from the outside. There was a bathroom and four bedrooms upstairs, although one of them was little more than a box room. Mum was allocated a double bedroom, Bryan a single and Vincent obviously had his own room, which we assumed was another double. Rosemary and I were allotted the box room with one single bed. Downstairs we would share the sitting/dining room and kitchen with Vincent and there was a downstairs cloakroom.

Vincent told us to make ourselves at home and use food from the fridge for our evening meal. He took bread, cheese and salad into his father for supper and left the house.

We eagerly had a similar meal and went to bed, having been told that the 'preacher's sister had been in to prepare our beds and so it transpired. We climbed into ready-made, clean beds, and fell fast asleep.

The following morning mum was up before 6am, tidied the kitchen and had our breakfast on the table when we came down at 7.30. Vincent devoured his full English and repeated his apology for misleading her with his letter and again pleaded with mum to stay. He had already discussed the matter with his father and mum would now receive £5 a week and not have to cook a Sunday lunch, unless she wanted to for the rest of us. Mum agreed she would stay for a month and see how things panned out, but, she wanted the first week's money in advance. Vincent agreed and immediately handed her five £1 notes.

Mum soon discovered the 'preacher' needed total personal care, which combined with everything else, was going to be a full-time job. The house was in need of a good clean, exactly what she would expect with two males, one a drug-taking alcoholic, living in their own mess. Her first day was taken up with getting the 'preacher' sorted out, which meant, blanket bathed, hair washed, bed sores dressed, his room cleaned and bedding laundered. She dispatched Vincent and Bryan to the shops for medical supplies, fresh food and whisky for the 'preacher'. Mum told me that she had a plan to help him reduce his dependence on whisky and drugs, but it had to be a slow, weaning off, process.

Rosemary was not happy there and that night she got into mum's bed, so I had the whole bed in the box room to myself. Luxury!

Bryan tolerated Vincent, but made it clear that he would not be staying. He was looking for a job and somewhere else to live. He didn't even unpack his bags!

I just felt it was good to be in Oxford, close to mum's friends and family. We even had a real grandma of our own close by, who we would soon be meeting and at least we had somewhere to live. Mum was giving it a month's trial, which gave her time to look for something better.

However, the 'preacher' was about to drop a bombshell. On the second evening, when mum went in to tidy up, he had obviously downed a few glasses of his favourite whisky and smoked several of his 'special' cigarettes, but he was nowhere near as bad as he had been when she first saw him and he spoke calmly to her.

"Mrs Williams, thank you for all you have done so far my dear, I'm impressed, however you do realise that my personal needs will have to be met?"

"What personal needs?"

"Well dear, I would like you to bring me comfort during the night".

"WHAT? Mum could not believe what she was hearing, "I certainly won't be bringing you anything at all during the night; I'm a nurse, not a prostitute!"

The 'preacher' was unfazed by her reaction.

"Come, come dear, you didn't honestly think you were getting a weekly £5 and free accommodation for nothing, did you?"

Mum exploded. "Nothing! I hardly call what I have done over this past, exhausting, 24 hours, nothing!"

Not knowing then what had taken place between mum and the 'preacher', I thought we were safe and comfortable, so I was taken aback when, after only two nights in the house, mum said it was not right for us and she was looking for another position.

That night, Rosemary was in with mum and I was drifting off to sleep, when my bedroom door slowly began to open. It was Vincent! He crept into the room, sat on the side of my bed and stared at me in a very odd way.

"I'm cold Betty, do you mind if I get in with you?"

Before I could answer he whispered, "Shhh! keep quiet or someone will hear us." He lifted the covers and tried to pull my nightdress up. Although I was young and totally innocent, I instinctively knew this was not right; I screamed at him and clawed at his face. He leapt up, yelled and holding his torn face, made for the door, but before he got there, Bryan came hurtling in.

"What the fuck!"

He grabbed Vincent by the hair, dragged him out onto the landing and punched him full in the face. This sent Vincent rolling and crashing down the stairs. He ended up in an unconscious heap on the hall floor outside his father's room.

The 'preacher' came stumbling out to see what all the commotion was about.

Mum rushed out from her room and joined me on the landing.

Bryan, who had followed Vincent down the stairs, was standing over him, fists clenched.

"Stand up you dirty bastard."

I thought Bryan had killed him. He yelled at the preacher.

"Your pervert of a son has just tried to rape my sister!"

Vincent stirred and Bryan kicked him in the stomach. Mum was mortified and ran down the stairs. Vincent started to get to his feet and as Bryan kicked him again, she stepped in.

"Bryan! That's enough, Bryan! Betty's OK and we'll be leaving here tomorrow."

The preacher pulled his son into his room and we could all hear him violently raging against him. I was alright, confused, but physically unaffected by Vincent's attempted abuse.

Mum and Bryan stayed up for the rest of the night discussing what we were going to do. They agreed that as I remained unhurt and there were no witnesses to support the attempted abuse, the police should not be called, but we would leave that day.

Vincent had left the house during the night and the preacher tried to pacify mum and Bryan, saying that if we stayed he would ensure nothing like that ever happened again. He was given short shrift by both of them and left in no doubt that we would be leaving that day.

Leaving Bryan to look after us, mum took a taxi to a friend's house in Cowley, it was a nurse she had lodged with before in St. Mary's Road, close to the hospital. On hearing mum's plight she insisted we leave Littlemore immediately and stay with her until mum could find another job. Her house was small, so mum, Rosemary and I would have to sleep in the same double bed, but there was no bedroom for Bryan who would have to bed down on her sitting room floor.

We had not really unpacked since the move from Yorkshire, so it only took a short time to collect all our stuff together and leave Champion Way to stay with mum's 'Angel of Mercy'.

Our temporary safe-house just happened to be directly opposite where Auntie Mary and Uncle Bill lived. Mary was the sister of one of Tom's sister's husbands. They had moved to Oxford from Redcar some years before and knew all about mum's marital history, thought Tom behaved very badly, but never openly took sides. After we settled in, mum crossed St. Mary's Road to call on them. They were delighted to see her and, when she explained our difficulties, insisted that Bryan should not have to sleep on the floor and could lodge with them. They had a teenage daughter and a son, also a Brian, the same age as our Bryan, who happily crossed the road, moved in with them, to become great friends with their son.

He used to see us on a daily basis and would bring mum copies of the local papers from Auntie Mary and go through them with her, hoping to find a suitable job for mum and odd jobs for himself. As he was not yet 15 he was supposed to be at school, not working, but he had missed so much schooling already he had dropped off the education radar.

After a week of not finding anything, mum visited the Oxford Labour Exchange to see if they had anything suitable and as luck would have it, there was an immediate vacancy for a live-in housekeeper to an elderly gentleman whose wife had recently passed away. It was music to Mum's desperate ears, especially when she was told that he was very respectable, kind and lived in Boars Hill.

Boars Hill was an attractive hamlet she knew well. It was only three miles South of Oxford and much favoured by retired, wealthy academics. Due to her experience and nursing qualifications, she was given an appointment, to meet Mr Philips, at his house and to take us along.

We boarded a No. 20 bus from Gloucester Green Bus Station the following morning, but without Bryan. He was happy where he was, Auntie Mary and Uncle Bill were happy to have him and it would be easier for him to search for jobs from their location.

We alighted from the bus in Boars Hill only a few yards from leafy Hamels Lane, which led up to the house. The homes either side of the lane were large, stylish, of individual design and set within their own, well-tended large gardens. Hamels Lane oozed wealth and 'establishment'.

As we walked, mum told us of the many happy days she had spent in Boars Hill during her youth and that if we did come to live there, she would show us where she enjoyed picnics with our father and Mr and Mrs Meads. Learning this made me feel we were close to her roots, her family and good friends.

'The Chalet' the house we were seeking sat behind a wide, five-bar gate. It was charming, quite large, but not intimidating and the front garden was a riot of spring flowers. We walked over the gravelled drive to a brightly painted, yellow front door which looked as if it had been hand carved especially for the house. It was opened by a tall, thin woman with her hair tightly rolled up at the base of her neck and tucked beneath a brown hairnet. We were invited into a hallway, and the woman tapped on a door.

"Mrs Williams is here to see you Mr Philips, with her two daughters."

We heard a man's voice.

"Thank you Mrs Cross, please show them in."

Mrs Cross opened the door and beckoned us through. We entered the gentleman's study and an elderly man stood-up behind a huge, gold embossed leather topped desk to greet us. He walked with an enthusiastic spring in his step for one so old as he came around the desk towards us, followed by the big fluffy white dog, which had been sitting in its own chair next to him. He held a hand out to mum and gave her the warmest of smiles.

"Welcome Mrs Williams, I've heard so many good things about you," as he shook mum's hand, his pale blue eyes twinkled down at us and he added, "and your family."

"Thank you for seeing us at such short notice, Mr Philips," replied mum.

I immediately knew she was impressed by this well-spoken, courteous gentleman, who invited us to sit down in chairs which had been set out in a semi-circle. He pulled-up another chair to sit opposite us and the gorgeous white dog sat next to Rosemary and put its enormous head on her lap. Rosemary was in heaven!

"Ah, Rhona has chosen a friend," he chuckled before he gave mum an encouraging smile and asked her what had brought her to apply to be his housekeeper.

He listened, without interruption, as mum gave him an unemotional summary of our lives over the past few years. As she talked I looked around the room which was obviously his sanctuary. Darkly papered and curtained it had heavy, mahogany furniture. Book cases covered three walls and there must have been hundreds of books crammed into them. The wall space to the right of the door we came through, displayed several elaborately decorated shot guns, safely locked away within a glass fronted gun cabinet. Above the shot guns there were two mounted deer heads.

A highly polished, walnut card table stood against the wall on the other side of the door, with an array of gleaming, half-filled, crystal wine and spirit decanters, each with a highly polished silver label to identify the contents: Whisky, Sherry, Port, Brandy, etc. Etched glasses of differing sizes, but perfectly matched to the crystal cut of the decanters were arranged to the left and right of the decanters. They all looked so perfectly spaced and I was wondering if they were ever used, when mum stopped talking and Mr Philips gave a deep sigh.

"Life has been very tough for you and your family Mrs. Williams; we must hope there is better to come. Please allow me to tell you about the position on offer. I'm looking for a housekeeper who can cook to a good standard especially when members of my family come to visit. The pay is two pounds ten shillings a week, with a free, fully furnished, two bedroomed flat and all found. Every Friday and Sunday afternoon and evening will be time off. Mrs Cross, the lady who showed you in, is my regular cleaner and she will remain in post. Is this the sort of position you are looking for?"

Mum said it was, but obviously did not want to sound over enthusiastic in case he had other applicants. However, as they continued to chat for over half an hour, I began to think it sounded positive and was astounded to hear all that was being revealed about my mother's early life. Mr Philips talked of his wife, who had only recently died and said how much he missed her, then said, with a weary smile, "I think we have unburdened ourselves enough for one day, Mrs Williams, don't you? Would you care to join me in a glass of sherry?"

Mum returned his smile. "Thank you very much, Mr Philips that would be very nice."

As if by magic, as Mr Phillips set out the glasses to pour the sherry and they clinked together, the door opened and Mrs Cross brought in two glasses of orange squash for Rosemary and me.

Afterwards Mr Philips escorted us through the ground floor of the lovely house and around the enchanting gardens, which surrounded the house on all sides and extended to well over an acre. He took us up to the flat, situated above a large garage which was empty as he was too old to drive and had sold all his cars, the flat looked perfect for us.

When we had completed the tour and he escorted us back down the gravel drive to the gate, I thought he and mum seemed to get on very well but was unprepared for what came next.

"Well, thank you for coming Mrs. Williams," he said as he opened the gate for us, "and thank you for bringing your delightful daughters with you. If you feel that I am acceptable and the job is suitable, it is yours if you want it and you can move in as soon as you wish."

Mum appeared to be so happy, she looked as if she could have kissed him; but she merely replied, "It has been a great pleasure to meet you too Mr Philips and I would be delighted to accept the post, thank you".

"Splendid. Splendid." Mr Philips beamed and asked Rosemary and me if we would like to live there. We said that we would and he shook us both by the hand, saying he looked forward to seeing us again, very soon. I had to tug Rosemary away as she did not want to leave her beautiful new canine friend.

We were deliriously happy as we walked back to the bus stop and thrilled at the prospect of living in Boars Hill in our very own, comfortable flat. Mum was almost breathless as she confided in us.

"As soon as Mr Philips spoke I knew he was a real gentleman, a kind gentleman and I wanted to be his housekeeper. At long last, we have stability and I can see a light at the end of our tunnel."

However, I was old enough to know that old people do not live forever and fervently hoped the light at the end of our tunnel did not turn out to be the headlights of an oncoming train! But on such a happy day, I kept that negative thought to myself.

THE CHALET BOARS HILL

21

MR PHILIPS

When we all arrived at 'The Chalet' we were again shown into the study by Mrs Cross. Mr Philips was his same charming self and shook Bryan by the hand, smiling at him and saying how pleased he was to meet him. Then he quietly and respectfully outlined the rules of our residency. We all had full use of the garden and the small summer house, except when members of his family were visiting, when we would have to be discreet. Mum was the only one allowed into the main house, we could only go in if specifically invited and even then the study was definitely out of bounds. We all nodded although neither Rosemary nor I knew what 'discreet' meant. We could use any of the sundry items of food in his pantry, other than his, pineapple juice, cheese, meat, fish, marmalade, honey and his special collection of teas and coffee. Finally he smiled and his pale blue eyes looked kindly at us.

"Well, that's got that over, but it's as well to know where we all stand, so, welcome to 'The Chalet', I do hope you will be happy here and soon feel comfortable in your new home."

He turned his attention to mum. "Mrs Williams, it is indeed good to see you looking so relaxed. Obviously you will have full reign over the house and the help and cooperation of Mrs Cross, should you need it."

Mum returned his smile. "Thank you very much Mr Philips, I look forward to starting my duties at breakfast tomorrow morning."

With all the opening pleasantries concluded, Mr Philips opened the study door for us and we filed out. We had the rest of the day to settle in and explore so we immediately went up to our flat to unpack.

Bryan said he was impressed with the way Mr Philips had treated us and was delighted to learn that he had his own bedroom in our two bedroomed flat over the garage. We finally had an indoor bathroom with hot and cold water and a flushing toilet, even if it was located in a sort of lean-too attached to the main kitchen down stairs. There was also a small laundry room with a washing machine and electric iron. We also had the use of the warm, main kitchen as our sitting room. This housed an ancient, coke fuelled stove, large pine kitchen table, four cartwheel chairs and an enormous, comfy sofa. There was a radio in the kitchen, but no TV.

The acre or so of garden surrounding the house was simply lovely and we had free use of it when the family were not visiting. Bryan took 'discreet' to mean 'anywhere we could not be seen by anyone in the main house'.

It was late-spring of 1956. Bryan was fifteen and by law, should have been in full time education until the end of the summer term, but we had moved around so much and he had attended school so little, he was raring to find a job. Rosemary and I would be attending a school in Sunningwell, which was a mile and a half walk from Boars Hill.

Mrs Cross turned out to be very friendly and a font of information. She told us that Mr Philips was Eton educated, went to Oxford University and rowed for his college. His son, Michael followed the same route, but whereas Mr Philips never spoke down to anyone, Michael was very snobbish and dismissive. She introduced us to Ivan, the Polish gardener, who chose to remain in England after WW2. He was industrious and pleasant, the exact opposite of Mr Strong, who came each day to de-clinker the stove. He was fat and slovenly. 'Stove- man', as we called him, cycled slowly up the lane at six most evenings. Breathing heavily and without making an effort at conversation, he would slump to his knees to clear-out and de-clinker the coke-burning stove. This dated contraption provided the hot water and heating for the whole house and required maintenance every day. If this was not done, the leaking, asphyxiating smell of sulphur would make our eyes sting and give us sore throats, before going out,

335

leaving us with no hot water and cold radiators. 'Stove-man' was paid ten shillings (50p) a week, but often failed to turn up so mum or Bryan would have to rake-out the clinkers themselves. Mr Philips could see what was happening, so sacked Mr Strong and gave mum a ten shilling pay rise for a job she was doing most of the time anyway.

It wasn't long before Rosemary's craving for pets came to the fore and when she heard sorrowful meowing sounds coming from high up in a tall pine tree, saw an opportunity and came looking for help.

"Betty, Betty," she wailed, "come quick, there's a poor cat stuck in a tree and it's going to have to stay there forever as it can't get down."

I too had heard the meowing and knew the darned cat would come down when it was good and ready, so I refused. But eventually, her distress and my love of climbing trees, decided the issue and I agreed to climb up to rescue it. The branches were unevenly spread so it was a great challenge, but as I got closer, the cat climbed higher. It was really scared, but I managed to grab it by the scruff of its neck and somehow climb back down clinging on to it. Or rather, it clung onto me and its grasping claws went through my jumper. My shoulder was severely scratched but I was my sister's hero for a while. It was a lovely cat, but female and pregnant! Rosemary was in heaven!

Mr Philip's son, Michael, was a regular visitor and his young family occasionally accompanied him. Our bedroom window looked out onto the five bar gate at the entrance to the drive and we would secretly watch as this unconventional, very bohemian family, arrived from their fashionable London home. Their luxurious, silver Rolls Royce would silently glide into the drive and as it came closer, the only sound made was the crunch of tyres on the gravel. The family climbed out and stretched after their long drive from London.

The extremely graceful, blonde mother was a private GP. Michael, the pristinely bearded father, worked at the BBC. The three youngsters, Sebastian fifteen, Cordelia twelve and Saffron, seven, all inherited their parents good looks. Finally, the father reached into the back of the Rolls Royce and lifted out a carry-cot. In it was their beautiful, golden-haired, nine month old baby, Charles. They all wore the loveliest trendy clothes and Charles was always dressed in a blue, smocked, two piece romper suit, following the trend set by the Queen for her baby sons.

They, like the guests we had seen at Dyrham Park, possessed an in-bred sense of self- importance. In the early days, the family were for the most part indifferent to Rosemary and me, we were simply the bothersome children of the omnipresent, compliant, housekeeper. Bryan was hardly ever home, so he never saw much of them, or he might have had designs on Cordelia!

Their arrival meant we would see less of mum until they left. When they stayed we were supposed to steer clear of them as they needed to enjoy their rare moments of privacy. As always however, we bent the rules and found it interesting watching these much less inhibited, posh people enjoying their sanctuary. They behaved very differently from us, being less self-conscious and living a more liberal lifestyle. The parents made love in the summerhouse and under the arched, splayed cherry tree. They walked in the garden, nude, whilst enjoying a cocktail or two. The children were allowed to drink a glass of wine with dinner. Mrs Cross told us that none of them wore any underwear – all very entertaining, and unquestionably enlightening for us.

Sebastian, reserved, good-looking and dark, more often than not, stayed in London with their housekeeper and his friends. Cordelia, cool and quiet, was very attractive with long, naturally blonde hair, spent most of her time reading from the vast library of books in her grandfather's library.

Saffron, who everyone called, Saffy, was very bubbly, with curly blonde hair. She adored her grandfather and was always by his side.

But, Charles became mine! I began looking after this blue-eyed, blonde baby one day when his mother arrived feeling particularly tired and asked mum if I could take him for a walk or play with him for a couple of hours whilst she got some sleep. Charles gurgled and giggled happily when he was in my charge and it became a regular and wonderful 'chore' for me whenever they came to visit. I loved having him and took him for long walks across the open National Trust Common which enjoyed clear, distant views, of 'Oxford's Dreaming Spires'. I was also allowed to bathe and feed him. I looked forward to his visits and we had a wonderful time but were both upset when the family, inevitably, had to leave.

When family or friends visited, they enjoyed the best of food, wine and hospitality and mum prepared the most marvellous dinners, such as roast pheasant, with tail feathers placed appropriately and all the trimmings. Home-made soups, pate`s, lobster, game and delicious desserts of all kinds.

The 'silver-lining' of this opulence was that we got to enjoy the left-overs. We would help to clean up after they had all gone to bed or home, which was always late. Mum and I would very often be washing-up at midnight.

Mr Philips soon became totally reliant on my mother; she became his nurse, cook, confidant and friend. She seemed to be content with this and fully accepting of her situation, but never forgetting 'her place'.

Rosemary and I loved it there, especially the large, interesting garden. We climbed the tallest trees and made camps in the shrubs and bushes. There was a highly productive vegetable garden with a long, heaped-up, asparagus bed. A soft fruit garden and tucked away, out of sight of the house, a large chicken coop and run, which housed twenty chickens and three geese. The knowledgeable Polish gardener, Ivan, cared for all of this as if it were his own. I got on well with him and he taught me a lot about how to look after plants, chickens and geese. There were always eggs for the house and an abundance of vegetables and fruit for the kitchen.

Mr Philips would often stroll into the garden to ask us how we were getting on. He was always immaculately dressed, perhaps in a bespoke suit or a sports jacket and cavalry twill trousers or if it was a warm sunny day, jacket-less. But no matter what, he always wore one of his plain woollen ties with a check shirt.

One day he invited Rosemary and me to follow

him over to an empty hut which stood at the side of the vegetable garden. It was timber framed with corrugated iron walls and roof. The front had glass panels which looked out onto a small orchard and it had once been used to store apples, pears, plums and such. He smiled and posed a question.

"How would you girls like to have this as your very own Wendy house?"

Of course, we were delighted and left him in no doubt that we loved the idea. He called Ivan over and asked him if he could clean it out and give the inside a coat of paint. We could not believe our luck! Ivan got it cleared and decorated within a few days and he moved some bits and pieces in there, a small table, two scruffy chairs and a small metal set of three shelves for our seedlings. It was a sanctuary for us and we more or less lived in it and hated the idea of going to a boring school when the summer holidays were over.

As I had left the small school in Sunningwell in the July I had to move to the senior school in Boxhill, Abingdon, in September 1956. I was initially placed in the 'Junior Remove' (bottom class), but moved up into the 'A Stream' after a week. I obtained a free school bus pass and caught the bus every day with Heather Strange, whose mother worked at a huge country mansion called 'The Hamels' at the bottom of Hamels Lane. It had its own private driveway down a long winding lane and as you rounded the final bend the vast, old, wooden framed mansion came into view. It had its own lodge cottage at the drive entrance which housed the Strange family.

There was a lake with huge Coy Carp of every colour and size, water snakes which zipped across the surface and most of the birds we had enjoyed in Dyrham. Heather's father, the gardener/chauffeur, turned a blind eye when we went swimming as long as Heather was with us and we stayed well away from the main house. Heather's mother, like mine, was a fabulous cook and always had cake or biscuits on offer.

Their employer was an infirm elderly lady, who we never saw, but she owned an Armstrong Siddeley Sapphire which had a silver phoenix emblem on the bonnet. It was a big, shiny, grey and black car which purred its way up and down the lane. People stopped to admire it as it went by, perhaps hoping to catch a glimpse of the elusive old lady, but invariably the only person in the car was the chauffeur, off on some errand or other.

Rosemary and I mixed with some of the local children from the large posh houses. We became well known in the village and if anyone objected to their children playing with a housekeeper's children, we never heard of it. The only thing I noticed was that other children were called in to have lunch at midday and dinner in the evening. For us it was dinner at midday and supper in the evening.

We also got to know many of the housekeepers from the large houses owned by what was called 'old money'. One such lady, Mrs Brown, worked for Sir Alan, a retired judge. Mrs. Brown and her husband came from Austria and she made the second most delicious chicken soup we ever tasted. We were baffled to see that she put the chicken's head and feet into the pot and always ate the parson's nose herself. As we pretended to vomit she would say, "Vot's the matter vith you? It's cook's privilege to eat ze soft fruit nose."

Her husband's job was to look after the garden and care for the fowl, but it was always the cook's job to kill, pluck and dress the chicken ready for the pot or oven. She would select a bird from the free range run and then chop off its head, which could be a messy business if the headless chicken ran around spurting blood all over the place. Wringing its neck was her preferred method. To do this she held the bird upside down, rendering it unconscious, then quickly twisted and snapped its neck. Not only did it die instantly, she could then roast the bird with its head still attached. Rosemary and I watched her once as she did this and I thought it cruel. Mrs Brown shrugged.

"Vell, you both eat chicken, don't you?"

She never wasted a thing from fowl or garden produce, cooking anything and everything. As we knew from Dyrham Park, cooks made their own jams, jellies and bottled their own fruit besides baking their own cakes and biscuits. Cooks, housekeepers and head gardeners of the elderly middle-class property owners in Boars Hill took great pride in the work they did for their employers and in turn, they were highly valued and treated well. With few people opting to go 'into service' following the Second World War, they were a dwindling breed and replacements hard to find.

By Christmas time, Rosemary and I were well known by housekeepers and cooks in the big houses and made plans to go carol singing to selected homes We practised our carols at home until we knew them by-heart, so by the first evening of our venture we were well rehearsed and left the house carrying a lantern, a small brass bell and a paper, church collection box. We thought a collection box would encourage more 'donations' and stuffing money into our pockets would look unseemly.

We would sing two rousing and cheerful carols; Good King Wenceslas and God Rest Ye Merry Gentlemen. Then knock on the door and ring our bell. If no one came to the door we would sing another carol, knock and ring their bell. We always ended with Silent Night, which usually got a response, but if not we would quietly leave. If someone came to the door, we would sing a few more carols, ending with a reprise of Silent Night, which could see us collect anything up to a ten shilling note, which is only 50p today, but back then it was a knockout amount.

Sometimes we were invited inside and asked to sing to family and friends. As it was evening time, they would be gathered around the fireside or dining table, anticipating a bit of unscheduled entertainment. This could be nerve-racking, as some could be a bit tipsy after, cocktails, wine, or both. This, mixed with our singing, could make them; melancholy from missing family and Christmases gone by; brash and noisy; or induce a tendency to overload our modest collection box. We both knew which reaction we preferred!

On one evening we were invited into one of the grandest houses in the area and ushered into the most splendid dining room where everyone was formally dressed, the table was laid with beautiful bone china dishes, highly polished crystal glasses and huge Christmas crackers. It was the setting for a high class dinner party and through the sweeping bay windows, the illuminated garden, with lights shining up into the trees provided the back-drop. For me, Christmas lights on an outdoor tree and a large indoor tree meant they had more money than the Queen.

We had already sung our complete repertoire outside in the cold and were about to start again when one of the guests volunteered to accompany us on the grand piano in a corner of the room; he beckoned us over to stand next to him. Everyone turned their chairs to face us and my throat closed up, as it always did when I was nervous. However the pianist played so beautifully no one seemed to notice that only Rosemary was singing the first verse of the carol, I just mimed it and my voice began to come through as we both relaxed. In the end we were judged to have been a great success and raised a colossal £2 for our Christmas Fund.

We made a fair sum with our carolling, more than twice what mum earned in a week! Bryan was only on five shillings a week as an apprentice gardener. Of course, our carol singing had a short season, but it helped pay for a brilliant Christmas.

One winter's night, we were all woken-up by loud banging on our stairs and Michael Phillips shouting for my mother.

"Mrs Williams, could I see you down here, right away?"

Earlier that day Ivan asked Mum to look after some day old chicks he had bought. They needed to be kept warm overnight. Mum, put them in a cardboard box, topped up with cotton wool and after Mr Philips had retired for the night, she placed the box in front of the dying embers of the log burner in his main sitting room. Her thinking was that they would be kept warm overnight and be ready for the gardener to collect first thing in the morning, well before Mr Philips came downstairs. But it was just mum's bad luck that his son chose to pay one of his unexpected visits that night.

When Michael Philips opened the sitting room door he found the baby chicks happily chirping away in their warm haven. He failed to see the funny side of it and angrily berated mum and made her collect the chicks and put them back in the box.

Mum knew it was pointless trying to explain the situation to him; he was one of those people who loved wielding power over others. He watched mum carry the box up the stairs to our flat before storming off.

We had no heating up there, but by placing the box under blankets and surrounding it with hot water bottles, all the chicks survived.

I was helping mum during breakfast service the following morning when Mr Phillips, winking at mum remarked. "Oh, how lovely, two freshly laid boiled eggs for breakfast today! Oh, by the way, Mrs Williams, how are the chicks this morning?"

Mum, returning his amused smile, responded.

"They're quite chirpy, thank you, Mr Philips."

Bryan could not stand the way mum was treated by Michael Phillips. On one occasion he came into the kitchen whilst mum was up to her neck in steaming food and busy getting their dinner ready, demanding to know why they had not been served. It was 7pm! I heard her explain that when his father had guests, he always liked dinner served at 7.30pm."

"Well, I'm here now and jolly hungry. Get it out now!"

There was no please, no thank you, he was like a petulant child always wanting his own way. Mum stood her ground. "It's impossible to serve it now, unless you want everything undercooked. It's all timed to come together for 7.30."

On another visit he saw me in their part of the garden and strode into the kitchen demanding to know what I was doing there. Mum would not be bullied and replied, "Looking after your baby son for your wife, I shouldn't wonder."

Mum always commented on how relieved she was when he returned to London. Bryan knew mum could stand-up for herself, but for him, life in 'The Chalet' still smacked of servitude. By the summer he was hardly ever home and beginning to lead a life of his own with an army of new friends. His job as an apprentice gardener at a large house near Jarn Mound came with a free bicycle, but he was still only on five shillings a week. He moaned about it as we were cutting some asparagus

"I'm just a dogsbody where I work Betty. I slog away for a pittance, for a posh chap who calls me 'Barry', if he ever calls me anything at all. I loathe him and his bloody job."

I tried to cheer him up. "You're learning the names of lots of plants and mum lets you keep all your earnings."

"Yea, all five bob of it!" He gently shoved me into the fine, feathery asparagus ferns, an action which broke his self-pitying mood and he grinned as he tossed a huge, slimy worm at me.

I put some fresh herbs mum had asked for into the trug basket with the asparagus and took them to the kitchen. Mr Philips was in there discussing a lunch he wanted to give for his younger brother. He took the basket from me and gave me a quizzical look, before handing it to mum.

"Follow me Betty; there is something I want to show you."

I looked at mum. She smiled and intimated that I should follow him. Mr Philips led the way up the plush, green carpeted staircase and turned to the right onto a spacious landing. He opened a door leading from it and we stepped into the most enchanting room I had ever seen: it was his deceased wife's bedroom.

Mrs. Cross told me that Mr Philips and his wife had slept in separate bedrooms for years before she died. His bedroom, which I had seen when mum asked me to take him up some extra juice for his breakfast, was, like his study, another manly room. Called the 'Green Room', it was compact with a high single bed, two generously sized, free standing, dark-mahogany wardrobes and a matching dressing table covered in silver framed family photos, silver brushes, pots and some leather bound diaries. A set of glazed French doors led out onto a wooden balcony overlooking the garden, where he sometimes took breakfast during the warmer months.

As I stood in the doorway of his wife's bedroom, the 'Pink Room', I gawped at the beauty of it. Her splendid and spacious boudoir and en-suite bathroom were kept as a shrine; nothing had been allowed to be moved since her death. Mrs Cross kept it spotlessly clean and, on the pain of being sacked, altered nothing. It smelled of fresh wax polish and expensive cologne. This truly sumptuous room was completely dressed out in silks and taffetas in the palest greens, creams and pink. The huge, sunny, south facing bay window looked out over the garden and woodlands beyond, It was exquisite, like something from a film set. French antique furniture was inlaid with the finest woods, delicately painted with birds and flowers. Every door or drawer had coordinating, ornate brass or china handles. The wall-sweeping bay window had theatrical, double layered silk curtains, held back by large tasselled tie backs. Inside these were pale cream lace drapes. A sumptuous four poster bed was the main focus of the room; it had a deep base-mattress with the softest of feather overlays. Green silk drapes hung from the ornately carved canopy and a pale, flowery eiderdown lay over a fringed bed cover. There were mountains of soft pillows and cushions with all the colours of the room matched to perfection. The covers were turned back on one side, exposing the Egyptian cotton, satin bound sheets. An enormous, delicately coloured tapestry rug was laid on top of a deep pile, pale green carpet. As if to complete some fairy tale, lying across the top of the opened bed was a pale pink, hand-embroidered negligee.

All the elements combined to give the eerie, sensory illusion that the lady of the house would arrive at any moment, remove her evening gown and slip into this dream attire ready to drift into bed. It was a truly enchanting room and I was totally fascinated by it. Mr Philips obviously recognised how spellbound I was. He smiled and ruffled my hair.

"You like it then?"

I was so absorbed in taking in the wonder of that room, I just nodded. He walked me back to the open door and allowed me one last look before he closed the door and watched as I walked back down the stairs, in a daydream. Mum, who had followed us to the bottom of the stairs asked what I thought of the room and I heard myself reply.

"I think it is the most beautiful room I have ever seen; I wish I had a bedroom like that. One day I will." I couldn't have known the repercussions we would all suffer as a result of that visit!

Afterwards, when no one was about, I would secretly slip into that enchantingly peaceful room and sit serenely in the huge comfy armchair, bask in the warm sunlight coming in through those sweeping, bay windows and pretend it was my room and re-promise myself that one day I would have a bedroom just like it. No one ever knew I was in there, or, if Mr. Philips did know, he never let on.

One day, I was in the 'Pink Room', totally absorbed in my fantasy, when I heard the door open and someone creep into the room. I quietly rose from the chair. "Christ Almighty!" yelped Bryan. "What the hell are you doing in here?"

"What are you doing in here?" I retorted.
Recovered from his fright, he whispered, "Don't look so worried, I'm just having a sniff about; I won't touch anything."

He began to drift around the room picking things up and putting them down again, in the wrong position! I began to feel uncomfortable; it was as if he was violating the dead lady's memory.

"I think we should leave before anyone finds us in here."

He ignored me. "Have you looked in the cupboards or drawers?"

"No, of course not, we should leave and not riffle through things that don't belong to us."

I was cross that he had spoiled my daydream. He went over to a tall boy with a set of ten drawers and tried to open the top drawer, but it was locked. There was a large, intricately carved, wooden box sitting on the top of the tall boy, he lifted the lid. It was empty but he began randomly pressing buttons he discovered inside, then, to his amazement, and my consternation, a secret drawer shot out from the front of the box. It contained a small, gold key. He picked it up, grinned triumphantly at me, unlocked the tall boy and slowly pulled open the top drawer.

"Jesus Christ! Betty, come and see."

I scampered over to his side and was stunned by what I saw. The drawer was crammed full of large, white, five pound notes. We just stared at the wads of cash. Bryan was the first to break the silence.

"Bloody hell Betty, if we took one for mum, no one would ever know." He lifted out one five pound note, shoved it into his pocket and crept out of the room before I could stop him. I was terrified by what he had done and just knew retribution would befall us if we got caught. I closed the drawer, re-locked the tall boy, replaced the key in its not so secret drawer, closed the box and furtively followed him out from the room.

Bryan was waiting for me at the bottom of the stairs to our flat and we both went up as if we had just come in from a walk. Bryan pulled the five pound note from his pocket and gave it to mum, telling her we had found it lying on the road. She totally accepted the fib, thanked providence and innocently accepted the 'windfall'.

The following Friday she took the bus into Oxford and bought some clothes for us from Marks & Spencer. Rosemary and I each had a royal blue, zip front cardigan and Bryan had a jumper and shirt.

Michael Phillips arrived alone and unexpectedly from London that very weekend. He had only been in the house for a few hours when he stormed into the kitchen demanding that mum should go to the sitting room, immediately. When she got there, she was faced by a grim looking Mr Philips and his son, who was quite beside himself with rage. Rosemary and I could hear him yelling at mum from where we were in the kitchen. Someone had been in his mother's bedroom and photographs had been moved into different positions. He accused her of stealing the £5. For a few moments mum didn't have a clue what he was talking about and then the penny dropped. She must have been totally stunned by this news, delivered to her as brutally as it was, but she never told them about us. She totally accepted the blame and the son insisted the police must be called. We heard Mr Philips disagree.

"No, on no account will we involve them Michael. This is a private matter and that is how I will deal with it. Mrs Williams has been very attentive and cared for me with diligence and I will not have you intervening. I had no idea that money was there and don't care if five pounds out five hundred has disappeared."

Rosemary had no idea what it was all about, but I breathed a sigh of relief on hearing the opinion of Mr Philips. Then Michael Philips dashed my hopes.

"Pa, we cannot look lightly on this; if you won't deal with it, I will." I heard him pick up the phone and call the police.

"They'll be here as soon as they can. In the meantime Mrs Williams, you're not going anywhere, you're to sit down and await their arrival."

Rosemary and I had crept into the hallway outside the sitting room and that's where Mr Philips found us. He spoke directly to me.

"I'm so sorry Betty, but will you please take Rosemary up to your flat and stay there until I call you."

I heard the son shout at mum in the sitting room.

"Where do you think you're going?"

But mum obviously ignored him as she followed Mr Philips into the hallway.

"I'll take my girls up to the flat, Mr Philips and I will be there when required."

With that, she took our hands and led us out of from the hallway, through the kitchen and up to our flat, where she settled us down. She asked me to tell her exactly what had happened and why.

When two policemen from Abingdon arrived mum was called downstairs. After about an hour she quietly came back into the bedroom and asked us to sit next to her on the bed.

"I have to go with the two policemen and explain what happened, but you're not to worry. They think I took the money and that's how it must stay. Do you understand Betty?"

I nodded, too racked with guilt to utter a word.

"Tell Bryan I will explain when I get back and he is to say nothing, not a word, to Mr Philips or his son. Look after your sister until Bryan gets home, I'll be back before too long."

As she descended the stairs she called back, "Love you girls and see you soon."

We watched from the bedroom window as mum was taken to the police car and driven away. I could hear raised voices from downstairs, but was afraid to go down to hear what the father and son were arguing about.

When Bryan arrived home, we told him what had happened. He was stunned and despite relaying mum's message that he was not to say anything to Mr Philips or his son, he immediately went to find them, to tell them what really happened. When he returned after only a few minutes, he looked crushed.

Mr Philips and his son were having a huge row in the sitting room and when he went in to own-up to the crime, he was told, forcibly, to, "Get out and stay out!" by Michael Philips.

Knowing it was his fault, he was gutted and beside himself with guilt and remorse. It was the first time I had seen him cry since St. Ediths.

Mum was detained all night, charged with theft early the following morning and bound over to appear in Court in Abingdon the following week. When she returned she came straight up to the flat. Bryan told her she must tell them he was responsible for taking the £5 note, but mum would not hear of it.

"Absolutely not Bryan. If you incur a police record, you will never get a decent job and never be free of the stigma of being a thief. No! You will say nothing! Promise me, here and now, that you will say nothing, ever."

Bryan sobbed as he promised and I sobbed because I knew I was culpable too. Mum put her arms around both of us.

"Stop crying, pull yourselves together and make sure you both learn from your mistake, okay?"

We stifled our sobs and nodded meekly.

Later Bryan told me mum was probably right; he had just applied for a new job at the Oxford Football Club as a groundsman, it was decent money and he would have no chance of getting it if he was charged with stealing and got a lifelong police record. He reckoned mum would get a 'slap on the wrist' and no formal charges would be made.

The cardigans were returned to M & S and a full refund received. That money was promptly given to the son and mum told him she would pay off the outstanding amount from her wages over the next few months. He accepted this, saying he hoped the Court would be lenient with her. Mum never said a word about our involvement to anyone and held us to our promise. She went back to her duties and although the upcoming court case hung over us, Mr Philips did not mention it again until the day of the Hearing.

22

TAKING THE RAP

On the day of the court case Mr Philips arranged for a taxi to take mum to court and Bryan went with her. Rosemary was kept busy by Mrs. Cross and Mr Philips came into the kitchen and asked me to go into his sitting room. He was a very unhappy man and wanted to apologise.

"I did not want this to happen to your mother, Betty, but my son has such a quick-temper and could not be placated. He was absolutely determined that your mother should beheld accountable and once the police were informed and he pressed charges, the decision was taken out of my hands. I am so very sorry it has come to this."

I recognised his genuine distress and wanted him to know that the woman he had trusted so completely had not let him down, so I told him the truth. He was horrified.

"If I had known that, Betty, perhaps I would have been able to stop Michael calling the police. But, it's too late now, what's done is done. You must never tell my son, let sleeping dogs lie and never mention it again to anyone, do you promise?"

I promised. It was my second promise and I had already broken the first one I gave to my mother, but I felt she would perhaps forgive me for telling the old man that his implicit trust in her had not been broken.

Mr Philips then told me he had sent a letter to the Court, in which he fully supported my mother and explained that she had already started to repay the money. At that point we heard his son's car pull into the drive and he quickly thanked me for confiding in him. He was extremely relieved and pleased to know that the trust he had in my mother was not misplaced.

I was leaving the room as his son entered, glowering at me as he pushed past. Mr Philips called after me. "Please don't worry, Betty, I'm sure your mother will be home very soon."

He was right, mum and Bryan were back within two hours, looking chastened, but relieved. The Court had taken into account Mr Philip's highly supportive letter and sentenced mum to six months' probation.

After the court hearing mum dutifully began preparing food for Mr Philips and his son and Mr Philips came into the kitchen.

"Welcome home, Mrs Williams, I'm pleased the matter was dealt with in the way you thought best. It's now in the past and will never be mentioned again."

Mum looked straight at me and I could see she knew that he knew the truth, but she smiled and as she kissed me she put her finger to her lips and I knew no more would be said.

The Court Case was fully reported in the local newspapers on the following Friday.

The awful headlines read something like, 'Deceitful housekeeper steals from frail elderly employer.'

When I arrived at my school in Abingdon the following Monday, the school bullies had seen it and were waiting to pounce. The first cat-calling started even before I got in the school gate.

"Whose mother's a thieving bitch then?" shouted one.

"Stealing from a poor old man who can't protect himself!" shouted the ring-leader.

I told her to shut her mouth, but kept moving.

The whole pack joined in as I walked up the path towards the school entrance. For some reason, I had not expected I would become their target, I naively thought no one would be any the wiser. It was such a shock, I thought I was going to be sick, my head felt like it was about to explode and my legs felt weak, but, I managed to keep walking. Then to my relief, Miss Baxter, the Deputy Head, came out and told the mob to get themselves into class, immediately.

Miss Baxter ushered me into her office. She was known to be firm but fair; she had helped me before when I found that 'big-school' rough and daunting in my early days at Boxhill. She told me not run away, but stay and accept the teasing. They would soon get fed up with it and pick on another child to intimidate, that was the way bullies operated.

I thanked her for intervening and told her I had no intention of allowing that lot to affect my schooling, I was going nowhere. I had my own small circle of friends; Josie, Susan and Kathy who helped sustain me through that time. The teasing went on for a week or so, but a lot worse had happened to me over the last few years and as Miss Baxter predicted, the mob soon got bored and turned on someone else. That someone turned out to be, Ann the Head Girl who we were all envious of. She was pregnant and had to leave the school!

However, the once quiet and easy going Rosemary reacted very differently at her school in Sunningwell. She was teased as well, but one girl, Judy Dean, went too far in her taunting and Rosemary, with just one blow of her little clenched fist, knocked her spark out.

The unfortunate recipient of my sister's rage just happened to be the cosseted daughter of a local farmer, so this was not likely to blow over too easily.

My mother was summoned to the school and the police were called, but thankfully, this time, the police were at a loss to see why they had to be involved. They assessed the situation and told the authorities they should have stopped Rosemary from being tormented. She was much too young for any action to be taken anyway, so they should all make friends and get on with life. Rosemary became the school heroine and was never bullied again.

Bryan became withdrawn after the court case. He said he knew he was responsible for what had happened to Mum, but he was also very angry about the way Michael Philips had overruled his father and involved the police. I could hear the growing resentment in his voice as he told me he wanted to take revenge. I didn't take this too seriously so I asked what he meant by revenge?

His response frightened me. He stared directly ahead and his eyes looked cold.

"Someone should scare the shit out of him."

I didn't see my brother for a day or two after that, I assumed he was out with his friends. But a few nights later, I was fast asleep when I felt a tug on my shoulder and a finger lightly pressing on my mouth.

"Shush, or you'll wake mum up." Bryan removed his finger from my lips. "Get up and follow me."

I could see he was serious and as nothing like this had happened before, thought it best do as he asked. I crept into his room; it was only then that I noticed he was dressed all in black and holding a large spade.

"Betty, do you trust me?"

"Of course I do."

"Well then, will you come up to Bagley Woods and help me retrieve a gun?"

"Will I go where and do what?" I blurted.

"Christ, it's only a bloody mile or so and keep your voice down," he hissed, "you'll be back and in bed within an hour."

For a moment I couldn't for the life of me think what he was talking about and then the realisation dawned.

"You really do intend to shoot Michael Philips. No, forget it. I'm not going anywhere to help you get a gun."

"You idiot, don't be so stupid! It's not to GET a gun, it's to put one back!"

He went on to explain that on the evening after he talked about taking on the son, he crept into Mr Philip's study, found the key to the gun cabinet and removed a shotgun from the rack. He put it in a sack and fled to Bagley Woods, where he buried it until the time was right to use it.

However, he was thwarted in his aspiration for revenge, when early the next morning, Mr Philips realised the gun was missing and confronted him in the garage. He did not have to ask if Bryan had taken the gun, he could tell by his guilty body language.

"Bryan, I know you have been into my study and taken a shot-gun. If it's not replaced by midnight, I will call the police and report it as missing. Do you understand what that means, Bryan?"

"I only borrowed it to shoot a few rabbits," protested Bryan.

Mr Philips shook his head in despair. "You can't go around taking things young man, especially a gun, without serious repercussions. And, we both know what that means, don't we Bryan?"

That was the moment Bryan realised Mr Philips knew about the money. He clammed-up and Mr Philips continued on a lighter note.

"Anyway, Bryan, there isn't any ammunition. Not much point in trying to shoot rabbits without any ammo, is there dear boy?" He gave Bryan a paternal pat on the shoulder. "Gun back by midnight, don't let me down."

"Why did you snitch on me to the old boy, Betty?" whispered Bryan

I whispered back, "Because I didn't want him living the rest of his life thinking mum had stolen from him. If you want me to go with you to retrieve the gun, shut-up and let me go and get dressed."

A few minutes later, clad in warm, dark clothes I followed him out from the house. It was pitch-black as we hurried the mile or so to the woods and every time we heard a car coming we hid in a gateway or hedge. When we got to the boundary of the woods I breathed a sigh of relief.

"Okay, I'll wait here"

"You've got to come with me; I need you to hold the torch and sack."

"What sack? We haven't got a sack."

"The sack's in there!" he yelled in frustration. "Jesus, just get going will you? PLEASE!"

We had to leap over a ditch, then wriggle under barbed wire fencing. We were scratched and torn as we forced our way through dense bracken and undergrowth, hearing all sorts of scuffling and night-time animal sounds, which scared me as I knew the area wasn't called 'Boars Hill' for nothing. I moaned at him.

"Why bring the gun all this way? Why didn't you hide it in the garden?"

361

"Ivan's always poking about and could have found. Much better to hide it here, I didn't know how long it would be before I wanted to use it."

"What do you mean 'use it' Bryan?"

He hissed, "I don't mean kill him stupid; I was only going to scare him, that's all. The darn thing hasn't even got any bullets."

It was then that I knew my brother really would have gone that far, had Mr Philips not discovered the gun was missing.

A sack hanging from a tree marked the spot. I held the torch as Bryan began to dig between the roots of a very large tree. Within minutes he pulled out the shot gun, which was wrapped in Rosemary's doll's cot blanket. We put it into the sack and began to retrace our steps, but lost our bearings and it took over an hour to find our way out from the wood onto the main road and by that time I was angry, cold and fed-up. We then had to be very careful. There were many attempted burglaries in the wealthy area of Boars Hill and police cars regularly carried out night patrols. Had we been caught in the middle of the night with a shot gun in a sack, there would have been hell to pay! Just what poor mum needed to finish her off!

Mum and Rosemary were still asleep as I quietly changed and climbed back into bed.

Bryan replaced the gun and returned the case keys into their hiding place. As he left the study he saw Mr Philips standing on the landing at the top of the stairs, silently staring down at him.

He laughed later as he told me, "I nearly shit myself, Betty. I thought it was a bloody ghost!"

362

Mum never knew Bryan had 'borrowed' the shotgun and what his intentions were, until many years later. As I said, Mr Philips was very kind, probably too much of a gentleman to be put-on by Bryan and his juvenile antics.

Mum was expecting to lose her job after the court case, but Mr Philips pleaded with her to stay. He told her how fond he had become of us as a family and how much he relied on her. However, mum was in two minds. What was done could not be undone and perhaps it was time to move on.

Michael Philips heard that she might be about to leave and called her into his father's study and offered her a glass of sherry. He awkwardly apologised for the trouble he had caused.

"I admit that I was too hasty in calling the police Mrs Williams; my father was right, it should have been dealt with privately. The family would be most grateful if you would stay on and continue to look after him."

Mum disliked this arrogant man intensely. It had obviously dawned on him that his father would soon have no one to care for him and the responsibility would fall on him and his wife.

Mum pointedly ignored the offered glass of sherry.

"I will give the matter further thought, Mr Philips."

Mum was about to leave when the son motioned her to remain seated.

"Please hear me out, Mrs Williams. I have a proposition for you. I will make you a cash payment of two hundred and fifty pounds if you agree to remain with my father until his death."

Mum was flabbergasted, it was a huge sum, but she settled coolly back in the chair and took a sip from the previously ignored glass of sherry. She knew he was expecting her to bite his hand off, but made him wait. She thoughtfully took another sip of sherry.

"Mrs Williams?"

He was getting agitated and mum enjoyed watching him squirm as she took a larger sip and savoured its warming sweetness.

"Mrs Williams! My proposition?" He returned to character and spoke sharply, but mum ignored his tone, he was never going to change. But two hundred and fifty pounds was a colossal sum, especially when you were only earning three pounds a week. She finished the sherry in one swig, placed the expensive glass back on the table and stood-up.

"Thank you, Mr Philips." She paused long enough to read the doubt in his face. Was she thanking him for the sherry, or his offer?

"Thank you Mr Philips, I will stay on to look after your father until the end and accept your offer."

A relieved Michael Philips actually smiled as he shook my mother's hand to seal the deal.

The following day, he called her into the study, handed her the telephone and left the room. It was Mr Philip's younger brother, who mum liked and made a bit of a fuss when he came for lunch or supper.

"Hello Mrs Williams, I'm calling to tell you how much I appreciated the care and affection you have shown to my brother and indeed to me on my frequent visits. I can't begin to think how he will be able to cope without your skill and understanding. I know you have been through a lot just lately, but you have my complete admiration for the way you shielded your son from a criminal record. I understand from Michael that after much deliberation, you have decided to stay on to care for Charles and I would like to offer you one hundred pounds for making what must have been a tough decision."

Mum could not think of anything to say, she was overwhelmed.

"I hope I haven't upset you Mrs Williams, I can assure it's not a bribe, just a way for me to say thank you for all you do and the comfort and reassurance you will provide for Charles."

"I'm not upset Mr Philips, merely stunned. Thank you so much for your kind words and generous offer, but I would be staying anyway."

"I know, but it's a tangible way of showing how much I appreciate what you do. Goodbye, I hope to be the beneficiary of one of your delicious luncheons, in the not too distant future." Mum walked out from the study as if I in a dream. To be offered £350 to carry on doing a job she loved seemed unreal, but to know Mr Philip's brother rated her so highly made her very happy and that meant we were too.

Every Tuesday, regular as clockwork, Mr Philips would collect two string shopping bags from the kitchen and catch the No.20 bus into Oxford. He was off to do his personal shopping and would return on the 3.30pm bus, with his bags loaded. As time passed and he struggled with the weight of the bags, he asked me if I would like to accompany him. I was always eager to go, depending on school commitments.

Mr Philips was a creature of habit so we would always follow the same route. We would alight from the bus in Gloucester Green and walk to Mac Fisheries in George Street. They had live fish in tanks under large, iced display counters at the entrance to the shop. Wet black and white tiles covered the floor, the fishmonger decked out in wellingtons, white overalls and a heavy, navy and white striped apron. Mr Philips always asked for fresh herrings and mixed crab meat.

On the first visit, mum gave me enough money for some cod, so I asked Mr Philips if he could order it for me. He agreed and with one of his famous smiles said the would pay for it. The shop felt icy cold and the smell of fish overpowering to my nose as the fishmonger selected, gutted and wrapped the fish. As we waited, I watched the fish in their tank and thought they were a bit like turkeys at Christmas. Wonderfully oblivious of their fate!

Next stop was the Co-op butchery department, for a sheep's head, lamb chops, liver and seven ox hearts for Rhona. Mr Philips had a Co-op members 'dividend-number', which he always gave as it saved him one shilling and three pence in the pound. I was surprised at his thrift, thinking it was only the working class who were attracted to the 'Co-op Divi'. He handed money to the butcher who put it into a cylinder attached to a wire which whizzed through the air to the cashier's cubicle. She took the money out and sent a receipt and the change back.

From there it was a short walk along Cornmarket Street to the famous food emporium of Grimbly Hughes for Coopers Oxford Marmalade, Twinings Tea, two half- pound rolls of fresh butter, tinned pineapple juice and coffee.

By that time both bags were full and Mr Philips carried one in his right hand and we carried the heavier one between us. The amazing aroma of freshly ground coffee wafted over us as we walked down the street towards the Cadena Café. It had been popular with academics, students and shoppers for over fifty years and it was Mr Philips weekly indulgence. I passed under the distinctive white canopy, joined to Mr Philips by the string bag, it was almost like holding hands. As we went through the swing doors, I was wide eyed in wonder at the vast ornate interior. Mr Philips was instantly recognised and given a warm welcome by Rudolf, the immaculately groomed Maître d'. Rudolf, a Jewish refugee who had fled Germany before the Second World War, waved an authoritative hand at a waitress wearing a black and white dress, starched apron and cap. She led us to Mr Philip's favourite table, which was beautifully laid out with a pristine white linen table cloth, napkins and Cadena's own delicate china cups and saucers.

As we made ourselves comfortable in the deep, wicker chairs, the waitress handed Mr Philips a fresh copy of that day's Oxford Mail and a menu. He asked me what I would like and I ordered a strawberry milkshake and a cream filled, chocolate topped doughnut, a popular house speciality. They became my favourites.

Having dealt with my order he gave his own

"My usual coffee, two boiled eggs, soft, with extra brown bread and butter and a pot of your own heather honey." I noticed that although he smiled at the waitress, he never added a "please" or "thank you" which he would have done with mum.

As we waited, Mr. Philips began to read his newspaper and I listened to a small court orchestra playing popular light music. I took in everything: the sound of animated conversation: the smell of expensive perfume: the small army of primly dressed waitresses as they flitted from table to table under Rudolf's watchful eye and the sheer opulence of that beguiling place. It was a different world and I vowed to myself, that one day, I would have enough money of my own to take mum there and buy her a pot of tea and a doughnut.

Most evenings, after the last early-evening meal was cleared away, we went for walks through the lanes of Boars Hill or disappeared up to our flat and listen to our transistor radio, either BBC or Radio Luxemburg, as we did jigsaws, knitted or sewed.

One night mum was awoken with a dreadful head pain and deafening sounds in her ear. She was not one to submit to pain, but it was so bad, she hurriedly dispatched Bryan, a mile across Boars Hill, to alert, Doctor Naismith, Mr Phillip's private, elderly lady GP, who lived in 'Badgers Holt' a lovely old house, surrounded by tall pine trees. She arrived in her Austin Seven accompanied as always by her small grey poodle called 'Phup', before Bryan had managed to cycle home.

Following a lengthy examination she told us mum was suffering a minor breakdown and needed rest and quiet for a few days. After the doctor had gone mum still had the dreadful pain and asked me to warm a few drops of olive oil to pour into her ear. As I tipped the oil in her ear she screamed with pain and we both thought we had made a dreadful mistake. But then, from feeling her ear drum was about to burst, the pain suddenly stopped and as she tipped her head to one side, a dead, oil-soaked moth fell out. It had obviously crawled into her ear during the night and must have been trying to find its way out by desperately clawing at her eardrum, the very one which remained sensitive due to her mastoid operation years before.

When Dr. Naismith, aged 86, was told about this she was very apologetic, saying that it must be time for her to retire and within three months she did so.

That bizarre incident saw the beginning of a sustained period of instability for us.

Very soon after the moth incident, mum began to suffer pain in her lower back. Following a referral to the Radcliffe Hospital, she was told she needed a full hysterectomy. At the time it was major surgery and meant two weeks in hospital, followed by rest and recovery in a government funded Convalescent Home.

These sanctuaries could be located either by the sea or in picturesque countryside, but mum was transferred to Osler House, Oxford. So, no sea or country air, but a welcome respite nonetheless and of course, totally free for NHS patients.

During our first summer with Mr Philips we were introduced to his sister, Miss Sallugh, when she attended his birthday luncheon. After that she became a regular guest for tea and one day confided in me.

"I would happily jump on the No. 20 bus for a piece of your mother's black tea fruit cake, dearest one."

She called everyone, 'dearest one', but would never consider hopping on a bus, her only mode of transport was a chauffeur driven limousine. She was certainly a one-off, with lots of very long, fine silver hair, held up in a bun by a large tortoiseshell comb with a pearl and diamond decorated handle. Her diminutive figure disguised a strong, somewhat domineering nature and although she appeared, to me, to be at least 200 years old, she was actually in her mid-90's. She always wore floor length, darkly coloured silk and lace dresses which 'swished' as she passed by and carried a slim, ivory and silver stick, apparently given to her by a member of the royal family.

"I have never suffered a day's illness, or been seen by a doctor, in my entire life, dearest one," was one of her favourite mantras. I found her fascinating and I looked forward to her next visit, yet, when Mr Philips told us that his sister was going to move in to take charge of the household whilst mum was away, both Rosemary and I feared her semi-permanent arrival into our world.

We were right! She was continually correcting our grammar, keeping tabs on what we were up to and carrying out embarrassing daily checks to ensure our bedrooms were clean and we had emptied the chamber pot of what she called "slops" into the downstairs toilet. This assertive lady was constantly on my case and I did not like that one bit. If it wasn't emptying the potty it was taking our cups and plates down from our bedroom into the kitchen, washing them, drying them and putting them back in the cupboard. I could just about understand that, but expecting me to help mum's stand-in, Mrs Cross and her daughter, was a step too far! I could not understand why I should help when they were being paid to carry out mum's domestic duties. By dint of constant explanation, Miss Sallugh convinced me that we all had to help fill the huge gap left by my mother. She did such a good job of it that I, in turn, persuaded Rosemary and Bryan to help.

Miss Sallugh turned out to be firm, but tolerant of our faults and over time began to enlighten me on the inborn ways of the affluent set. I felt emboldened to ask a question.

"What did you do in your younger days?"

She gave me a strange look. "What do you mean, DO?"

I explained, "What did you do for a living?"

"Nothing dearest one, I didn't work, if that's what you mean. I inherited wealth and privilege from my parents and family. But, those golden days of inherited wealth and privilege are in their twilight, the war and taxes have seen to that. I have been most fortunate, apart from living through two world wars and consequently losing many friends. But, you should not fret about not been born into a privileged status, dearest one. You and your siblings are in the dawn of a new era and if you apply yourselves, many opportunities will come your way."

At the time I did not understand what she was wittering on about, but many years later I recognised how shrewd, far sighted and encouraging she was.

Eventually Mum returned and picked up her duties and as Miss Sallugh left, she gave me a box of luxuriously expensive chocolates to thank me for the work I had done whilst mum was away. Her chauffeur driven limousine arrived and she left us in a swirl of silk and lace to return to her 'historically significant' house, which apparently overlooked Folly Bridge, beside the River Thames in Oxford City.

It was wonderful to have mum back, but all too soon we discovered that she had not fully recovered. I awoke one morning to find her lying motionless in her bed. This was not at all normal as she was always up early to take Mr. Philips his early morning tea tray and have our breakfast on the go by the time we scrambled down stairs. However, on that day she could not speak or move. I ran to fetch Mrs Cross who took one look at mum and called for an ambulance.

I managed to get my unresponsive mother into her dressing gown, brushed her hair and with Bryan's help, gingerly walked her down the stairs and into the toilet, just before we heard the ambulance pull into the gravel drive. I told her it was time to go but she didn't respond, merely stared vacantly at the toilet door, her face ghostly white. The only acknowledgment she had heard me was to squeeze my hand, very, very, hard. I was terrified she was going to die and we were about to lose her.

The two ambulance men came in with a wheelchair and gently wrapped her in a red blanket with "HOSPITAL" stamped on it. As they wheeled her to the ambulance, I hurried upstairs to pack her a toilet bag and ran to give it to Bryan, who had hopped into the ambulance with her.

She was taken to the Radcliffe, where Bryan was able to explain to an amazed medical team the problems she had faced over the past few years. She was assessed there and then with a mental and not medical problem and quickly transferred to the Warnford Hospital, where she was to be treated for a full mental breakdown. It was assessed she would have to stay there for several weeks of specialist treatment and care.

This time, a temporary cook/housekeeper, was brought from London by Michael Philips and diligently looked after all of us. Hooray, no more chores!

Another big hooray! Miss Sallugh returned, but this time, instead of 'being on my case', she took me 'under her wing' and shared her stories and thoughts.

She turned out to be a highly intelligent and extremely well-travelled lady who had lived in a straw and bamboo house in China for ten years and shipped back rare objets d'art of great value which seemed to be the source of much of her wealth.

As a daughter she was given an excellent education and a substantial yearly allowance, but she always knew the inherited wealth would go to her brother, Charles, because that was the way things were.

She had taken steam ship journeys to India and Africa and had friends who were passengers on-board the Cunard Royal Mail Ship, Carpathia when it went to the rescue of survivors from the Titanic in 1912. Her tales about her travels were spell-binding to a girl like me, who already spent most of her days dreaming about what might be? She taught me so much, for which, in later years I became extremely grateful.

The first time Bryan and I were allowed to visit mum, we were warned by a nurse that she was sedated and we would most likely find her asleep. But no one warned us of what to expect when we entered the bleak ward she shared with fifteen other patients, all suffering from some kid of psychiatric disorder. A few patients were quiet and still, but most were highly agitated, waving arms and legs and calling out to us. They all wore the same cream, heavy cotton gown with ties on the back at neck and waist level, most of which were undone, exposing private parts of their anatomy. They lay in or sat on single, metal beds, some strapped to them. We were both scared witless as we hurried past.

When we arrived at mum's bed, we found her lying very still, staring up at the ceiling in a sort of trance. Although we spoke to her, she did not acknowledge our presence and seemed locked within her own mind. We were only allowed to stay for a few minutes before being taken to see the senior psychiatric nurse, who could clearly see how distressed we were. She was very kind.

"You are not to worry. I promise you, your mother will recover, but she needs total rest and that takes time."

"How much time?" asked Bryan?

The nurse shrugged. "I can't say, but what I can tell you is that your mother's brain has found the last few years of trauma and strife just too much to handle and it has shut down. She is in a stress-induced, wakeful coma, which happens when our brain needs to protect itself from irreversible harm. She will come out of the coma when her brain is ready."

The senior nurse's diagnosis proved correct. On our second visit, three weeks later, mum was up, dressed and sitting in a communal day room. She waved as we walked in and was so pleased to see us. Although she looked frail and spoke very quietly, she was obviously on the mend and we were very thankful for that. Mum remained there for another two months and on our final visit we joined her for a cup of tea in the garden and she told us she was feeling much better and looking forward to coming home.

Life at 'The Chalet' continued; Miss Sallugh took over the companionship of her brother and the London cook/housekeeper did a fine job of caring for us all. I spent a lot of time with Miss Sallugh and always looked forward to her company.

"Have you seen the piano in the Music Room Betty?"

The question from Miss Sallugh surprised me. Was she trying to find out if I had ventured to parts of the house I had not been invited to? I replied cautiously.

"No, I have heard someone playing one, but I've never seen it."

Her eyes sparkled and she held out a hand.

"Ah, then come with me dearest one."

We went together through the sitting room and on towards the previously out of bounds Music Room, which meant going through a library which I never knew existed. I thought all the books in the house were on the packed shelves in Mr Philips' study, but in the library there were hundreds more and shelves full of piles of sheet music.

The musty floral scent which hit me as we entered the sanctum of the Music Room was intoxicating. It was a mixture of the fragrance from the Wisteria and White Jasmine, which cascaded around the open French windows, combined with real wax polish and pipe tobacco. This was obviously a place for informal, musical enjoyment and a home for objets d'art and worldwide travel paraphernalia.

Paintings and historic photographs of family members adorned the walls and suspended on brackets from the ceiling were monogrammed, highly lacquered oars used by Mr Philips during his University days as an eminent oarsman. Winner's cups, trophies and university shields were on display, but in pride of place stood a shiny black 'Steinway' grand piano, which, Miss Sallugh told me, Mrs. Philips, a highly gifted pianist, played for most of her life.

As we drifted around the room Miss Sallugh told me the history of some of the treasures and watched as I gently caressed some of the fine figurine antiques. When she asked if I would care to listen to her play something on the piano, I eagerly said I would.

It was unforgettable for me when she took her seat at that stunning piano and played Beethoven's 'Moonlight Sonata' and 'Fur Elise'. She trained at The Royal Academy of Music and was an extremely talented musician.

After that magical first visit, I was allowed to spend many contented hours quietly ensconced in that fragrant room. I looked through magazines and books with Miss Sallugh whose companionship and stories helped to widen my very narrow view of life. She taught me the rudiments of playing the piano, but I'm sad to admit I never progressed much beyond, 'Chopsticks' and 'My Bonnie Lies Over the Ocean'.

Michael Philips did not visit very often and his family visits had dwindled to almost nothing by then.

Rosemary spent a lot of her time with Mrs Cross and her family at their home in Bayworth, about a mile away. She came with Mrs Cross every day to care for her cats and Rhona. Bryan was either at work or with his friends and only came home to check on us and occasionally stayed overnight.

When mum was discharged from Warnford Hospital, Mr Philips arranged for a taxi to take Bryan there to collect her. When she climbed out from the car she looked extremely fragile. Rosemary and I ran to greet her but refrained from hugging her too tightly, lest we harmed her in any way. With Bryan holding her arm, she walked to the kitchen to be welcomed by Mr Phillips, Rhona and Miss Sallugh.

After tea and cake she asked if she could walk in the garden which she had missed so much. Bryan, Rosemary and I walked with her, delighted to have our beautiful mum home again. That evening, when we told her how much we had missed her and how we would help ensure she would never fall ill again, mum laughed and simply said, "We'll see."

It was not long before mum was back in harness and we returned to some form of normality, but with a lot more help from Mrs Cross and us.

The regime imposed upon us from Miss Sallugh during her first stint, stood us in good stead. Mrs Cross kept up her increased hours, Bryan took over the stove maintenance, I started to assist more with the cooking and washing up and Rosemary continued to care for and feed Rhona and her cats.

Miss Sallugh sadly passed away quietly during an afternoon nap, a few months after my mother's return.

Mr Philips was noticeably affected by the loss of his beloved sister, becoming reclusive and disinterested in the world around him; even his family could not distract him from his grief. He became forgetful and absent minded.

On a defining occasion, he was brought back from one of his rare solo visits to Oxford by the police. He had been found wandering around Carfax in the city centre and could not remember his name or where he lived, luckily he had his wallet in his pocket and they were able to identify him from the information stored in there. It wasn't long before he was diagnosed as having dementia.

As the weeks passed he became more frail and confused. He suffered several TIAs (Trans Ischaemic Attacks or mini-strokes) which came on a regular basis. I was able to spot them coming an hour or so before they were upon him because he started to stammer, looked vague and became agitated. As soon as Mum or I spotted this, we would encourage him to allow us to escort him up to his bedroom, before he collapsed, became irrational and doubly incontinent.

For some months, mum and I cared for him day and night, without any outside help, other than Mrs Cross, until he was finally confined to his bedroom.

On the 20th June 1959, Mr Philips had his final stroke. Mum summoned his son and the doctor. The doctor arrived first and confirmed there was nothing more he could do: things must be allowed to take their natural course. Mum reassured him that she would remain with her patient until he passed and upon that assurance, the doctor left asking her to call him when Mr Philips had died.

Not long after, the son arrived and demanded to know where the hell the doctor was.

Mum calmly explained that the doctor had been, but as there was nothing more he could do and was assured by her that she would stay with her patient until the end, he left to await her call when the inevitable happened. The son became irate and shouted something indiscernible, before shutting himself in his father's study, where he remained, without visiting his father, until the early hours of the following morning.

Mum sat with Mr Philips all that night and as he entered 'Cheyne Stokes' breathing, which indicated imminent death, his son strode into the bedroom and angrily kicked open the French doors to the balcony, smashing glass in one door as it banged back against the wall.

He bellowed at my mother. "Get out! Get out now! Leave!"

Mum, was shaken by his action and command, but refused.

"Your father has not taken his last breath yet. I will not leave him until he has passed and his spirit has left his mortal remains." She frowned at him. "Now, behave yourself and show some respect."

He glared at her, but remained quiet. It was only a few moments before Mr Philips died and mum could leave his side. Without another word she stood, made a sign of the cross and left the room to telephone the doctor.

Following a visit from the doctor, who certified death and amid frequent interruptions by an emotionally charged Michael Philips, mum 'laid-out' his body. His death was confirmed on the 21st June 1959. The longest day of the year.

Caring for people who had died and preparing their body for funeral, was something my mother had done many, many times and in many situations. She always regarded it as an important and meaningful part of her profession. When she had completed her last task for Mr Philips, she obtained the son's permission to take us up there to pay our last respects.

We followed her up to his room. I was amazed to see how clean and comfortable he looked. Many years had slipped away from his face and he looked younger and at peace. We all mourned the passing of this kind and gentle man.

As we came back down the stairs we were met by Michael Phillips who seemed more angry than upset. Taking two steps at a time, he pushed passed us, then stopped and turned to look down on us.

"Now my father is dead Mrs Williams, you will vacate the flat as soon as possible. I'm selling this house and I want you gone by the end of July."

He spoke with loathing and no hint of compassion. Mum looked as if he had slapped her in the face. She was shocked and stunned. I looked from her to him and thought what an unbelievably cruel and heartless man he was. Mum said nothing; I don't believe she was able to. We continued our way down the stairs and up to our flat where mum broke down and sobbed her heart out.

Following the death, the family and friends came in droves, most were kind to my mother and wished her well for the future. Some were indifferent, others dismissive. We were not invited to attend the funeral, but as mum said, "Never mind, we did all we could for him whilst he was alive, he does not need us now."

Supported by Miss Booth and Dr. Naismith, Mum applied to Abingdon County Council for a council house and within a week we were invited for an interview at the Council Offices. The Housing Officer told her that vacant properties were as rare as hen's teeth, but as she had two girls less than 15 years of age and was being made homeless through no fault of her own, she would be high on their waiting list. He warned her that if and when we were offered one, we would have to accept within twenty four hours or it would be offered to the next family on the list.

We waited for three weeks before we were called back to the Council Offices. We sat patiently for over an hour before being called in by a female Housing Officer. She smiled as she told us that a house had suddenly become available on a council estate in Wootton. We knew this large village well, having often shopped there and more or less knew where the house was.

It was impossible to disguise our relief. Mum's voice went completely as she began to weep and Rosemary and I laughed and hugged each other. This highly emotional reaction brought the officer from behind her desk to comfort my mother. She put a hand on her shoulder.

"I take it that you want to accept the property then Mrs Williams?"

Mum, wiped her eyes and managed to confirm that was indeed the case. The Housing Officer said we could view it that weekend. It was in a poor state, as left, but the property would be completely refurbished before we moved in.

As we caught the bus home, mum said, as she had said many times throughout our travails, that she always knew God would open another door for us.

BETTY & MUM, ROSEMARY AND BRYAN AT NUMBER 26

23

HOPE SPRINGS

Two weeks after the funeral 'The Chalet' was all ours for a few days, which gave us the time to think about and prepare for our next move. We were buoyant in the knowledge we had been awarded a council house and there was the three hundred and fifty pounds mum was promised for staying on to care for Mr Philips. We were full of hope for a brighter future.

Mr Philip's brother was as good as his word. When he made a final visit to have lunch with Michael

Philips, he went into the kitchen, where mum and Mrs Cross were washing-up the dishes and asked mum to accompany him to his car.

"I didn't want to say anything about the one hundred pounds I promised you for staying on to care for Charles in front of Mrs Cross, Mrs Williams. I've left an envelope with Michael, as I wasn't sure I would have the opportunity to give it to you in person. Thank you for all you have done and may I give my very best wishes to you and your family for a bright future."

Mum thanked him and waved as he drove away.

I went out and took mum's hand in mine and we walked back into the house. We met Michael Philips in the hallway, still holding my hand, mum asked if she could have the envelope his uncle had entrusted to him.

"Ah, that." He smirked as he pulled an envelope out from his inner jacket pocket. Staring directly into mum's eyes he tore the envelope open and pulled out a thick wad of one pound notes. He teasingly waved them in front of her before calling Mrs Cross from the kitchen and handing the money to her. An astonished Mrs Cross put it in her pinafore pocket. She grinned broadly at mum before she turned back to face him.

"I have worked for your father and your dear mother before her passing and never, ever, have you so much as given me a thank you. As far as I'm concerned this is too little too late." She turned to mum. "Ethel, I know you're a religious person so please forgive me for what I'm about to say, but I have to get it off my chest." She turned back to Michael Philips.

"Michael, you are the nastiest piece of work I have ever known, God alone knows how two such lovely people as your parents could produce such a shit as you. I won't be staying on to help clear the house; you can shove the bloody job where the sun don't shine. I wouldn't work for you if you begged me. So there!"

Satisfied to have said what she had obviously been rehearsing in her mind for weeks, Mrs Cross gave mum a kiss, said she would miss working with her and, unknowingly, walked out with her cash.

Michael Philips was totally unabashed by what Mrs Cross had said, in fact he seemed to revel in it and take it as a compliment to his superiority. As if to endorse her opinion, he spoke dismissively to mum.

"I'm not allowing you to have that money, Mrs Williams, because of all the time you needed off work for your illness last year."

Mum was dumbstruck and just stared at him. It was the stare I remembered from her breakdown and I was frightened she was heading for another one. Unable to utter a word and with legs, she later said, felt as if they might give way at any moment, she left the room and went upstairs into our flat, where she cried tears of exasperation at his spitefulness – and the loss of £100!

We knew Mrs Cross could not have known the money had been promised to mum, but that did not soften the blow.

After she recovered from the shock, mum decided it was best if Bryan was not told about what had happened as he might do something we might all live to regret.

On a happier note, viewing day for our Council House arrived. Rosemary and I walked the three miles with mum to see our new home. We were brimming over with joy as we walked through Boars Hill, past Jarn Mound and down the country lanes into Wootton, but, we became nervous as we entered the large Council Estate. We felt hundreds of pairs of eyes were watching our every step and they all knew we should not be there. Mum no longer had a proper job and we were scroungers, depriving some hard working family of a home. The scars left by working for the rich and living in tied houses, travelled with us.

The house was identical to every other house in the road, the only difference being a right or left side semi-detached. Ours, being an even number, 26 Matthews Way, was on the right side of a pair. The previous occupants, an elderly couple one of whom had died and the other moved into a care home, had not been capable of keeping the place clean; it reeked of urine and blocked drains. We made a quick walk through and tried to see past the detritus and keep an open mind and anyway, we had a long history of moving into far worse! However, we were assured the house would be cleaned, redecorated and any remedial works completed within two weeks, after which we would be free to move in.

We walked home, not too sure that would be the case, but it was a house and we would make it our home. However, as good as their word, two weeks later we were invited to collect the keys.

On the day we were moving out from the flat, Michael Philips could not hide his relief and actually smiled as he ushered us into his father's, already mostly cleared, study and invited us to take one thing from the few oddments remaining to remind us of his father.

Mum said we wanted nothing as we had our memories and that would suffice, but Rosemary had other ideas.

"Please, could I have Rhona?"

I suppressed a giggle, but Michael Philips could not see the funny side of it.

"Certainly not, I will be taking Rhona to London for my own children."

Rosemary's bottom lip trembled. Mum put a comforting hand on her shoulder and looked at me. Take her out please, Betty, I won't be a minute."

She closed the study door behind us, but, as ever, we put our ears to the door and listened.

"Mr Philips, why did you not honour your uncle's wishes and give me the one hundred pounds he promised?"

"I think, Mrs Williams, my father was overly generous in continuing to pay your weekly wage," came his pompous reply.

"That was not your decision to make," mum said firmly. "I want the money your uncle expected you to give to me."

"But, I gave that to Mrs Cross and that, in my opinion, was the right decision. The two hundred and fifty pounds I owe you is more than enough for what you have done."

Mum stood her ground. "No! That can't be right, Mr Philips, a promise is a promise and that money was not yours to give."

Michael Philips responded in the only way he knew and shouted angrily. "I decide what is and what isn't right, Mrs Williams and I have decided that two hundred and fifty pounds will suffice. Now please leave, before I decide to give you nothing at all!"

Mum was left with no option other than to stifle her mounting rage and leave the room before she lost everything!

All our worldly belongings were tightly packed into a small car one of Bryan's friends had managed to borrow. At the last moment he loaded in Rosemary's three cats and left us to walk to the house, saying he would have a cup of tea on the go when we arrived.

Rosemary went to say a tearful farewell to Rhona as mum and I surveyed the flat which had been our home for four years. We would be taking a mixed bag of memories with us, plus the physical bag we each picked up to carry to our new home. We assembled on the front drive, where mum asked us to wait whilst she went back into the house to ask for the two hundred and fifty pounds. She was worried that he might have thought up an excuse not to pay the full amount, but apparently he smiled as he counted out fifty pristine white five pound notes from a large wad, most likely the stash Bryan and I found in the Pink Room!

We walked into number 26, Matthews Way, on the afternoon of August 1st 1959 with nothing other than our toiletries, clothes, the brass tea caddy, the crucifix and three cats. We were overjoyed! Our new home was wonderful, marvellous, fantastic and, immaculately clean!

The smell of fresh paint lingered in all the rooms. Downstairs we had a front room, a back room and a kitchen and upstairs, three bedrooms and an indoor bathroom, complete with a fitted bath, flushing toilet and hot and cold running water.

We had a garden, front and back and outside the back door a second toilet and a coal store. There was a brick-built garden shed in the back garden. The garden itself was a bit of a tip, but we didn't care about that. We were simply over the moon and could not believe the lovely, spotless home was ours and no one would take it away.

The RSPCC came to our aid once more with free furniture, beds, bedding and utensils

We laid cheap linoleum covering on the upstairs floors and the kitchen and in a sale, bought offcuts of a red floral patterned Axminster carpet for the stairs, hall and sitting room.

The council paid for five sacks of coal, which were delivered through the back garden gate into the purpose built coal store, no carrying it through the house, which was a memory mum shared with us from her time in Wales. The council also put enough shillings in the gas and electric meters, to cope with our lighting, water heating and cooking needs for a month. But they did not stop there! They supplied us with a gas cooker, a copper boiler and a mangle for squeezing water out of our laundry, before hanging it out on the clothes line, which was already in place in the back garden.

There was, of course, no central heating, just two open coal fireplaces and an electric fire set into the wall in the rear dining room.

The two hundred and fifty pounds in cash was a small fortune for us, equal to over sixteen months' salary for mum. It was ceremoniously hidden in the old brass tea caddy, to be used sparingly for things we needed to complete our new home and to save for a rainy day.

We had yet to tell Bryan about the missing one hundred pounds. We thought it best to wait until 'The Chalet' was sold and Michael Philips was well clear of the area.

26 Matthews Way was our Utopia, where we were finally free of bondage, orphanages, employers, landlords and our deceitful, bullying father. I was fourteen, Rosemary twelve, Bryan eighteen and Mum fifty. We had survived with our spirits intact and were finally at liberty to be ourselves for the first time in our lives. Our destiny was, finally, in our own hands.

Post Script

As I collated all the information together to write about my mother's life experiences, it became painfully obvious I had not asked enough questions when I had the opportunity. However, given her hard life, I believe I did ask her the most important question of all.

"Mum, do you think you would have fought so hard to survive had you known the trials and tribulations you would have to face for most of your life?"

She smiled. "Yes, Betty my love, because life is a precious gift and no matter what challenges come our way, we must fight to survive."

My mother firmly believed in God, the Holy Spirit and the Church. She felt that God has a reason for putting the tests we face through life in our path, although she did admit to sometimes wondering what those reasons could be? However, she possessed an absolute faith in Heaven as the next stop on our journey and our earthly death is not the end, just the beginning.

****

Ethel May Bryan/Williams (born 1.2.1909) died in Betty's
private nursing home 2001

Thomas Samuel Williams (born 8.7.1913) died whilst
sitting on his mother's sofa, in 1961

Ellen Harriet Bryan/Couldrey (born 1889) died at
No.26 Wootton in 1960

Herbert Arthur Bryan (born 1897) died in Oxford in 1909

Ruby Florence Bryan/Parker (born 1908) died in Ethel's
private nursing home in 1973

Bryan Thomas Williams (born 1940) died in Liverpool
Hospital of heart failure in 2004

Rosemary Margaret Williams/Knight (born 1947)
died of cancer in Oxford 2018

****

Printed in Great Britain
by Amazon